T0347303

TRANSNATIONAL BUSINESS AND CORPORATE CULTURE

PROBLEMS AND OPPORTUNITIES

edited by

STUART BRUCHEY
ALLAN NEVINS PROFESSOR EMERITUS
COLUMBIA UNIVERSITY

SMALL BUSINESSES TRICKLING UP IN CENTRAL AND EASTERN EUROPE

GALEN SPENCER HULL

Routledge
Taylor & Francis Group
New York   London

First published by Garland Publishing, Inc.

This edition published 2011 by Routledge:

Routledge
Taylor & Francis Group
711 Third Avenue
New York, NY 10017

Routledge
Taylor & Francis Group
2 Park Square, Milton Park
Abingdon, Oxon OX14 4RN

Library of Congress Cataloging-in-Publication Data

Hull, Galen.
    Small businesses trickling up in Central and Eastern Europe /
Galen Spencer Hull.
        p.   cm. — (Transnational business and corporate cul-
ture)
    Includes bibliographical references and index.
    ISBN 0-8153-3236-X (alk. paper)
    1. Small business—Europe, Eastern. 2. Europe, Eastern—
Economic conditions—1989–   I. Title. II. Series.
HD2346.E92H85 1999
338.64'2'0947—dc21

                                                    99-19279

To the memory of my father
Norman Everette Hull

Contents

Contents

Acronyms and Terms

AFD	Alliance of Free Democrats (Hungary)
BGK	Bank Gospodarstwa Krajowego (Poland)
BIC	Business Information Center (Poland)
BIC	Business Innovation Center (Romania)
BNB	Bulgarian National Bank
BSC	Business Support Center (Poland)
CARESBAC	CARE Small Business Assistance Corporation
CBE	Center for Business Excellence (Romania)
CDR	Romanian Democratic Convention
CEE	Central and Eastern Europe
CEEPN	Central and Eastern European Privatization Network
CDP	Civic Democrat Party, also ODS (Czech Republic)
CMEA	Council for Mutual Economic Assistance
CERGE-EI	Center for Economic Research and Graduate Education—Economics Institute, Charles University, Prague
CHAMP	Change Management Project (British Know-How Fund in Hungary)
CRIMM	Romanian Center for SMEs
CSD	Center for the Study of Democracy (Bulgaria)
CSO	Central Statistics Office
EBRD	European Bank for Reconstruction and Development
EC	European Commission
ECE	Economic Commission for Europe
ECU	European Currency Unit
EICC	Euro-Info Correspondence Center (Bulgaria)
EU	European Union

FESAL	Financial and Enterprise Sector Adjustment Loan (World Bank)
Fidesz	Alliance of Young Democrats (Hungary)
GNP	Gross National Product
HDF	Hungarian Democratic Forum
HSP	Hungarian Socialist Party
HUF	Hungarian Florints
IFC	International Finance Corporation
ILO	International Labor Organization
IME	Institute for Market Economics (Bulgaria)
IMF	International Monetary Fund
IPF	Investment Privatization Fund (Czech Republic)
ISBD	Institute for Small Business Development (Hungary)
ISO 9000	International Standard Series
MPP	Mass Privatization Program (Czech Republic, Poland, Romania
NADESME	National Agency for Development of Small and Medium Enterprises (Slovak Republic)
NATO	North Atlantic Treaty Organization
NBP	National Bank of Poland
NBS	National Bank of Slovakia
NIS	Newly Independent States (former Soviet Union)
NPF	National Property Fund (Czech Republic)
NSF	National Salvation Front (Romania)
NSI	National Statistics Institute (Bulgaria)
NTF	National Training Fund (Czech Republic)
OECD	Organization for European Cooperation and Development
PHARE	European Union Program of Assistance to CEE Countries
PDSR	Romanian Party of Social Democracy
PPF	Post-Privatization Fund (Romania)
RAEF	Romanian-American Enterprise Fund
RAIC	Regional Advisory and Information Center (Romania)
RDA	Romanian Development Agency
ROM-UN	Small Business Center (Romania)
SBA	Small Business Administration (United States)
SDK	Slovak Democratic Coalition
SECI	Southeast European Cooperative Initiative

sejm	Polish parliament
SME	Small and Medium Enterprises
SDP	Social Democratic Party (Czech Republic)
Solidarity	Polish political party
SP	Socialist Party (Hungary)
spolka	limited liability or joint-stock company (Poland)
STRUDER	Structural Development in Selected Regions (PHARE Program)
TQM	Total Quality Management
UDF	United Democratic Front (Bulgaria)
UNDP	United Nations Development Program
UNIDO	United Nations Industrial Development Organization
UPEE	Union for Private Economic Enterprise (Bulgaria)
USAID	United States Agency for International Development
VOSZ	National Association of Entrepreneurs (Hungary)
VuB	Vseobecna uverova banca (Romania)
WTO	World Trade Organization (Geneva)

Preface

Small Businesses Trickling Up in Central and Eastern Europe argues that micro-, small, and medium-sized enterprises in selected countries of Central and Eastern Europe (CEE) have been the key to economic growth rather than privatized large-scale enterprises. Small businesses have come to constitute the most dynamic element of growth in the emerging markets of the CEE region in the last decade. In 1989, most of the countries of the region were still under the political and economic domination of the Soviet Union. Since then a process of liberalization has been unleashed in the region to dismantle statist economic policies and replace them with free market policies. This has involved programs of privatization and restructuring of state-owned enterprises, as well as the promotion of policies to enable a private sector to develop. Small businesses are creating thousands of new jobs while large companies are retrenching and downsizing their workforce.

In some countries of the region this process is much further along than in others. In each country, however, the small and medium enterprise (SME) sector has developed at a more rapid pace than has the privatization of the large public companies. The privatization of small and medium-sized state-owned enterprises has been rather more successful. With the economic transition there has been a flurry of new enterprises springing up throughout the region, some registered as legal entities but many micro-enterprises often remaining unregistered in the informal sector. Micro-enterprises are increasingly seen as an important element of this SME sector, although they were traditionally treated separately as belonging to the informal sector and a detriment to economic growth.

These small and medium-sized businesses with fewer than 250 employees are "trickling up" in a frequently hostile environment against tremendous odds, and yet have managed to have a pronounced impact on their respective economies. Small businesses have taken over in sectors that used to be the exclusive domain of state enterprises, especially in services and consumer products. They have provided a crucial outlet for pent-up entrepreneurial talent that had remained dormant during the long period of state domination.

The introductory chapter to this book presents six propositions that provide the framework for looking at small businesses in the CEE region. The first concerns the transition of countries in the region from communist systems dominated by state enterprises to free market systems. The second examines the assumption that privatization was the primary key to economic growth. The third examines the nearly universal interest of countries in the region in joining Western European institutions. The fourth proposition is that small businesses have provided the impetus for economic growth in the region. Clearer policies to promote the small business sector are needed to accelerate economic growth. The final proposition is that the growth of small businesses in the CEE region reflects a global trend.

Six countries in the region are selected and a chapter is dedicated to each of them: Bulgaria, the Czech and Slovak Republics, Hungary, Poland, and Romania. Each chapter reviews primary characteristics of the country in eight sections: the historic and economic setting, privatization and economic growth, integration into Europe, the role of SMEs in the economy, financing SMEs: bank and nonbank sources, government and donor agency assistance to SMEs, a profile of entrepreneurs, and the potential for SME development. The eighth chapter revisits the six propositions and summarizes their relevance to the six countries.

The final chapter offers an agenda for small businesses in the CEE region. An action agenda is located first in the context of integration into Europe. Legislators, policy makers, and development agencies alike should take account of the importance of the small business sector in the legislative and planning process. Given a more favorable environment, these small businesses will provide even greater impetus for economic growth. Equally important is that entrepreneurs themselves be convinced of the rightness of their path in societies that traditionally looked down upon profit seekers as unscrupulous under the communist system. If the CEE region is to achieve its full potential of economic growth, policies and support mechanisms to promote the SME sector will be needed.

Acknowledgments

The idea for this book evolved out of several trips which I made to Central and Eastern Europe from the fall of 1996 through the spring of 1998. During this period I traveled to all of the countries covered in the book, some of them three times. I was serving as a consultant on a USAID-funded contract to monitor and evaluate grant activities being carried out by U.S. universities to assist universities in the CEE region in developing their capacities in economics and management education. It was an exciting and challenging assignment which afforded me the opportunity to experience a new region of the world for the first time.

The ultimate beneficiary of these programs was often owners and managers of private firms, most of them small or medium-sized. Our work entailed numerous interviews with small business owners and managers, several of whom are profiled in these pages. This experience ignited my long-standing interest in the role of small business in development. I found people in every country—in universities, government agencies, and private firms—who were quite helpful in providing me with useful references and documentation.

Many of my colleagues in the U.S. and in Central and Eastern Europe, have been supportive of my efforts. I would especially like to acknowledge the support and encouragement of Ikbal Chowdhury, Luba Fajfer, Lee Preston, Kevin Sontheimer, Heather Sutherland, and Felipe Tejeda. Peggy Ferrin was very helpful in reading and editing a first draft of the manuscript. I would also like to recognize the kind assistance and guidance provided to me in my initial dealings with Garland Publishing by Deane Tucker, who has since left the company. His successor, Damon Zucca, was equally helpful in bringing the whole project together. I should especially like to express my deep appreciation to my wife and partner, Mani Sangaran, for both her editorial assistance and moral support.

Small Businesses Trickling Up in Central and Eastern Europe

CHAPTER 1

Historic and Economic Trends in Central and Eastern Europe

Small Businesses Trickling Up in Central and Eastern Europe examines the economies in transition of a representative sampling of countries formerly under Soviet hegemony: Bulgaria, the Czech Republic, Hungary, Poland, Romania, and the Slovak Republic.[*] The term *small business* is used to include micro-, small-, and medium-sized businesses and these categories are subject to close scrutiny. While the countries selected share many historic, geographic, and economic similarities—especially years of communist domination—they are also unique in many ways. Four of them—the Czech Republic, Hungary, Poland and, in economic terms, the Slovak Republic—are by now considered to have been relatively successful in the transition to market economy, while Bulgaria and Romania have lagged behind. Six propositions are presented and explored in this chapter which provide the framework for examining the six countries.

---

[*]A journalistic distinction in vogue (*The New Europe*) divides the region as follows: Central: Poland, Hungary, Czech Republic, and Slovakia; Eastern: Russia, Belarus, Ukraine, Latvia, Lithuania, Estonia, and Moldova; the Balkans: Romania, Bulgaria, Yugoslavia, Croatia, Slovenia, Albania, and Bosnia. However, Bulgaria and Romania are also often classified as belonging to Eastern Europe and are referred to as such in this book.

The Central and Eastern European (CEE) region has been in a transition from a communist command economy to a free market since 1989.

It has been argued that the transformation of the centrally planned economies to free market economies beginning in the early 1990s is the most fundamental economic phenomenon of the second half of the twentieth century. Among the first economists to assess these trends was Andras Koves (1992). Koves examined the same six countries as those in our study (Czechoslovakia was divided into two separate republics in 1993). He noted that what was unforeseen in their systematic transformation was the depth of the economic deterioration and inability of the governments concerned to control the decline or to slow the accumulation of social and political tensions. The rapidity of the decline in economic activity and living standards in the late 1980s as well as the increase in uncertainty for most of the population of these countries was unprecedented by any standards.

For example, in 1990 Bulgaria, Romania, and Poland experienced a 10 to 14 percent decline in total output in a single year. Industrial output dropped by 20 to 24 percent in Romania and Poland. The following year proved to be an even greater shock, contrary to expectations. In that year the drop in industrial output ranged from 12 to 15 percent in Poland and Hungary to as much as 20 to 24 percent in Romania, Bulgaria, and Czechoslovakia. The decline in gross domestic product (GDP) ranged from 8 to 10 percent in Hungary and Poland to 10 percent in Romania and Czechoslovakia, and more than 20 percent in Bulgaria. Consumer prices increased by 35 percent in Hungary, more than 50 percent in Czechoslovakia, and 70 percent in Poland. Triple digit inflation was the norm in Romania and Bulgaria. Unemployment became a critical problem throughout the region. Whereas unemployment rates ranged from 1 to 2 percent in 1990, by the end of 1991 in many countries of the region they were reaching 10 percent. None of the countries had an infrastructure capable of managing unemployment.

The socialist systems in the Central and Eastern European countries shared many features but were also dissimilar in many ways. Hungary, for example, abolished mandatory planning and central allocation of resources as early as 1968. By the late 1980s, Hungary had also progressed toward domestic and foreign economic liberalization. In Poland, progress was much more constrained and the tasks undertaken after the political change more difficult. But like the case of Hungary, the Polish system was fundamentally different from the variants of the classical Stalinist economic system in the other countries of the region.

The living conditions of the population, as well as the degree of political freedom in these countries, were quite diverse. In Hungary, the 1960s and 1970s were regarded as decades of the greatest increases in living standards in history, even though in Hungary they were still well below Western standards. In Czechoslovakia, the consumer market was relatively well-balanced despite a rigidly planned economy. However, the general economic tendency in all of the countries during the decade of the 1980s was one of decline, and the respective governments were unable to cope with it. The decline was comprehensive, consisting of stagnating population growth, obsolete investment stock, damaged infrastructure, deepening ecological disaster, and falling standards in health and education.

As a consequence of this deteriorating economic performance, the role of these countries in international trade also dropped precipitously. Their share of world exports declined from 4.3 percent in 1970 to 2.2 percent in 1989 and their share of imports declined from 4.1 percent to 1.9 percent for the same period.

The outset of the economic crisis was brought on by developments within the Soviet bloc to which all of the countries under discussion belonged. Beginning in the mid 1970s, the Soviet Union experienced economic and political decline leading eventually to an end to its hegemony in the CEE region. The five countries all belonged to the Council for Mutual Economic Assistance (CMEA). Contrary to a widely held view, trade within the CMEA was not characterized by Soviet subsidization of the CEE countries. Instead, the CEE countries suffered disadvantages from their involuntary participation in the Soviet bloc.

During 1990 and 1991, the Soviet economic collapse and the transition to dollar trade among the CMEA countries led to a decline in Soviet trade with the countries of the CEE region which in turn contributed to the region-wide recession. The CMEA as a system of economic relations among its members was abolished on January 1, 1991, and the organization came to an end six months later. This date, according to Koves, may well prove to be the most significant turning point in the modern economic history of the region. It marked the change from ruble to dollar payments and world market prices in trade among the former CMEA countries. It destroyed traditional trade flows and long-established chains of cooperation within the region. At the same time, it opened up new opportunities which tended to focus on "joining Europe," that is the European Union, a notion that has come to preoccupy all of the countries in the region.

In the light of these serious economic imbalances, macroeconomic stabilization became the main priority of most of the countries in the region. There was no exact formula for economic transition. However, the experience of Poland was most instructive because it was the first country in the region to announce a comprehensive program of stabilization and liberalization. On January 1, 1990, Deputy Prime Minister Leszek Balcerowicz initiated a program which was to carry his name and become associated with the "shock therapy" approach. Balcerowicz and his associates believed that the conditions for long-term stabilization could be established only at the cost of a short term recession and declining living standards.

In contrast to Poland, most of the other countries in the region chose a gradual approach to stabilization and liberalization. Czechoslovakia was a case in point. It was generally thought that conditions for economic transformation were more favorable here than in other countries of the region because of its traditionally prudent fiscal and income policies coupled with industrial development. Characterized as a "minimum bang" approach, the Czechoslovak program begun on January 1, 1991, featured monetary austerity, strong devaluation, and other measures much less drastic and less painful than those in Poland. This was not major surgery, since the problems to be dealt with were not as severe.

Hungary is another example of the gradual approach, which was deemed appropriate to its circumstances. Economic reforms that had been initiated in Hungary in 1968 had not brought about a free market, but had tempered the Hungarian economy; it was better suited to transition as a result of 20 years of reform than it would have been without it. Koves argues that this is true, in particular because the economic agents in Hungary had had more experience with a more open and business-oriented system. Romania and Bulgaria have only recently begun to undertake sustained economic reform efforts.

The basic assumption of policy makers and planners at the beginning of the transition was that privatization of state-owned enterprises would be the key to this process. In most countries this

process has been slow and ineffective and has not been the motor for economic growth.

What explains Poland's advantage? The answer is surely not privatization of state enterprises, because there has been little of this so far in Poland.

—Johnson and Loveman, *Starting Over in Eastern Europe,* 1995, p.5

Under the socialist blueprint, it was assumed that the productive capacities of the large state-owned enterprises would trickle down to the ultimate benefit of the population. Virtually all production was in the hands of the state, except for a small but increasingly important informal or black market in a few countries. The program of privatization of large state-owned enterprises, offered by economists as the main antidote for economic transformation and promoted in the countries of the CEE region beginning in the early 1990s, has generally met with disappointing results. The revitalization of large state enterprises has not been the key mechanism for reform at the enterprise level in the CEE region. The restructuring of these enterprises has proved to be a difficult task at best, often resulting in a decline in production and employment. The banking sector, which is critical to enterprise development, has generally been slow to make necessary adjustments to serve the nascent private sector.

The results of the privatization process in the CEE region have been uneven. For example, Czechoslovakia began the process from a position of virtually total state-ownership of the economy, unlike Poland and Hungary. As Jan Svejnar (1995) points out, in 1989 only 1.2 percent of the labor force, 2 percent of all the registered assets, and a negligible fraction of the Czechoslovak GDP belonged to the private sector. Yet extensive privatization became the cornerstone of the Czechoslovak (later Czech) economic transformation. By the end of 1994, the Czech Republic had carried out the most extensive privatization program among these six countries. The program consisted of restitution of property to previous owners or heirs and privatization of small units in public auctions (small scale privatization). Large and medium-sized firms were privatized as well. About 4,000 of the 6,000 large firms had been privatized in two waves of large scale privatization by 1994.

In Hungary, the small-scale privatization schemes in the first few years of the transition were not successful. This was due in part to the fact that it was only the rights to lease the shops that were privatized. Potential buyers were discouraged by the uncertainties involved in the scheme. Small scale privatization was obliged to compete with the development of new private activities which grew more successfully in Hungary. Efforts to sell off large, state-owned enterprises in Hungary were initially more successful than in any other CEE country, with some ten having been achieved by the first quarter of 1991. There was also considerable success with the privatization of medium-sized firms, usually initiated by enterprise management and workers together with outside investors rather than government officials. By the end of 1992, some ten thousand retail shops and restaurants had been transferred to private owners.

The transition process in Central and Eastern Europe has involved debate and experimentation with various forms of privatization. The term *privatization* has mainly been used in reference to the restructuring of state-owned enterprises. Privatization is often wrongly seen simply as the transfer of existing enterprises from public to private hands, but this transformation involves much more than the restructuring of public enterprises. Equally important is the promotion of new enterprises and the creation of an environment that will enable them to grow and thrive. It is unfortunate that it is the former interpretation that is most often used and the one that has been the preoccupation of both donor agencies and governments of the countries in transition. The development of SMEs is, however, bound up with privatization in general and the success of transition depends upon it (Dembinski, 1995).

In the CEE region, the privatization of state-owned enterprises has tended to be divided into small and large scale. Small-scale privatization has meant selling public retail shops, restaurants, and other services that had been units of larger state-owned trading or service chains. Schemes of this sort have had varied success within the region but have nevertheless been a very important part of the process. Large scale privatization is the most commonly used form and probably the most fiercely debated. It has typically been a more difficult undertaking than expected from the outset. Sometimes the greatest problems have been encountered in those countries where the strongest need for privatization prevails. Rarely has the process happened quickly, partly because of the complete absence of legal and institutional foundations for privatization. It has involved determining who can sell what property under what conditions.

In recent years trends in the economies of the region have tended to illustrate the growing importance of the private sector (European Bank for Reconstruction and Development, 1995 Annual Report). Investors in the region have seen marked improvement in the business environment over the past three to four years. Market-oriented reform has been advancing, inflation has come down sharply, and positive growth is returning to parts of the region. The countries that embarked on transitional adjustment the earliest are beginning to see the benefits of reform. This is in contrast to most of the countries in the former Soviet Union, where reform has only started in earnest in the last few years.

Most countries in the CEE region have implemented widespread liberalization of prices, external trade and currency arrangements, and privatization of small-scale units. These are considered to be the necessary conditions for private sector development. Progress in large-scale privatization and enterprise restructuring has been slower. These initiatives require more preparation to build the necessary political consensus and to create the implementation infrastructure.

There has been considerable variation in the implementation of privatization programs within the CEE region. Several have by now privatized a sizeable number of their large scale enterprises, including the Czech Republic and Hungary. The private sector share of GDP in these countries in 1995 was as follows: Czech Republic, 70 percent; Estonia, 65 percent; Hungary and the Slovak Republic, 60 percent; Bulgaria, 40 percent; and Romania 35 percent. In fact, the average for the region was around 55 percent, which was also the highest percentage among the former Soviet Union (the case of Russia).

The first noncommunist government in Poland assigned the highest priority to laying the rules for a British-style privatization program. Privatization of large firms through case-by-case sales was anticipated. With an initial goal of 150 privatized enterprises, however, only 26 had been sold by the end of 1991. Even though some 2,813 of the 8,500 state enterprises had begun some form of privatization by 1994, only 121 had actually involved the sale of equity to those who did not work in the company. Public reaction was against alleged sweetheart deals in which managers would agree with workers to sell their own firms directly to foreign investors.

All the countries in the CEE region aspire to join the North Atlantic Treaty Organization and the European Union, a process involving certain standards, including a healthy private sector.

The former communist countries of Eastern Europe, having thrown off statist economic policies, are looking to join the fraternity of nations embodied in such institutions as the North Atlantic Treaty Organization (NATO) and the European Union (EU), where they perceive economic advantage and security. In July 1997, Hungary, the Czech Republic, and Poland were invited to begin negotiations for admission to NATO, seen as a first step toward a historic expansion that in time could stretch from Estonia to Romania.

In March 1998, the same three countries, plus Estonia and Slovenia, formally began talks about joining the European Union. The EU, for its part, was faced with having to adjust its own policies and finances to accommodate the new members. Among the most contentious were proposed changes in farm subsidies that take up half the EU budget. Thus, the countries in the Central and Eastern European region jostled with each other for European attention, going through the arduous process of "harmonizing" policies and procedures to bring them into accord with NATO and EU standards. Among the CEE countries on the fast track to enter Europe, Poland with its rapid economic growth and large population, was clearly the front runner. Despite its claims to be the region's "tiger," Poland still had to drastically reshape its economy in order to cope with EU membership. Poles talked optimistically of completing negotiations by 2000 and actually entering the EU a year or two later, forgetting that it took Spain and Portugal seven years to accomplish this task.

However, the dispassionate observer looking at economic trends in Western Europe might well ask: What is the rush? Is Europe the model for what these countries want to become? The London-based magazine, *The Economist,* ran a cover story entitled "Europe Isn't Working," (April 5, 1997). Despite the promises of Europe's political leaders to create employment, some 18 million people in EU countries were looking for work. Most of the countries in the EU were suffering high rates of unemployment (an average of 11.3 percent) and lackluster economic growth. More than 40 percent of the unemployed in Europe had been out of work for more than a year, compared with only 11 percent in the United States. European youth had been especially hard hit by unemployment.

Is there a better model for growth and equity that the CEE countries can emulate? Few of the Western European countries offer a favorable example of an entrepreneurial economy. The one that comes closest, according to The Economist, is the Netherlands where unemployment in 1997 was a modest 6.2 percent, just over half of what it had been in 1983. Dutch economic reform since the 1980s has been persistent and far-reaching, accomplished with little conflict and without sacrificing the goal of redistributing resources from rich to poor. Fifteen years ago journalists were writing about the "Dutch disease," not the Dutch model. However, in the last year or so Holland, a country of 15 million, has become an economic paragon. One of the keys to Dutch economic success has been the promotion of small businesses. Whereas the Dutch economy has traditionally been characterized mainly by large multinational businesses such as cosmetics-maker Unilever and manufacturer Philips Electronics, the government is now promoting entrepreneurship. The Dutch government is promoting a flexible work force and at the same time encouraging people to start their own companies.

Western European nations are coming to recognize the importance of the role of small businesses in a healthy economy as a source of competitiveness and employment creation. Until fairly recently, the EU defined enterprises according to three categories: micro (fewer than 10 employees), small (between 10 and 99 employees), medium (between 100 and 499 employees), and large (over 500 employees). Then, in April 1996, the European Commission adopted a recommendation to change the definition of SMEs. The medium enterprise category would be from 50 to 250 employees, the small from 10 to 50 employees, and the micro-enterprise up to 10. In the United States, small business has been defined as having fewer than 500 employees.

The European Observatory for SMEs publishes an annual report providing a comprehensive analysis of the scope and structure of SMEs in Europe. The Third Annual Report (European Network for SME Research 1995) identified trends during the period from 1988 to 1995. At that time in Europe economic stagnation severely hit the labor market. But while employment in larger enterprises increased only marginally, the SME sector grew at a rate of 2 percent. Likewise, SME labor productivity increased annually by 2 percent, accelerating since 1990. The relatively high growth rates in export-oriented sectors such as extraction, manufacturing, transport, and communications applied to both the SME sector and larger enterprises was an important indicator for international integration. It was clear that the SME sector was becoming an important factor in the economy.

The largest share of new enterprises was established in the service sector. On average, of all European start-ups, 87 percent had survived their first year, 68 percent survived for at least three years, and 55 percent stayed in business for five years. New enterprises accounted for a significant amount of job creation in most European countries, although large differences existed among countries. But the expansion of existing SMEs in most European countries was a more important source of job generation. The report noted that in recent years SMEs, and especially microenterprises with fewer than 10 workers, had created the most jobs in industrialized economies. It acknowledged the concern of the Organization for European Cooperation and Development (OECD) and others that these claims are subject to problems of data acquisition and analysis which might have led to an over estimation of the SME role in job creation. Methodological problems concerning this issue were reviewed in the report.

The European Observatory grapples with policy issues that are derived from analysis of the SME sector in Europe. These issues refer to the basic relationships between SME performance, the functioning of markets, and the business environment of the more unified Europe. The report concluded that more policy attention should be devoted to such issues as the legal framework in which SMEs are obliged to operate, the administrative burdens on them, and the supply of management and entrepreneurial training.

The main impetus for economic growth in the CEE region has come from the private sector, which is predominantly comprised of small and medium sized enterprises (the SME sector)

Not too long ago it was fashionable to argue that economic benefits in capitalist societies could "trickle down" from the barons of industry—accumulators of wealth—to the working poor. To stand this metaphor on its head, it is now possible to think of the productive energies of small and medium-sized enterprises "trickling up" to generate economic growth and to account for the largest portion of economic growth in the Central and Eastern European region.

To the surprise of many economists and policy makers, the most important factor in the transition process from command to market economies has been the emergence and growth of small private businesses. In most of the countries of the CEE region the private sector—now accounting for over half of the gross national product—has been nearly synonymous with the small and medium-sized enterprise sector. Employment in the state sector has fallen, while private sector employment has risen. Entrepreneurship has proven to be a powerful mechanism for redirecting incentives toward the efficient use of resources. It is ideally suited to the circumstance of these economies in transition.

Among the six countries examined in this study, Poland has emerged as the most successful example of economic reform, due in large part to the role of its small business sector. Poland has privatized proportionately fewer of its large state enterprises than other post-communist counties which have fared less well economically. However, beginning with an insignificant small business sector at the beginning of the transition in 1990, Poland has achieved impressive economic performance due to firms founded from scratch, not as a result of privatization. Even among those countries in the region that have failed to achieve appreciable economic growth, it is the newly created small business sector that has accounted for much that has occurred.

What, after all, is an SME? Only in the past two decades or so has the term SME come into vogue. Today, however, this acronym has taken its place in the English language lexicon of economic terminology alongside such familiar terms as GDP and GNP. It has become so commonly used that nearly everyone dealing with economic development takes SME to be more or less synonymous with small business, without bothering to determine its exact dimensions. Only when it is examined in microscopic detail is the term SME found to have a complex and changing referent. Now that SMEs have been acknowledged by governments and donor agencies to be crucial to the growth of countries in transition from socialist to capitalist economies, the definition is becoming more important. Indeed, in the view of many economists who study this region, SMEs are thought of as synonymous with the private sector, and by extension with entrepreneurship.

While there is no single agreed upon definition, the European Union adopted a breakdown of enterprise categories in April 1996 (see Table 1.1). In the countries in transition there is a disparate range of definitions, and even within the same country there may be several definitions depending upon whether it concerns such matters as qualification for bank loans, tax regulations, supporting consulting service, or application of new technologies. In both Albania and Uzbekistan a small enterprise is defined as one with three hundred or fewer workers, and there is no distinction between small and medium. In the Czech Republic there is no formal SME definition, although the government has created the legal basis for granting subsidies in the form of credit guarantees or favorable interest rates to enterprises with fewer than five hundred employees.

Table 1.1: European Union Categories of SMEs Recommendation as of April 1996

Micro-enterprise	1-9 employees
Small enterprise	10-99 employees
Medium-sized enterprise	100-249 employees
Large firms	above 250 employees

However the term may be defined, it is now clear the SMEs are beginning to play an important role in the countries in transition. Under the centrally planned economies, SMEs played a marginal to non existent role in total economic output. However, as the central controls began to be lifted, the Council for Mutual Economic Assistance (CMEA) was abolished, and the size of the Soviet market diminished, firms in the transition economies began to search for new markets where they could perceive a comparative advantage. For example, in the manufacturing sector of the Czech Republic, firms with fewer than 25 employees comprised 0.8 percent of all firms and accounted for none of the manufacturing output in 1989 (Svejnar 1995). Four years later, however, these firms constituted 90 percent of all manufacturing firms and accounted for 10.6 percent of manufacturing output. While smaller companies accounted for most of the economic growth in the Czech Republic, large state-owned enterprises frequently encountered serious adjustment problems and actually declined in production.

The exact size and scope of the small and medium enterprise sectors in the countries of the region remains uncertain and subject to change. Data collection and analysis on the SME sector is still in an undeveloped stage. In one of the most extensive efforts yet, the United Nations Industrial Development Organization (UNIDO) undertook to examine SME policies and programs in Central European Initiative (CEI) countries, in response to a request from the CEI Working Group on Small and Medium Enterprises requested (UNIDO, 1996). The

UNIDO approach was to collaborate with the national institutions and agencies involved in SME development. Country reports were prepared for six countries: Czech Republic, Hungary, Poland, Romania, Slovakia, and Slovenia.

The UNIDO study report concluded that there is generally not a shortage of information about SME development in the CEE region. The problem, however, has to do with information being provided in a sufficiently consistent form to be of value to policy makers and interested stakeholders. One of the objectives of the UNIDO study was to attempt to benchmark progress in the CEE countries against the "norms" of the Western countries in regard to the SME sector. The study also drew upon data from the European Foundation for Entrepreneurship Research to address the attitudes of small firms toward government policies and benefits from various forms of assistance.

The UNIDO report, presented in three major parts, notes that data on firm size, employment and contribution to the gross national product is not readily available. The study reviewed the various definitions of SMEs and their size within the economy, beginning with the European Union. In 1994, fully 92.4 percent of all enterprises in the EU were in the micro category, compared with 7 percent for small, 0.5 percent for medium, and only 0.1 percent for large firms. Using these categories as benchmarks for comparison, the countries in transition tend to have a higher percentage of enterprises grouped at the micro end of the spectrum. For example, Poland has a large proportion of enterprises in the 6 to 50 employee range (18 percent) while Hungary (0.8 percent) and Slovakia (0.65 percent) have a comparatively high percentage of medium sized enterprises. Romanian data in the UNIDO survey reported no enterprises at the medium or large-scale level.

There has been a tremendous explosion of the micro-enterprise sector (10 employees and under) in all of the countries selected, as reflected in the distribution of establishments by employment size similar to that of the European Union. On average, 90 percent of all enterprises in each of the countries now fall into this category, even when differences in size are taken into account. It is difficult to make comparisons of the small enterprise sector (11-99 employees) because of the noncomparability of data in several of the countries. In the medium firm sector (100-499 employees) there is a generally higher percentage of employment than in the European Union. This may reflect the slow growth of privatization in this sector or, conversely, a stronger sector.

The large enterprise sector in the CEE region generally still has a larger share of employment on average than in the European Union. This may indicate that the contraction of the state-owned sector still has a way to go in these countries, even though it has been substantial already. Data on birth and death rates of enterprises and the portion of inactive enterprises that are registered are especially difficult to come by. The informal sector is particularly hard to account for. While it is clear that micro-enterprises have grown substantially, the incidence of inactive registered businesses is also very high. For example, in Hungary and the Czech Republic it is estimated that nearly 30 percent of those on the register are inactive. The informal sector (defined as unregistered businesses) is estimated to account for between 10 and 30 percent of the gross domestic product in these countries. In sum, the UNIDO study concludes that the distribution of businesses in all the countries in the region is moving towards the norms of Western Europe.

In order to understand fully the contribution of SMEs to total GDP growth and employment, it will be necessary to have more reliable data on the SME sector than is currently available. The Economic Commission for Europe (1996) is beginning to track statistics on the contribution of the SME sector to total employment. Again, figures vary drastically from country to country in the region, but the SME contribution to total employment ranges from a small fraction to nearly half. At the end of 1994, the Czech Republic registered a total of 5.2 million employed in the economy, of whom 2.2 million were in SMEs in industry, construction, and trade (but not services). In Poland, roughly four million workers were employed by SMEs out of a total of fifteen million in the economy. The SME sector in Slovakia accounted for 790,000 workers out of a total of 1.9 million and nearly half of all employment in Croatia. By contrast, in Kazakstan it was a mere 32,000 out of 2.5 million.

Policies and institutions that promote the SME sector are needed in order to accelerate economic growth and social development in the CEE region.

Governments of most countries, whether they be industrialized or developing, have traditionally paid little attention to devising policies specifically for the promotion of small enterprises. Free market purists tend to believe that if all the macroeconomic policies are in place, conditions will be right for businesses of any size to grow and flourish. The small businesses that do not succeed are considered to be obeying the rules of the marketplace. Some countries have begun to monitor the growth and development of small businesses and have established a fairly extensive system of support for them. But government agencies established to promote small businesses are often out of sync with their needs and thus not very helpful to them. And small business owners the world over are known for their antipathy toward government red tape.

The UNIDO study (1996) noted that in most of the countries surveyed, the government was still in the process of formulating policies for small enterprise development. Most have not attempted to identify the contribution that SMEs might make to broader national goals of growth, productivity, and social justice. There are no clearly established criteria for intervention in the market. Some of the countries in the region have developed a broad sectoral focus, such as Poland's emphasis on tourism and international trade and Romania's focus on textiles and furniture. One common policy preoccupation, both explicit and implicit, is to bring the very substantial informal sector—in some cases accounting for as much as 30 to 40 percent of the GDP—into the formal sector. However, micro-enterprises are inclined to prefer the informal sector because of corporate and employment taxes levied on registered firms.

In some instances, there are policies that affect SMEs which do not, however, constitute an SME promotional strategy. As early as 1994, the Polish government elaborated a small business policy embodied in the national strategy document which set forth targets for a higher than average increase in SME turnover as well as growth in the SME sector. In the Czech Republic, the Ministry of Economy was given responsibility for small business development but little power to control it. (Eventually the Ministry of Economy itself was abolished.) Reflecting the Czech government's free market orientation, interventions focused on SMEs have been minor. In 1992 the Czech government issued an annual report setting forth policy on SME assistance and justifying support for SMEs in terms of preserving market forces. While the main focus of the policy statement was to bring the Czech Republic into harmony with European Union practice, it provided no SME industrial development policy.

In Slovakia, the SME policy focus is within the framework of a broad government statement of support issued in 1993 which included no detailed targets. The policy implementation structure in Romania is being altered to incorporate SMEs within the National Agency for Privatization, with a greater focus on medium-sized rather than small and micro-enterprises. In Hungary, there has been little official reference to SMEs in economic policy, although there have been broad statements calling for the removal of barriers to SME development such as social insurance, financing systems, and information.

In nearly all instances there is recognition of the importance of the relationship between small and large businesses and between small businesses and government agencies as providers and customers. This is manifested in several ways. Improved methods of facilitating subcontracting between large and small firms are being explored. Restructuring of large firms can involve a process of spinning off small units within the firm that become small businesses. This has become commonplace in the CEE region, although it is considered illegal in some countries because of the dubious practices associated with it.

With a proper mix of policies and regulatory reform, it is possible that the small business sector in these countries will provide the even greater impetus for growth with equity that is hoped for. Legal systems still remain inadequate to stimulate and protect small and medium enterprises and facilitate their growth. Access to finance is an abiding issue for small-scale entrepreneurs, often linked to the financial instability of the countries in which they operate. Entrepreneurs need advice and help in marketing their products to overcome the deficiencies of the distribution system and insufficient development of business linkages. The support framework needs to be assessed to ensure that local and regional support institutions are to be encouraged where there is sufficient demand for services. Training for SMEs is important, especially in marketing, financial accounting, and entrepreneurship development. More focus must be given to developing local case study materials and linking training with business consultancy.

Development planning and research in recent years has become increasingly focused on the small enterprise sector and its role in development. In fact, there is a growing number of international development agencies, business centers, and non governmental organizations involved in small enterprise promotion. In the past few years several of them have commissioned SME sector strategy studies.

Research institutions in the region are also beginning to pay attention to the importance of the SME sector. Most of these have focused on the programmatic imperatives of donor agencies for promoting SME assistance programs rather than the dynamic of economic growth and the role of SMEs in that process, which is presented in this book.

The growth of SMEs in the CEE region reflects a global trend: the bigger the world economy, the more powerful its smallest players become.

> The study of the small economic players, the entrepreneur, will merge with the study of how the big bang global economy works.
>
> —John Naisbitt, *Global Paradox*, 1994, p. 6.

> On my tombstone they'll write, "David Birch discovered that small firms create most of the jobs." God gives you one sentence—that's as much as people can remember about anybody—and that's the one they'll be writing about me.
>
> —David Birch interview with *INC Magazine*
> (*State of Small Business in the U.S.*, 1997)

John Naisbitt, author of *Megatrends*, puts forth several propositions in a more recent study entitled *Global Paradox* that emphasize the importance of small actors in the global economy. He argues that we have moved from economies of scale to diseconomies of scale, from bigger is better to bigger is inefficient, costly, wastefully bureaucratic, and inflexible. The entrepreneur is the most important player in the building of the global economy because he is the cornerstone of a healthy domestic economy. The bigger and more open the world economy becomes, the more small and middle-sized companies will dominate.

While big companies and economies of scale succeeded in the relatively slow-moving world until as recently as the mid-1980s, today only small and medium-sized firms—or big ones that restyle themselves as networks of entrepreneurs—will survive as we enter the next century. Meanwhile, the giants are downsizing, reengineering, and dismantling their bureaucracies. In order to survive, they are deconstructing themselves and creating new structures, often as networks of autonomous units. It is axiomatic for Naisbitt, then, that the bigger and more open the world economy becomes, the more small and middle-sized companies will dominate. In the years ahead, big companies will find it increasingly harder to compete with smaller, more speedy, and more innovative firms. In the CEE region, small businesses are just beginning to spread their wings, demonstrating the same innovation and responsiveness to consumer demand.

Naisbitt sees a global trend pointing overwhelmingly toward *political* interdependence and self-rule on the one hand, and the formation of *economic* alliances on the other hand. Naisbitt contends that the more people are bound together economically, the more they want to otherwise be free to assert their own distinctiveness. Regardless of the speed and extent of European integration, the emerging markets of Central and Eastern Europe are obliged to seek closer union in order to grow.

In examining the role of small businesses in Central and Eastern Europe, it is helpful to place it in a comparative context. The experience of the United States is particularly instructive. If Naisbitt is the avatar of global trends, it is David Birch who has taught us the most about the role of small business in the United States. He was the first to point out how important small businesses are in the American economy. In his pioneering research in the late 1970s Birch discovered that a large proportion of the new jobs being created in the U.S. were not to be found where economists and policy makers had traditionally looked for them. Jobs were not being created by the Fortune 500 companies but rather by small and medium-sized businesses.

If we are looking for a way to explain the process of transition from state- controlled to market economies in Central and Eastern Europe, it should be clear by now that privatization has not provided the principal answer. Rather, it is in the growth of an indigenous private sector characterized by millions of micro, small, and medium-sized businesses, that is creating sustained economic development.

In recent years economic trends in other parts of the world have occasioned cause for re-thinking the basic tenets of growth and development. As recently as 1993, the World Bank was busy documenting and codifying the *East Asian Miracle* in a comprehensive study (World Bank 1993). Looking at Japan, the "four tigers," (Hong Kong, Taiwan, South Korea and Thailand) and three newly industrializing economies, the policy research report concluded that their success was due to the relationship between public policies and rapid growth. This would be the model for other developing economies.

However, four years later these very same East Asian economic giants had been shaken to their very core. Economists were now beginning to analyze what went wrong. Is it possible that they will discover that a missing ingredient in the "success" of these countries was the promotion of a culture of indigenous entrepreneurship?

REFERENCES

Blanchard, Olivier, et al. 1991 *Reform in Eastern Europe*, Cambridge, MA: MIT Press, published by The World Institute for Development Economics Research (Finland), a center of the United Nations University, Tokyo, Japan.

Blanchard, Olivier, and Kenneth Froot, and Jeffrey Sachs eds. 1994 *The Transition in Eastern Europe Volume 1: Country Studies*, Chicago: University of Chicago Press.

Clague, Christopher, and Gordon Rausser eds. 1992 *The Emergence of Market Economies in Eastern Europe* Cambridge, MA: Blackwell Publishers.

Dembinski, Paul 1995 *From Post Communist Privatization to SME Support* Paper presented at the ECE Workshop on Economic Aspects of the Implementation of New Technologies in SMEs Moscow September 12-13.

Economic Commission for Europe (ECE) 1996a *Small and Medium-Sized Enterprises in Countries in Transition* ND/AC.3/1 Geneva: Regional Advisory Services Programme, Industry and Technology Division, February.

Economic Commission for Europe 1996b *Small and Medium-Sized Enterprises in Countries in Transition in 1995* IND/AC.3/3 October.

(The) Economist 1997 "Europe Isn't Working: Europe Hits a Brick Wall" April 5.

European Bank for Reconstruction and Development *1995 Annual Report.*

European Network for SME Research 1995 *The European Observatory for SMEs: Third Annual Report 1995* submitted to Directorate-General XXIII (Enterprise Policy, Distributive Trades, Tourism and Cooperatives) of the Commission of the European Communities, February.

INC Magazine 1985 Interview with David Birch, April.

INC Magazine 1997 "Face to Face: An Interview with David Birch," State of Small Business in the U.S.

Johnson, Simon, and Gary Loveman 1995 *Starting Over in Eastern Europe: Entrepreneurship and Economic Renewal* Boston: Harvard Business School Press.

Koves, Andras 1992 *Central and East European Economies in Transition: Their International Dimension* Boulder, CO: Westview Press.

Levitsky, Jacob ed. 1996 *Small Business in Transition Economies* London: Intermediate Technology Publications.

Naisbitt, John 1994 *Global Paradox* New York: Avon Books.

Podkaminer, Leon et al. 1997 "Year-End 1996: Mixed Results in the Transition Countries," WIIW Research Report No. 233 February Vienna: Institute for Comparative Economic Studies.

Spolar, Christine "Poles Enthusiastic About NATO Entry, Czechs Ambivalent" *The Washington Post* June 18, 1997.

Svejnar, Jan ed. 1995 *The Czech Republic and Economic Transition in Eastern Europe* Orlando, FL: Academic Press.

Swardson, Anne "A Model of Economy: Dutch Growth While Preserving Social Benefits in the Envy of Stagnating European Neighbors" *The Washington Post* July 17, 1997.

Szabo, Antal 1997 *Microcrediting Small and Medium-Sized Enterprises in Countries in Transition,* paper prepared for the Microcredit Summit Washington, D.C., February 2-4.

United Nations Industrial Development Organization (UNIDO) 1996. *A Comparative Analysis of SME Strategies, Policies and Programmes in Central European Initiative Countries,* a study undertaken by UNIDO at the request of the Central European Initiative (CEI) Working Group on Small and Medium Enterprises.

Vienna Institute for Comparative Economic Studies 1996 *Countries in Transition 1996: Handbook of Statistics,* Bratislava, Slovak Republic: Vienna Institute for Comparative Economic Studies, supported by Bank of Austria.

World Bank 1993 *The East Asian Miracle: Economic Growth and Public Policy*
World Bank Policy Research Report Oxford University Press.

CHAPTER 2

Bulgaria

BULGARIA

Bulgaria Profile

Area: 110,910 square kilometers, slightly larger than Tennessee

Bordering countries: Greece, The Former Yugoslav Republic of Macedonia, Romania, Serbia and Montenegro, and Turkey

National capital: Sophia

Population: 8,290,988 (July 1997 est.)

Population growth rate: -0.63% (1997 est.)

Ethnic groups: Bulgarian 85.3%, Turk 8.5%, Gypsy 2.6%, Macedonian 2.5%, Armenian 0.3%, Russian 0.2%, other 0.6%

Religions: Bulgarian Orthodox 85%, Muslim 13%, Jewish 0.8%, Roman Catholic 0.5%, Uniate Catholic 0.2%, Protestant, Gregorian-Armenian, other 0.5%

Languages: Bulgarian, secondary languages closely correspond to ethnic breakdown

GDP—real growth rate: -10% (1996 est.)

GDP—per capita: purchasing power parity ($4,630 1996 est.)

Inflation rate—consumer price index: 311% (1996)

Unemployment rate: 12.5% (1996 est.)

Administrative divisions: 9 provinces (*oblasti*, singular—*oblast*)

Natural resources: bauxite, copper, lead, zinc, coal, timber, arable land

Independence: September 22, 1908 (from Ottoman Empire)

National holiday: Independence Day, March 3 (1878)

Chief of state: President Petar Stoyanov (since January 22 ,1997),

Head of Government: Prime Minister, Ivan Kostov (since May 19, 1997)

Source: U.S. State Department

Bulgaria

THE HISTORIC AND ECONOMIC SETTING IN BULGARIA

Bulgaria is variously considered as part of Eastern Europe and the Balkans. In the context of this book Bulgaria is taken as belonging to Eastern Europe, with Romania bordering it on the north, Greece and Turkey on the south. Due partly to its mountainous terrain in the Balkan Peninsula, the country's population density is one of the lowest in the CEE region. Two-thirds of the people now live in urban areas, compared to one-third after World War II. Sofia, the capital, is the largest city. The principal religious organization is the Bulgarian Orthodox Church, to which most Bulgarians belong, although Islam, Roman Catholicism, Protestantism, and Judaism claim adherents. Bulgarian is the primary language spoken in the country, although some secondary languages closely correspond to ethnic divisions. Russian is also widely understood, and English is increasingly used in business. The most important ethnic language is Turkish, which is widely spoken by the Turkish minority. From 1984 until 1989, the government banned the use of the Turkish language in public, although the ban is no longer in effect.

Bulgaria's name is derived from the Bulgars, a Turkic people who originated in the steppe north of the Caspian Sea. Although the name Bulgaria is not of Slavic origin, the Slavic people who had earlier entered the Balkan Peninsula absorbed the invading Turkic people and were the precursors of the present-day Bulgarians. Bulgarian kingdoms continued to exist in the Balkan Peninsula during the Middle Ages, after which the Ottoman Turks ruled Bulgaria for five hundred years. In

1885, the union of the Principality of Bulgaria with Eastern Rumelia south of the Balkan Mountains created an autonomous Bulgarian state with roughly the same borders as those of present-day Bulgaria. A fully independent Bulgarian kingdom, proclaimed in 1908, participated in an anti-Ottoman coalition that defeated the Ottoman Empire in the First Balkan War (1912). It later allied itself with Germany in World Wars I and II and suffered defeat both times. Bulgaria's involvement in these wars was partly due to its ambitions for an outlet to the Aegean Sea.

Communist rule in Bulgaria began September 9, 1944, when a communist dominated coalition seized power from the coalition government formed to arrange an armistice with the Allies. At the same time, Soviet forces were marching into the country without resistance. Communist power, consolidated over the next three years, led to the adoption on December 4, 1947, of a constitution modeled after that of the USSR. Following Stalin's death and separation in the USSR of the positions of party leader and head of government in 1954, Todor Zhivkov became head of the Bulgarian Communist Party (BCP). Zhivkov blamed his predecessor for the "Stalinist excesses" and "violations of socialist legality" which had characterized the 1948-1953 period. Zhivkov soon took on the additional post of premier, thus combining the positions of party leader and head of government. In 1971, he gave up the premiership and took on the newly created and more prestigious position of Chairman of the State Council (chief of state). He held this position and that of Bulgarian Communist Party (BCP) secretary general until November 1989.

Zhivkov's removal from government and party positions on November 11, 1989, began a period of significant change in Bulgarian political and economic life. On January 16, 1990, the National Assembly removed the paragraphs in the Bulgarian Constitution that guaranteed the "leading role in society" to the BCP. Until this time, the BCP, with nearly a million members, controlled all phases of Bulgarian life. Petur Mladenov, former foreign minister, took over from Zhivkov as Head of State and Secretary General of the BCP. In the period that followed, six of the nine full Politburo members were dismissed, as were three of the six candidate members. In most cases, these had been individuals closely associated with Zhivkov or with his most unpopular policies. There were also changes in the Central Committee membership of the BCP which were widely viewed as an effort to bring more liberal and reform-minded party members into responsible positions. Most important, however, the Central Committee voted in December 1989 to relinquish its monopoly on power.

In 1992, Zhivkov was convicted of embezzling $24 million of public funds spent on luxury apartments and western cars for his family (*New Europe*, September 28—October 4, 1997). In January 1997, the Bulgarian Supreme Court overturned that sentence, although Zhivkov remained under house arrest on charges connected to his assimilation policy against ethnic Turks. At the age of 85 he lived comfortably in his granddaughter's villa in Sofia's wealthy Boyana suburb. During his rule, Bulgaria's more than one million ethnic Turks had been forced to give up their Islamic names and religious traditions, leading to an exodus of three hundred thousand to Turkey in 1989. While their rights were eventually restored, many Turks have not forgotten the episode and continue to live in fear.

The other political party that had functioned in Bulgaria during communist rule was the Bulgarian National Agrarian Union (BANU). A coalition partner of the BCP, it could not have an independent program. Its leadership also changed in November 1989, and some of its members began to take the initiative in the National Assembly and elsewhere to assume a more independent position. Other political parties have been formed since Zhivkov's dismissal, initially without benefit of legal guidelines, but have been permitted to function without government interference. Among them was the Bulgarian Socialist Party, formed from the remnants of the communist era.

By 1996, Bulgaria was suffering through a severe political and economic crisis. The ruling party—the Democratic Left—was comprised of a coalition headed by the Bulgarian Socialist Party that badly managed the crisis. An opposition party, the Union of Democratic Forces (UDF), led 30 days of mass protests fueled by the economic hardships which eventually toppled the ruling Socialists in February 1997. An interim government undertook certain macroeconomic reforms in anticipation of elections on April 19.

On March 17, 1997, the caretaker government presented the main features of the stabilization program on national television, admitting it could cost as many as fifty- eight thousand people their jobs. (Unemployment reached 13.4 percent in January, the highest level since July 1994.) All prices would be fully liberalized except for the temporary continuation of subsidies for bread, milk, white cheese, and chicken. Earlier the government announced a 257 percent increase in the prices for heating, electricity, and coal. Services offered by the

Bulgarian Telecommunications Company were to be raised eightfold. (World Bank, 1997).

The caretaker government promised to increase wages by 70 percent as of April 1, and to create a new social security system by the end of June. The average monthly wage was to reach $72 in April and $112 in December, the average pension $22 in April and $34 in December. The government would try to find ways to compensate the country's poorest citizens. Some 20 million ECU (European Currency Unit) provided by the European Union were to be distributed among one hundred fifty thousand families. Eighty-nine percent of Bulgarians said that they were poorer than they were the year before. The number of those living off their savings had doubled since 1995. According to the National Statistics Institute (NSI), almost every fourth Bulgarian had run up debts.

Then, in a historic shift, the results of the April 19 election brought a non Socialist party to power for the first time in Bulgaria since the communists seized power. The United Democratic Front (UDF) and its allies won 52 percent of the vote and 137 seats in the 240-member parliament. The leader of the UDF, Ivan Kostov (a former professor of economics), was installed as prime minister and the new parliament was convened for the first time on May 7. Kostov formed a cabinet which he said would rely on the reform majority in society to support reforms (*New Europe*, May 4-10, 1997).

In anticipation of the election results, the International Monetary Fund agreed to bail out Bulgaria with a $657 million loan (*Daily Chronicle*, April 14,1997). Bulgaria also won pledges of $285 million from the European Commission and support from the World Bank, a total package of about $1.2 billion. This represented a little more than the total foreign debt payments owed by Bulgaria. The accord was intended to stimulate investment through cash privatization and new jobs as well as to lower emigration. The agreement also targeted a budget reduction and a decrease in inflation. At the same time unemployment was expected to increase by the end of the year, as loss-making state enterprises were closed or restructured.

The Bulgarian Economy: Belated Market Reforms

At the end of World War II, Bulgaria was one of the least industrialized European countries. In 1948, only 18 percent of the workforce was employed outside the agricultural sector. The national income grew rapidly in the 1960s and early 1970s, averaging more than 6 percent annually during the 1960s and reaching 9 percent in 1975. Economic growth slowed markedly beginning in the late 1970s and was averaging only 1 to 3 percent in the late 1980s. Bulgaria's gross national product was $67.6 billion in 1988, or $7,540 per capita. The national currency, the *lev*, is not a convertible currency and has been tied to the Soviet ruble. The official *lev*-dollar exchange rate is, therefore, not necessarily an accurate index of the true value of the Bulgarian *lev*.

A major factor in Bulgaria's postwar growth rate was Soviet assistance which included raw materials at favorable prices, technical assistance, and substantial credits, partly in hard (convertible) currency. In contrast to some more developed Eastern European countries, which have suffered economically from their dependence on the Soviet Union, Bulgaria's ties with the Soviet Union brought economic benefits during most of the post World War II period. However, during the 1980s, reduced deliveries of Soviet raw materials and fuels, coupled with higher prices, reduced these benefits to Bulgaria.

Bulgaria's command economic system was patterned on the Soviet model. From 1948 on, the BCP government pursued a policy of rapid industrialization, so that about 80 percent of the workforce was employed in sectors other than agriculture. Industry remained the motor of Bulgarian economic growth until the early 1980s, when it became clear that this policy had carried the Bulgarian economy about as far as it could. Bulgaria has since launched a campaign to modernize its aging industrial base, increase efficiency, and introduce new technology such as robotics. The largest industrial sector is "machine building" (heavy industry), which accounts for more than a quarter of industrial production. The largest single industrial plant is the Metallurgical Combine at Kremilkovtsi (near Sofia), one of the largest iron and steel mills in the Balkans.

Economic reforms have not met with great success. For several years in the mid-1960s, it appeared that Bulgaria had launched a program of reform involving decentralization of decision making, a greater reliance on market forces, and even embryonic workers' councils. By 1968, however, fears aroused by the course of developments in Czechoslovakia and by domestic abuses in the use of decentralized authority prompted the BCP to reverse the trend toward decentralization. Beginning in 1971, productive enterprises were grouped into more than 60 state economic amalgamations responsible for almost all nonagricultural production. In the agricultural sector, state and collective farms began to be combined into "agrarian-industrial complexes" averaging forty four thousand to sixty six thousand acres. Beginning in 1979, halting attempts were made to decentralize the economic planning and decision making processes in both the industrial and agricultural sectors.

Despite its lower priority, agriculture has remained a key component of the economy. Although only about 40 percent of the land is arable, Bulgaria has one of the highest ratios of arable land to population in Eastern Europe. Small private farms exist, mainly in the uplands. The size of the private plots is based on the size of the household: one-half hectare is the maximum in most places; in mountainous areas, one hectare. Climate and soil conditions are suitable for raising livestock and for growing various grain crops, vegetables, fruits, and tobacco. More than one-third of the cultivated land is devoted to growing the principal grain crops—wheat, corn, and barley. Bulgaria is a major tobacco producer, the fourth largest exporter of tobacco, and the largest exporter of cigarettes in the CEE region (mainly to the former Soviet Union).

Bulgarian economic policies after 1990 initially created relatively favorable conditions for private sector development. Prices were liberalized, the state monopoly in foreign trade was abolished, real estate was restored, and privatization initiated. After steep declines in the early 1990s, Bulgaria's economy appeared to be rebounding, with a modest 2.4 percent growth in 1995. The internal transition to a market economy proceeded by fits and starts. By the end of 1995 the private sector was contributing just over 35 percent to the GDP, among the lowest percentages in the region. Per capita income had increased slightly over the past two years in nominal terms.

In September 1994, Bulgaria reached agreement with commercial bank creditors on debt and debt service reduction. The impact was to reduce the external debt from $12.5 billion at the end of 1993 to $10.4 billion at the end of 1994. The up-front costs of the buyback option of the debt agreement amounted to $716 million, which was funded by foreign currency reserves as well as loans from the IMF and World Bank. A third rescheduling of official obligations with the Paris Club was completed in April 1994, easing the country's liquidity problem.

But the Bulgarian economy was by no means out of the woods. Key laws related to finance and banking, the environment, nongovernmental organizations, and social programs had not been passed by the government. Weak control over the banking system, currency policies, and an increasing tax burden tended to undermine private sector growth. Socialist government policies led to inflation peaks of over 450 percent in 1991 and 300 percent by 1996. Consumer goods prices had risen over three hundred times since 1990.

These trends would culminate in the political and economic crisis beginning in early 1996. The GDP fell by 10.9 percent in 1996, compared with a decline of 2.5 percent in 1995, making the Bulgarian economy the weakest in the region. The long-awaited mass privatization was just getting under way. The proximate cause of the crisis was a run on the local currency in April 1996, prompted by growing instability in the banking sector and foreign exchange markets (*Business Central Europe*, 997). Interest rate hikes failed to restore confidence in the currency. Once forex reserves were exhausted, the *lev* plunged and inflation soared.

The crash of the banking system and the increase in inflation was felt most strongly in the summer of 1996. There ensued many bankruptcies of state as well as private enterprises as the crisis deepened. Small businesses in particular found it extremely difficult to rely on long-term planning and to secure funding and markets. Nevertheless, while the public sector of the economy shrank by more than 3 percent in the first seven months of 1996, the private sector actually grew by the same amount.

The establishment of the International Monetary Fund (IMF) -mandated currency board, an old colonial invention designed to make monetary policy in the colonies manageable, was one of the most important anticipated reforms under the new government formed after the elections of April 1997. A modern form of currency board had been used in Argentina in 1991, serving as a self-regulating mechanism to deal with hyperinflation and economic chaos. In the CEE region, Estonia and Lithuania have both implemented currency boards. A currency board puts monetary policy on automatic pilot, tying local interest rates and therefore inflation to an international anchor economy (typically the dollar or deutschmark). The new parliament is under intense pressure to implement these reforms and thus save the Bulgarian economy (*Business Central Europe*, 1997).

Jeffrey Sachs, Director of the Harvard Institute for International Development and prominent Bulgarian presidential adviser, expressed the opinion that the Bulgarian government should seek ways to restructure its heavy debt burden over both the short and the long term. He told a news conference in early March that a country with hyperinflation could not be expected to make net payments to the outside world to any significant extent. Sachs claimed that the country's small foreign reserves (about $400 million) cast doubt on the efficacy of a currency board. Noting that annual debt service was about 10 percent of GDP, Sachs lambasted the West in the spring of 1997 for being more concerned about the welfare of Western creditors than about the Bulgarian people.

PRIVATIZATION AND ECONOMIC GROWTH

The government decree on Economic Activity and Regulations in January 1989 provided for the restructuring of economic organizations as companies in Bulgaria, with varying forms of ownership and liability to bankruptcy. Theoretically, companies became free to engage in foreign trade, thereby ending the state's monopoly. The beginnings of a commercial banking system had come in late 1987 with the creation of eight new commercial banks, which initially functioned only as investment banks. Price controls were lifted in stages through the end of 1990. A new basic legal code for self-managing entities became effective in January 1991. However, reform since 1992 has slowed in critical economic restructuring areas such as public services pricing, industrial and agricultural privatization, and the banking sector.

Privatization in Bulgaria began in 1992, but the government has been slow to privatize state-owned assets on a case-by-case basis. Recognizing that traditional methods of privatization would not likely achieve the desired rapid expansion of private ownership, in 1994 the government initiated a Mass Privatization Program (MPP) using vouchers. Under the MPP, all Bulgarian citizens over the age of 18 were declared eligible to receive vouchers worth 25,000 *leva* (roughly $450) which could be redeemed for shares in companies directly or for shares of privatization funds set up for this purpose.

By the end of 1995, the legal framework for the MPP was successfully established, including a list of 1,063 enterprises approved for the first wave of privatization. The list represented some 35 percent of the total amount of Bulgaria's state-owned capital, 40 percent of which was expected to be privatized in the first wave. Registration for participation did not begin until January 1996, and privatization auctions were scheduled for later in the year. A newly established Securities and Exchange Commission was charged with the licensing and regulation of privatized funds.

The privatization program begun in 1995 differed substantially from those of previous years, and seemed to stand a chance of becoming a watershed year in Bulgaria's privatization history (Prohaska 1996). There were a number of favorable circumstances and reasons for this: clearly stated political support, as confirmed by the ambitious annual privatization program adopted by the parliament; intensifying activity on the part of the executive power in preparation for the launch of mass privatization; and significant amendments to the Transformation and Privatization of State-Owned and Municipal Enterprises Act.

For the first time, the program consisted not only of an agenda, but of conceptual elements as well. The document set forth annual objectives by sectors and branches, privatization techniques, financial instruments of payment, and organizational measures on the part of the authorities engaged in the preparation of privatization and the conclusion of transactions. In the beginning of 1996, a serious discrepancy had already emerged between the ambitious content and scope of the program and the actual results. For example, while the latter targeted tourism, the largest number of transactions concluded involved commercial companies.

With respect to the kinds of privatization transactions carried out, emphasis was placed on employee and management buyouts. Privatization practice in Bulgaria was still limited to a few time-consuming and highly bureaucratized techniques. There was a tendency for smaller entities and separate parts of enterprises to be sold through auctions, while the larger transactions were negotiated with potential buyers. This methodology conforms least to market principles and is only applied in exceptional cases in the advanced countries. When used as a privatization method, it is inevitably subject to bureaucratization. On the other hand, it is interesting to note that none of the "major" transactions concluded by the Privatization Agency in this manner have avoided becoming the object of public controversy.

Small-scale privatization was the second method prioritized in the Bulgarian privatization program. This term has not been legally defined either. Following the 1994 changes in the privatization law, small-scale privatization under Article 35 was defined to include trade, services, and small manufactures. Out of a total of 254 concluded transactions for the privatization of state-owned enterprises, 143 were carried out under Article 35 of the Transformation and Privatization of State-Owned and Municipal Enterprises Act.

By June 1996 there had only been 109 privatization transactions involving enterprises typical for Bulgaria in terms of size and economic significance. Only 65 of those involved whole enterprises, of which 18 were sold by the Privatization Agency. Those figures indicate that the actual scope of "real" privatization had been quite modest in terms of the number of transactions concluded. In fact, the privatization transactions carried out in 1995 amounted to just a little over 11 percent of the 584 transactions envisioned in the program, besides those carried out under Article 35. The increase in the number of transactions and the total amount of revenue surpassed the results of the previous two years, but the pace remained unsatisfactory.

In contrast, the status of municipal privatization has been much more promising than privatization of state enterprises. The decentralized approach at the municipal level under the Municipal Privatization Program has been somewhat more successful. Local government leaders have emerged as catalysts for local privatization and private sector reform, in spite of structural weaknesses and a poorly defined enabling environment. This activity was intended to implement a quick grassroots, transparent privatization as part of a larger program of decentralization and local government promotion. One of the objectives of the program has been to institutionalize the capability at the municipal level to continue the program of privatization. This has included developing the legal and technological framework for privatization: an auction format, voucher design, computer and public relations tender specifications, criteria for enterprise selection, and the list of the 1,063 companies targeted for privatization.

By number of transactions concluded (1,487) municipal privatization has far surpassed privatization of state-owned enterprises. Auctioning is the principal technique employed (excluding sales under Article 35 of the Privatization Law). This is an aggressive market mechanism with the most immediate financial impact. Even though the average value of individual entities sold is under four million *leva*, municipal privatization generates significant revenues.

The term *enterprise* is quite ambiguous in the case of privatization in the municipalities. Municipal privatization really involves the sale of industrial and commercial entities whose fixed assets are transferred by inventory. Municipal privatization directly and immediately creates "real" owners and, mainly in the larger towns, forms the very basis for small and medium-sized business. Unlike state privatization, the relative pace and characteristics of municipal privatization in Bulgaria are similar to those in the Czech Republic, Poland, and Hungary.

In some towns and regions, the process is developing at a very fast pace, sometimes even raising doubts that the municipalities might hastily divest themselves of commercial entities which, for a number of reasons, they would be wiser to keep for the next few years. In 1995, favorable conditions—possibilities for using new types of financial instruments, the greater experience of privatizing authorities, readiness of employees, managerial teams, and potential investors to participate in privatization—failed to be adequately used in speeding up the privatization process in Bulgaria. Contrary to expectations, the techniques and approaches to the privatization of state owned enterprises did not undergo any significant development in the course of 1995. Furthermore, surveys tended to reveal that the public was not even aware of the imminent start of mass privatization.

In sum, market or cash privatization and private foreign investment were severely hampered by bureaucratic lethargy or opposition. A precarious situation in the banking sector and slow progress in privatizing costly and inefficient state-owned enterprises were major impediments to the structural reform process. Despite this, progress toward mass privatization demonstrated that momentum for reform could be maintained by the Bulgarian government.

LOOKING TOWARD EUROPE

> We would not like to let our economic crisis hinder development of foreign policy.
>
> —Foreign Minister Stoyan Stalev, following caretaker
> government vote to seek membership in NATO

Of all the countries in the CEE region, Bulgaria would appear to have the least chance of joining NATO or the European Union in the near future. Despite a 1993 parliamentary declaration stating Bulgaria's desire to join NATO, the ruling Socialist Party fudged the issue due to traditionally warm ties with Russia, which of course strongly opposed the eastward expansion of NATO *(Reuters News Agency*, February 18, 1997). Then, in early 1997, the Socialists were forced to step down after a month of mass protests which had been fueled by the economic hardship. Immediately after taking office in January, the newly elected

President Petar Stoyanov stated Bulgaria's intention to seek membership in NATO during a visit to NATO headquarters in Brussels. The opposition Union of Democratic Forces had traditionally supported Bulgaria's bid to join NATO.

The new caretaker government then formally adopted an unambiguous declaration of intent to seek membership in NATO at the Madrid summit of July 1997. Foreign Minister Stoyan Stalev stated that Bulgaria would like to have its candidacy considered on a equal footing with those of other Eastern European countries. But Bulgaria had already fallen far behind the top contenders in the race for NATO membership. Besides, it had no patron to champion its cause as did Romania. Like other former communist countries, Bulgaria takes part in NATO's Partnership For Peace initiative which is designed to foster cooperation between NATO and former Cold War enemies. The foreign ministry was expected to work out a NATO accession plan which would include evaluation of the country's capacity to adjust to the standards of the alliance. However belatedly, Bulgaria joined the scramble to join Western European institutions.

THE ROLE OF SMES IN THE BULGARIAN ECONOMY

Like Czechoslovakia, Bulgaria embarked on the transition to a free market with an economy fully dominated by the state. The Bulgarian constitution did not allow for the right to private property. Private business activity was possible only under the heading of self-employment within strictly defined limits and sectors such as handicrafts, agriculture, cattle-breeding, and services. At the end of the decade of the 1980s, the share of the private sector in the Bulgarian GDP was no more than 5 percent, according to the National Statistics Institute (Stoyanovska and Krastenova, 1996). Within this rather hostile political and economic environment was born a modest private sector, composed largely of small and medium-sized enterprises.

During the early years of post-communist Bulgaria, the government of Bulgaria undertook a number of political and democratic reforms, passing over two hundred laws in the first few years after Bulgaria's 1989 political changes. Donor agencies began to help establish the underpinnings of a free market economy through liberalized pricing structures, expanded trade measures, right to private property, land restitution and liberal laws on privatization, and a legal framework for competition and foreign investment.

Bulgaria is lacking in consistent legislation regarding SME policy (Economic Commission for Europe, 1996). According to Decree No. 108 of 1991, small enterprises were considered entities and branches of traders and commercial companies and cooperative societies. Small businesses were defined as having fewer than 50 employees and maximum assets of 20 million Bulgarian *leva*. Under this law, small enterprises enjoy several advantages: they are eligible for loans with preferential interest rates, reimbursement of 50 percent of interest on loans used for investment purposes, and a single financial grant not to exceed 50 percent of their capital. There is no definition of a medium-sized enterprise.

More recently, the Law for the State Bank for Investment and Development (section 1.1) provided further definition of SMEs (Center for Study of Democracy 1997). In addition to the 50-employee limit, small enterprises cannot have a balance value of long-term material assets in excess of five thousand times the national average monthly salary. Medium enterprises are defined as those with no more than 100 employees and a balance of no more than ten thousand times the national average monthly salary. There is, however, no clear and appropriate Bulgarian definition of SMEs.

There have been laws promulgated that have bearing on SMEs. Registration of private companies in Bulgaria got under way following the adoption of the Council of Ministers' decree providing for business activity. There was an initial flurry of companies registered shortly thereafter; in fact, most of the firms registered in Bulgaria did so during the period from 1991 to 1993 in the hopes of obtaining financing. Every year since then, registration has declined. The exception to this trend was in the capital city of Sofia, where the peak period of registration was in 1993-1994. In the first years the highest number of registrations was in manufacturing and transport, whereas in subsequent years there have been more firms in commerce and construction.

The year of the company's registration does not necessarily coincidence with the date of start-up operations in the early years. One-third of the companies registered in 1990 did not begin their business activity until a year of so later. During the period of 1995-1996 the number of registrations declined, although the actual start-up date closely approximated the date of registration. More than half of those registered were in trade, while one-third of the firms were in industry, construction, and transport.

By 1995, fully 90 percent of the 194,800 economically active registered firms were micro-enterprises with three or fewer employees. Only 1 percent had more than 50 employees. There were over 1.2 million people employed in the private sector. By 1996 SMEs were contributing up to 30 percent of the registered GDP and were helping to compensate for five years of decline in the public sector. However, with the political and economic crisis, heretofore resilient small businesses began to register a downsizing of their activities for the first time since the transition began (Stanchev 1997).

The weaknesses and potential of the Bulgarian private sector are reflected in the fruits and vegetables industry (Grant 1996). Agriculture is very important to the Bulgarian economy; the vast majority of fruits and vegetable production is exported for hard currency. The Bulgarian export market has traditionally been oriented toward Russia and the countries of the former Soviet Union. In fact, exports to these countries as a percentage of the total actually increased from 1992 to 1995, with Russia accounting for 90 percent. Bulgaria has yet to develop market contacts outside of the former Soviet Union. With the reorientation of exports back toward Russia, Bulgarian exports to European Union countries and the Middle East have fallen correspondingly.

By 1996 processed fruit and vegetable production was only one-third the level of 1989, and exports declined accordingly. The private sector now accounts for about 25 percent of processed production. Nearly one hundred new private processing firms have started up over the past five years, many of them privatized former state and cooperative plants. Nevertheless, fully 75 percent of actual production and exports remains in the hands of 40 government owned factories. The latter continue to access scarce resources which are preventing the growth of private firms. Even though the subsector is export oriented, analysts say that the industry is in a state of collapse. Those same factors that have crippled it over the past five years are the ones capable of turning it around: privatization of the productive base, access to working capital from private firms, and land restitution.

Economic destabilization and deterioration of the Bulgarian business environment has greatly hampered the development of the SME sector. Not only has the sector suffered governmental neglect, it has been discriminated against by policies that subsidize the public state enterprise sector. Although all private enteprises have been affected by the macroeconomic failures, the SME sector has been particularly handicapped by its inability to access credit and information.

FINANCING SMES: BANK AND NONBANK SOURCES

For Bulgarians the road to a monetized economy has been a painful experience. To understand the evolution of Bulgaria's financial system, it is important to keep several things in mind (Miller and Petranova 1996). Under the old system, the Bulgarian currency, the *lev*, did not necessarily buy consumer goods. Banking was monolithic. And secondary markets for financial instruments did not exist. In a capitalist system money buys goods and resources that are directed toward those economic agents—enterprises and consumers—who have money. By contrast, in the communist system inputs to enterprise production were determined not by the money the enterprise had but by central planners using nonmonetary criteria.

In February 1991, prices in Bulgaria were freed. The economy was "monetized" over night, creating a new set of problems. Under the old system, many people had substantial savings because money had not been especially useful for purchasing consumer goods. When goods could finally be purchased with money, this created a large unmet demand for the exciting supply of goods. The ensuing sharp increase in prices generated an inflationary environment, which became an increasingly serious problem.

This basic change in the role of money entailed a redefinition of the financial arrangements and practices supporting a monetized economy. In June 1991, the Law on the Bulgarian National Bank came into effect, redefining the role of the central and commercial banks. The development of a financial sector in Bulgaria began with reform of the existing banking system. The monolithic bank was broken up into two tiers: a central bank and commercial banks. During the communist era, all banking functions had been handled by the Bulgarian National Bank (BNB) under the direct control of the Council of Ministers. Loans and accounts of the state enterprises were distributed among the new commercial banks. In addition to the BNB, the State Savings Bank was the only bank permitted to hold the accounts of individuals. The Bulgarian Foreign Trade Bank handled all foreign exchange operations for the country.

In 1981 Mineralbank was created, with the purpose of extending credits to small and medium-sized enterprises. Seven sector-specific commercial banks were set up in 1987 for lending long-term credits in such areas as the chemical industry or transportation. At the end of 1989, a major institutional reform took place in the banking system as it moved toward the two-tier system. The sector-specific banks were allowed to loan to all sectors of the economy. In addition, commercial banks were created from the 59 branches of the BNB, many of which were quite small. At the same time, new private banks began to operate; there were 22 by the end of 1994. Four foreign banks had opened branches in Bulgaria by the end of 1995. Two groups of banks began to emerge. One group is composed of the large state-owned banks and the First Private Bank, representing over 70 percent of the assets of the banking system. The other, consisting of all other small and medium-sized banks, although quite numerous, account for only one-sixth of the market.

The private sector is also gaining a modest share of the market, rising from just 1.5 percent of bank assets in 1991 to 15.4 percent in 1994. However, one negative aspect of the banking sector reform in Bulgaria was the distribution of loans of state enterprises to the newly formed commercial banks. The unfortunate legacy of these loans created a severe challenge for the banking system. The original loans to most state enterprises were not really loans at all. The money was extended without the risks of default on repayment being evaluated. Many of the state enterprises suffered from critical financial problems and were unable or unwilling to repay the credit. If they were written off, the banks holding them would be seriously threatened with insolvency. As time passed the problem worsened, because the state enterprises paid neither the interest nor the principal on the loans.

Two additional problems arose which made repayment of these loans difficult. When the economy suddenly moved away from central planning and the Council for Mutual Economic Assistance (CMEA) trade collapsed, state enterprises found that the demand for their products dropped precipitously. Even if they had been in a position to repay the loans before the transition began, it soon became impossible to do so. Many of the loans were in hard currency. During the latter part of the 1980s, Bulgaria borrowed heavily, creating a large foreign debt that was difficult to repay. The new commercial banks inherited the bad loan portfolios from the previous Bulgaria National Bank branches. If this had been an isolated problem for one or two banks it might have been resolved. However, it was widespread and thus threatened the viability of the entire newly formed system. Rather than force the collapse of the entire system before a solution to the problem could be found, banking authorities neglected to oblige the banks to do a careful accounting of their bad loans.

Furthermore, the problem of bad state enterprise loans was exacerbated by critical social and political factors. Many of the loans were given to large enterprises employing many workers. If they were forced to close, their workers would lose their jobs and unemployment would increase dramatically. Hence, these enterprises continued to approach the banks for additional loans even though they could not repay the old ones. There was a tacit understanding between the banks and the government that defaults would be covered by the government. Yet loans to the private sector received no such government protection. Indeed, it became harder for private firms to obtain bank credit because the state enterprise loans were perceived to carry less risk since they were implicitly backed by the government. Meanwhile, the commercial banks, whose principal function was to make loans to the business community, were extending very few loans to the private sector. In 1993, only 12 percent of total credit went to the private sector, and only a slightly higher percentage the following year. Since a quarter of the economy by then was accounted for by the private sector, this illustrates a continuing bias toward lending to the state sector to the detriment of the private sector.

GOVERNMENT AND DONOR AGENCY ASSISTANCE TO SMES IN BULGARIA

There are no well-established structures and institutions offering assistance to SMEs as yet in Bulgaria. No government agency exists to address the needs of SMEs as in other countries of the CEE region. As a result, the development of self-organized SME associations has become increasingly important. A few such associations have been formed and are beginning to offer business advisory assistance and to articulate SME policy advocacy. They are profiled below.

The Union for Private Economic Enterprise (UPEE)

Established in 1992, UPEE was the first organization with nonprofit status which was formed to defend and encourage the development of small and medium-sized firms in Bulgaria. UPEE's main objective is to assist private entrepreneurs to develop their businesses. The UPEE consists of a network of 40 regional and five branch structures throughout the country. In 1993, UPEE was acknowledged as an employers' representative and a member of the National Council for Tripartite Cooperation. UPEE has actively lobbied in favor of legislation to improve the lot of SMEs. The main premise is the creation of an institutional framework for an Agency for Small Enterprises that would be responsible for registering all companies. It would manage three funds: credit guarantees, small projects crediting, and training programs. UPEE participated in the European Union's PHARE Program survey of small businesses in Bulgaria.

Euro-Info Correspondence Center (EICC)

With support from organizations in the Netherlands and Belgium, the EICC began to evolve into an SME development group with UPEE in 1993. The focus was on training and consultancy, information, and business services. The consultancy unit focuses on providing advisory services to the entrepreneur. Training is also offered in start-up procedures and business planning. EICC publishes a biweekly information bulletin for its members. EICC has become part of the EU Network of two hundred fifty EICs and is registered with the PHARE consultancy register.

Association for Building Partnerships (BAP)

The US Agency for International Development (USAID) Mission in Bulgaria has assisted in the development of the Bulgarian Association for Building Partnership (BAP), a nongovernmental, nonprofit organization whose members are Bulgarian individuals and small businesses. The core of BAP organizers are former participants in a USAID participant training program. BAP is a fee-based membership organization with some one hundred dues-paying members, both individuals and firms.

The first BAP activity was a National Business Conference on SME Development held in Albena in November 1996, attended by two hundred fifty participants with the financial assistance of the USAID Mission. A report on the economic and legal environment for the development of SMEs was debated at the forum and subsequently incorporated into a legislative proposal. The Center for the Study of Democracy had sponsored the drafting of proposed legislation to promote policies and a legal environment favorable to small and medium enterprises. Delegates elaborated a ten-point plan for SME revitalization which was then conveyed to appropriate committees within the parliament. This advocacy effort was similar to that being promoted by UPEE. A second conference, attended by over two hundred participants and held in June 1997, also addressed economic and legislative issues related to SMEs. Over half of the participants were business owners and managers, while others were from government agencies, banks, and embassies.

Institute for Market Economics (IME)

The IME, established in 1993 as the first independent economic think tank in Bulgaria, is registered as a nonprofit organization. IME's mission is to assess the trends in emerging capital markets in the country. It undertakes independent analysis of government economic policies and serves as the focal point for exchange of views on market economics. Since its beginning, IME has been a partner in the International Council for Economic Growth network of public policy institutes. In 1995, IME launched a public debate on mass privatization in cooperation with the World Bank mission in Sofia. The same year IME initiated a project on strengthening business associations in Bulgaria in partnership with the Center for International Private Enterprise.

Center for the Study of Democracy (CSD)

Established as an independent public policy research institution with USAID funding in 1990, the Center has gained considerable experience in monitoring public attitudes, privatization, and economic reform, and media and audience behavior. Its policy paper on the legal environment for SMEs in Bulgaria is one of the most extensive studies of this type in the CEE region.

EU PHARE Program

In 1992, the European Union PHARE Program sponsored a 22.5 million ECU local structural development program, the only SME support program financed by the EU thus far in Bulgaria. This program has met with serious delays which has resulted in most of the funds being reallocated to other projects within Bulgaria (Center for Study of Democracy 1997). Only 7 million ECU was left for SME development, to be disbursed for direct firm-level financial assistance. However, by the end of 1996, less than 1 million ECU had been allocated. The problems associated with the PHARE program in Bulgaria are very much related to the lack of participation of commercial banks. Banks proved to be overly cautious in reviewing loan applications and extending credit. Likewise, there were few appropriate loan candidates who were able to fill out the applications properly.

The PHARE 9105 Project provided funding for the study of SMEs in Bulgaria which was conducted in 1996 and published in December of that year. Within the framework of that study, the Euro-Info Correspondence Center was created and the study carried out by its staff in cooperation with GfK Bulgaria.

PROFILES OF SUCCESSFUL BULGARIAN ENTREPRENEURS

A profile of the SME sector in Bulgaria is provided in surveys of Bulgarian business owners. In 1995 Jan Svejnar and associates undertook a comparative survey of SMEs in Bulgaria and Russia, using a sample of 221 in Bulgaria and 216 in Russia (Svejnar, 1996). In Bulgaria, the cutoff for SME size was two hundred employees. It included both private companies and 22 state-owned enterprises. The main purpose of the study was to examine the widespread belief that lack of credit was the most important obstacle to the growth of SMEs. The study attempted to provide a deeper understanding of constraints to SME development with a view toward informing policy. This was based on the assumption that it is necessary to understand the factors underlying financial constraints in order to design successful lending and other policies to support SMEs.

The profile of Bulgarian small businesses that emerged was overwhelmingly of individual or family ownership. Typically, the SMEs surveyed were characterized by a highly concentrated ownership structure. Virtually none had foreign owners. Nearly all the Bulgarian firms interviewed (82 percent) started as new companies as opposed to having been spun off from existing companies. Very few indicated that they had existed previously as part of a state-owned enterprise. Thus, it is not surprising that most of the companies were quite young. The average Bulgarian SME in the survey had started its operations in 1989 and obtained its legal status in 1991, while the average Russian SME had started in 1986. Virtually all the companies in the Bulgarian sample were independent companies rather than subsidiaries. In terms of corporate structure, 39 percent of the Bulgarian firms were classified as limited liability, followed by unlimited liability (single operator/family) companies, 37 percent; and partnerships, 19 percent. The average size of the firm in the Bulgarian sample had 27 employees.

The Svejnar study explored the obstacles and constraints faced by SME managers in Bulgaria. Managers in each company were asked to rate the severity of the various constraints. Responses were grouped into seven broad categories: procurement and production, including technology issues; sales; finance; infrastructure; regulation and taxation; labor; and business services. The main constraints identified in the area of production were linked to the inability of suppliers to deliver on orders. Also cited was the high rate of duties on imported goods. Nearly as important was the problem of prices of local goods changing in a frequent and unpredictable manner.

An EU PHARE-funded survey in 1996 also examined the role of small businesses in Bulgaria, drawing upon data from the National Statistics Institute (Stoyanovska and Krastenova 1996). Conducted in March 1996, the study surveyed 450 firms from a sample of small and medium-sized firms, based on the definition in the Official Gazette (issue no. 88 of 1995). Small companies were defined as those with 50 or fewer employees while medium-sized firms were those with 51 to 100 employees. The study included only private firms in which the share of state ownership was less than 49 percent. Three-fourths of all the firms interviewed defined themselves as small.

The prevailing legal form reported in the PHARE study was sole trader (60 percent), followed by limited liability (14 percent), sole limited liability (9 percent), partnership (8 percent), cooperative (5 percent), and joint stock company (2 percent). None was reported to be unregistered. Those firms operating as limited liability were mostly in Sofia and bigger towns and were mainly in manufacturing and construction. Business activity was most favorable for manufacturing firms in 1995 while construction and transportation companies showed a decline in turnover over the previous year. Those smaller firms with fewer than 20 employees were forced to reduce their activities whereas those with more than 20 employees tended to report a growth in turnover.

For 59 percent of the PHARE study respondents, their own savings was the main financial source for starting their businesses. Family savings was the main source of funding for 38 percent of respondents, and loans from friends for 26 percent. Only 30 percent of those interviewed said they had received credits from a bank for the start-up.

Only 17 percent of firms with fewer than 10 employees reported using bank credits for everyday activities, and 44 percent of those with over 50 employees did so. Clearly, there remains a low degree of support for small businesses among government agencies and the banking system, despite officially declared policies for assisting the private sector.

Bulgarian private business is still predominantly local, rarely going beyond the national borders. Local neighborhoods and nearby towns are the primary market for 59 percent of the PHARE study respondents. Only 37 percent operate on the regional level and 25 percent on the national level, while 12 percent have reached international markets. Very few of these, only 3.5 percent, have met the rigorous standards required by Western European markets. However, among manufacturing firms, one-fourth have gained access to foreign markets. The major clients of the typical Bulgarian small business are individual customers, at 59 percent; private merchants are the main clients for 42 percent of the respondents; and only 17 percent work with mainly with state-owned enterprises. Following are profiles of individual firms:

Finsys Consulting Company

Finsys is a Bulgarian consulting firm whose president is Dr. Nikola Hristovich. The company was able to literally capitalize on the mass privatization process in Bulgaria. As a result of attending seminars for privatization fund managers and private consultants, Finsys developed the most comprehensive computer database in the country, consisting of more than one thousand Bulgarian companies on the mass privatization list. The list yields comparative financial performance data over three consecutive years and generates profit/loss forecasts and analyses of the investment risk associated with the companies. It thus proved to be a great asset to privatization funds and investors during the mass privatization process. Finsys held a series of seminars with American and Bulgarian lecturers on Bulgarian business issues such as corporate governance of newly privatized companies, meetings of privatization funds, and portfolio management.

Favorite Vision

This is an independent Bulgarian limited company registered in 1990. It was founded initially as a video production company and has expanded to include film and radio production facilities. George Menev, the managing director, previously worked for a state-owned company and is assisted by Valery Petrov, general manager and director of photography. Favorite Vision employs a full-time financial director, production manager, and five executives as well as a number of freelance directors, actors, musicians, photographers, and editors as needed. The firm's clients have included such well known companies as McDonald's, Nestle's, Audi, and numerous local firms. Favorite Vision did filming on contract with the CNN television network for a segment on the Bulgarian elections in April 1997.

THE POTENTIAL FOR SME DEVELOPMENT IN BULGARIA

This is going to look like a great year for Bulgaria.

—Stuart Parkinson, Deutsche Morgan Grenfell
senior economist, April 1998

In August 1997, after 100 days in office, Ivan Kostov's new center-right coalition United Democratic Front government in Bulgaria appeared to be succeeding in facing the challenge of much-needed reforms (*New Europe*, September 7—October 13, 1997). Kostov, leader of the Union of Democratic Forces, had been forced to fight the economic malaise of hyperinflation, an obsolete state-dominated economic apparatus, and a quasi-legal business mafia. He had initiated sweeping price liberalization. An 18-month deal with the International Monetary Fund was signed, which had already produced its third tranche payment. The currency board appeared to have stabilized the currency and inflation. Interest rates had fallen and the banking system appeared stabilized.

The Kostov government had also managed to complete the first wave of mass privatization, which was long overdue. It was preparing to pursue the sale of large state enterprises to foreign investors. The parliament was beginning to address government legislative proposals for a wide range of policy reforms. New privatization amendments were intended to speed up trading in mass voucher privatization shares. Smaller enterprises were to be sold by the respective ministries, enabling the Privatization Agency to concentrate on the most profitable transactions. Public opinion polls conducted in August 1997 suggested that the government's initiatives continued to enjoy wide support. One of the reasons for the support may well have been the crack down on organized crime.

By April 1998 it appeared that the Bulgarian economy had pulled back from the brink of chaos (*New Europe*, April 5-11, 1998). Since February 1997, when hyperinflation and street demonstrations led to early elections resulting in the downfall of the government, the Bulgarian economy had begun a slow but steady recovery. Funding agreements with multilateral lenders helped the government to slash inflation and interest rates, which in turn began to restore financial stability. In some respects, the Bulgarian economy looked so good in 1998 because it had looked so bad the year before. The new government expected inflation to fall to as low as 16 percent from a high of over 500 percent in 1997. The economy was expected to grow by as much as 4 percent after an 8 percent decline in 1997 if reforms remained on track.

The economic devastation which the Kostov government faced was reflected in the fact that during the first half of 1997 the GDP fell by 9.8 percent. The World Bank praised Bulgaria's reform performance while pointing out that more work was needed to sustain the stability achieved (*New Europe*, October 5-11, 1997). The government and the Bank signed an agreement marking completion of targets for a $100 million Financial and Enterprise Sector Adjustment Loan (FESAL). This represented a landmark in the country's economic reform, the first stage of the structural reform program. The Bank earmarked an additional $80 million FESAL-2 loan upon completion of the second stage, which would include privatizing 40 percent of long-term state assets and selling six state banks.

SMEs are continuing to operate in a generally hostile environment in Bulgaria. Small businesses in countries such as Bulgaria are fewer in number and face more severe obstacles to development than do those in CEE countries further along in transition process. One of the most serious problems facing Bulgaria in the immediate future is likely to be an increase in the rate of unemployment as a result of the stabilization program and the downsizing of state-owned enterprises. Already in 1997 unemployment was projected to reach 25 percent for the year. This could be both a curse and a blessing. As state-owned enterprises are restructured, workers are laid off to join the ranks of the unemployed. For their part, small businesses can create new jobs if the proper incentives are provided for their growth and development, thereby turning adversity into advantage. However, there are a number of problems that must be dealt with for this to happen.

The economy is characterized by a weak system of incentives and institutional features designed to induce firms to maximize profits rather than output. The most important constraints identified by Bulgarian entrepreneurs to their operations in the Svejnar study were as follows:

1. *Suppliers are often not ready to deliver.* Weak suppliers are a particular problem for Bulgarian manufacturing firms, whose managers lack formal education, and where there is a relative lack of capital intensity and labor productivity.

2. *Firms are facing financing problems that hinder expanding production.* This constraint, while important both in absolute and relative terms, was not linked in the Svejnar survey to any of the observable characteristics of the firm, the manager, or the environment.

3. *Firms are faced with a high level of interests rates.* Policies must address the problem of high interest rates and lack of access to cheaper credit sources such as local government credit.

In sum, the Svejnar study noted that in the early stages of transition, the success of SMEs depends to a large extent on their ability to do business with the state enterprises. Findings indicated that these enterprises and government agencies tend to discriminate or project the image that they discriminate against the SMEs in awarding contracts. Their delinquency in payments also makes it difficult for SMEs to do business with the state sector.

Access to credit is a universal problem for small businesses, as reflected in the Svejnar study. The integration of SMEs into the formal credit system in Bulgaria remains quite limited. Only 37 percent of the Bulgarian firms interviewed had obtained a loan from a financial institution over the past three years. Only 25 percent of the firms indicated that they knew anything about financing programs for SMEs such as PHARE and only a handful (eight) had ever used such a program. The Bulgarian SMEs not only seek credit, but they also extend credit to their customers. This finding tends to contradict the anecdotal evidence of a cash-in-advance economy in transition. SMEs lend to some clients deemed to be creditworthy and not to others.

Miller and Petranov (1996) note that the Bulgarian government and the state enterprise sector continue to make such large demands on bank funds that little remains for the development of the private sector. Because virtually no private financial intermediation has developed as competition, borrowers who need large sums to start production projects have little recourse other than the banks.

Clearly, methods must be found to encourage banks to participate more fully in private sector development. From their point of view, it is difficult for banks to evaluate risks because of the high degree of uncertainty in the economy. Most bank loan officers lack the expertise and experience necessary to evaluate small business loan applications. At the same time, it must also be noted that the typical entrepreneur seeking a bank loan is likely to be similarly inexperienced, lacking the skill to write a business or marketing plan. The inability to obtain credit from the banks has forced most private entrepreneurs to finance their activities out of their own savings, thereby limiting the scope of their operations. This has made it difficult to start even modest production activities.

Miller and Petranov have suggested that an alternative means for pooling risks would be to develop nonbank financial intermediaries such as savings and loan associations. They note, however, that these institutions are difficult to establish since savers must have confidence in the management before they will trust them with their savings. They are just beginning to develop in Bulgaria and will enjoy the advantage of not having been associated with the state in the past. An unanswered question in Bulgaria is how the present growth of the small-scale private sector is being financed, since its access to banks has been so limited. Personal and family savings are not generally sufficient to finance substantial productive activities.

The Center for the Study of Democracy (CSD) in its policy paper entitled "The Policy and Legal Environment for the Growth of the SME sector in Bulgaria" (1997) spells out a series of actions necessary to promote SMEs. The CSD calls for the development of an "anti-crisis program" in which the role of SMEs is to be clearly stated. All measures identified in the paper aim at strengthening the SME sector to help stabilize the Bulgarian economy. In the first instance, the CSD calls for a strategy of full-scale privatization, with particular focus on SME privatization. Only a relatively small portion of state-owned enterprises are large (10 to 15 percent), the remainder consisting mostly of medium-sized firms. The authorities should give priority to selling off the SMEs (small-scale privatization) quickly and expeditiously as has happened in other CEE countries.

The CSD policy paper calls for decisive measures to establish steady tax policy and practices. Small businesses in general tend to complain about taxes. Often it is not so much the amount of taxes as the arbitrariness and cumbersomeness, the ineffective and inconsistent work of the tax authorities, that is at issue. It is imperative to abolish the practices of backdated taxes and the frequent amending of tax policies.

The CSD paper also calls for the development of a clear definition of SMEs along the lines of those proposed by the European Union, through which a proper framework of support for the sector can be based. This is necessary so that SME programs, policies, and laws can be implemented with distinct constituents. It is also important to begin to conform to international standards in order not to be excluded from capital and technical assistance accorded by donor agencies.

Coupled with this is the need to establish an institutional infrastructure, including a government agency for the promotion of SMEs. Two SME programs administered by the Ministry of Industry and funded by EU PHARE have been fairly successful, according to the CSD. Regional development agencies have been established in two regional towns to provide seminars and training and business centers set up in two others. Existing business advisory services like those profiled above are mostly centered in Sofia with very tentative outreach to regional centers. A special fund is proposed to provide for credit guarantees to SMEs, export insurance, business incubators, and innovation centers. Another element of public policy that hinders the development of SMEs is the inadequate cooperation with the international financial institutions. The European Bank for Reconstruction and Development, for example, has provided 90 percent of its support to the public sector and only 10 percent to the private sector, even though the bank was created to support the sectors equally.

Two developments offer some hope for changes that will encourage the SME sector. First, on October 23, 1996, a law providing for the creation of a state bank for investments and development was approved in the Bulgarian parliament. Next, a second bill on SMEs is under debate in the Economic Commission of the parliament.

REFERENCES

Business Central Europe "Bulgaria After the Storm" April 1997.
Business Central Europe "Political Mantra" April 1997.

Center for the Study of Democracy 1997 *Policy and Legal Environment for the Growth of the SME Sector in Bulgaria: Policy Paper* Sofia: Bulgaria, January.

Daily Chronicle "IMF Agrees $657 Million Loan to Bail out Bulgaria" Sofia, April 14, 1997.

Economic Commission for Europe (ECE) 1996 *Small and Medium-Sized Enterprises in Countries in Transition* ND/AC.3/1 Geneva: Regional Advisory Services Programme, Industry and Technology Division, February.

Grant, William 1996 "Bulgarian Processed Fruits and Vegetables Subsector Survey" Sofia: FLAG Consortium, October.

Miller, Jeffrey, and Stefan Petranov 1996 *Banking in the Bulgarian Economy* second edition Sofia: Bulgarian National Bank.

New Europe: Global Independent Weekly "Bulgaria's UDC Nominates Reformist Kostov as PM" May 4-10, 1997.

New Europe: Global Independent Weekly "100 Days Strong: Bulgaria's Government Finally Faces Up to the Challenge of Tough Reforms" September 7-13, 1997.

New Europe "Zhivkov's Release Revives Bitterness" September 28-October 4, 1997.

New Europe "Bulgaria to Meet Debt Payments" October 5-11, 1997.

New Europe "Is Bulgaria the Success Story of the Year?" April 5-11,1998.

Prohaska, Maria 1996 "Bulgarian Privatization Results" in Center for International Private Enterprise's *CEE Regional Newsletter* Budapest, June.

Reuters News Agency "Bulgaria Says It Wants to Be A Full NATO Member" February 18, 1997.

Stoyanovska, Antonina, and Elena Krastenova 1996 *SME Development In Bulgaria*

Sofia: Informa Intellect Ltd. part of PHARE 9105 Projet for developing SMEs in Bulgaria, with collaboration of the Union for Private Economic Enterprise and the Institute for Marketing Studies.

Stanchev, Krassen 1997 "Bulgaria's Caretaker Cabinet" Institute for Market Economics Newsletter Vol. 4, No. 1, January-February, 1997.

Svejnar, Jan, Francesca Pissarides, and Miroslav Singer 1996 "Small and Medium- Sized Enterprises in Transition: Evidence from Bulgaria and Russia" (mimeograph) Prague: CERGE-EI.

World Bank 1997 "Milestones of Transition" *Transition Newsletter*, Vol. 8, No. 3, April.

CHAPTER 3

The Czech Republic

CZECH REPUBLIC

The Czech Republic Profile

Area: 78,703 square kilometers, slightly smaller than South Carolina

Bordering countries: Austria, Germany, Poland, and Slovakia

National capital: Prague

Population: 10,298,324 (July 1997 est.)

Population growth rate: -0.13% (1997 est.)

Ethnic groups: Czech 94.4%, Slovak 3%, Polish 0.6%, German 0.5%, Gypsy 0.3%, Hungarian 0.2%, other 1%

Religions: atheist 39.8%, Roman Catholic 39.2%, Protestant 4.6%, Orthodox 3%, other 13.4%

Languages: Czech, Slovak

GDP real growth rate: 5% (1996 est.)

GDP per capita: purchasing power parity ($11,100 1996 est.)

Inflation rate—consumer price index: 8.7% (1996 est.)

Unemployment rate: 3.3% (1996 est.)

Administrative divisions: 8 regions (*kraje, kraj*—singular)

Natural resources: hard coal, soft coal, kaolin, clay, graphite

Independence: January 1, 1993 (from Czechoslovakia)

National holiday: National Liberation Day, May 8; Founding of the Republic, October 28; Constitution ratified December 16, 1992; effective January 1, 1993

Chief of state: President Vaclav Havel (since 26 January 1993);

Head of government : Prime Minister Vaclav Klaus (from June 1992 until November 1997); Josef Tosovsky, caretaker Prime Minister to June 1998 elections

Source: U.S. State Department

The Czech Republic

HISTORIC AND ECONOMIC SETTING IN THE CZECH REPUBLIC

> The fall of the Communist empire is an event on the same scale of historical importance as the fall of the Roman Empire. And it has similar consequences, both good and extremely disturbing.
>
> —Vaclav Havel, *Toward a Civil Society,* from a speech at George Washington University, Washington, DC, April 1993, p. 224.

Sandwiched between Germany and Austria, with a population of just over ten million in an area of 30,450 square miles, the Czech Republic is among the smallest European countries. In terms of population, it is similar in size to Austria, Belgium, and Hungary . The vast majority of the population are ethnic Czechs (95 percent), with small minorities of Slovaks, Poles, Germans, and Jews. The Czech language is part of the family of west Slavic languages (together with Polish and Slovak). The golden era of Czech history dates from the House of Luxembourg in the fourteenth century when Bohemia was the center of the Holy Roman Empire. Prague was renowned as one of the great cultural centers in all of Europe. Eventually the Czech kingdom became absorbed into the Austro-Hungarian monarchy (CERGE-EI 1997).

After World War I, Czechoslovakia emerged from the ruins of the Austro-Hungarian empire as a modern democratic state consisting of Bohemia and Moravia, Slovakia, and Carpatho-Russia (part of modern-day Ukraine). It was the most industrially developed part of the former Austro-Hungarian monarchy, competing with the most advanced countries in Europe. By the 1930s, Czechoslovakia ranked among the top 10 most industrialized countries in Europe. Close financial and industrial links with the rest of Europe were forged and trade expanded. By 1921, already one-third of the working population was employed in the industrial sector. By 1937, this sector accounted for as much as 35 percent of the national income. In 1939, Slovakia separated from Czechoslovakia; the Czech part of the country was occupied by the German army and incorporated into the German Empire. In 1945 Czechoslovakia was liberated by the Soviet and American armies. The Czechoslovak state was subsequently restored, without Carpatho-Russia, which joined the Soviet Union.

In February 1948, the Communist Party gained power in a formal constitutional arrangement, and Czechoslovakia remained under Soviet domination for the next 41 years. By 1952, the new government had nationalized all sectors of the economy, taking over all commercial and industrial enterprises with over 50 employees. By 1960, private enterprises with employees had been officially abolished and collectivization of agriculture was nearly complete. Modest reforms were introduced in 1965 with the introduction of firm-level decision-making based on profitability and wage differentials. But further efforts to liberalize the economy led to the Warsaw Pact invasion of 1968 (Webster and Swanson 1993). Czechoslovakia went further in eliminating the private sector than did Poland and Hungary. By 1989, only 1 percent of the population was privately employed. Small craftsmen who remained in the private sector were tightly controlled, highly taxed, and subject to local officials.

During the 1970s and 1980s, Vaclav Havel, a Czech dramatist born in 1936, gained fame around the world as the leader of a dissident movement in Czechoslovakia. In 1989 he founded Civic Forum, a broad democratic coalition of political parties which fomented the Velvet Revolution of 1989. Following the Velvet Revolution, Soviet control came to an end, and Czechoslovakia embarked on the road to a free market and democratic order. However, the relationship between the Czech and Slovak regions of the country had been occasionally tense over the years. A federal constitution had been introduced in 1968 in response to the Slovak desire for greater self-determination. In 1990 Havel became president of federal Czechoslovakia and served in that capacity until the dissolution of the federation in 1992. From 1990 onward, the Czech and Slovak political parties negotiated the future form of the federation. Following the parliamentary elections of 1992, the decision to divide the country into two separate republics was made.

The political evolution of the Czech Republic in the transition years differed significantly from that of other countries in the region. While voters elsewhere were bringing in majority coalitions headed by former communist parties opposed to major economic reforms, in June 1992 Czechs chose a center-right majority coalition that had campaigned on a platform of rapid and basic economic transformation. At the same time the Slovaks were choosing a left-of-center coalition.

On January 1, 1993, the Czech and Slovak republics were peacefully established as separate and independent states. Vaclav Havel became the first president of the Czech Republic, although with no party affiliation. Vaclav Klaus, a former professor of economics and founder of the Civic Democratic Party, became the first prime minister of the new Czech government, having served as minister of finance in the federal government. His right-of-center conservative party was the driving force of the economic and political transition during the period from 1992. Klaus became renowned for his dedication to free-market capitalism in the Thatcher tradition.

The main opposition was the Social Democratic Party (SDP), a left-of-center party which was the successor to the Czechoslovak Social Democratic Party founded in 1948 and forced to merge with the Communist Party in the same year. The Social Democrats were restored in March 1990. The Czech and Moravian Communist Party, the unreformed post-communist party, was founded in 1990 as successor to the former Communist Party which had been founded in 1921.

Jan Svejnar and his colleagues at the Center for Economic Research and Graduate Education-Economics Institute (CERGE-EI) of Charles University in Prague have documented the evolution of Czech macroeconomic policies and outcomes during the initial transition period (Svejnar, 1995). They note that before World War II, Czechoslovakia had a GDP per capita comparable to that of Austria, with great potential for growth. However, with the annexation of the country by the Soviet Union in 1948, the economy was progressively underdeveloped. By 1990, the GDP per capita was estimated at $3,300, comparable to that of Venezuela and Yugoslavia. As in other transition economies in the region, the first several years of the Czechoslovak transition were marked by a significant decline in economic activity.

Nevertheless, the country enjoyed a number of advantages—some of them derived from the policies of the former communist government—that would benefit the new government. Under the communists, the country had had a long history of nonexistent inflation and low foreign debt. The country had mastered the planning process so that shortages of goods and monetary "overhang" were not as pronounced as in other Soviet bloc countries. The ancient city of Prague became an instant magnet for Western tourists, generating income and fueling potential for rapid development. Prague's Velvet Revolution became a cultural icon attracting thousands of youth from around the world. The country's proximity to Western European countries also facilitated the flow of goods, capital, technology, and people. These factors conspired to give the country a fairly favorable basis for launching economic transformation.

The principal aim of the Czechoslovak policy makers who came to power during the Velvet Revolution was to maintain macroeconomic stability while introducing a market economy. The government that was brought to power in the wake of the Velvet Revolution declared the twin aims of introducing a market economy and achieving integration into the Western economies to be of prime importance for reestablishing economic prosperity. After a year of debate and preparation, in the fall of 1990 the government gradually began to introduce a major set of reform measures. There was a general reduction of the role of the state in the economy, including a strong push for privatization accompanied by a decrease in government subsidies to state-owned firms. The Czechoslovak crown was immediately devalued vis-a-vis the dollar. Producer and consumer prices were liberalized and wage controls were introduced.

In several respects, the measures introduced by the Czechoslovak authorities resembled those initiated by the Polish government the year before. There were, however, significant differences. In 1990 the Czechoslovak economy was much less market-oriented than that of Poland. On the other hand, Czechoslovakia enjoyed a stable macroeconomic position characterized by low inflation, budget deficit, and foreign debt. The Czechoslovak government pursued restrictive fiscal policies resulting in budget deficits of less than 3 percent of the GDP in 1991 and 1992, at a time when almost all transitional economies were experiencing significant budget deficits. Indeed, the Czech Republic was the only country in the region that managed to maintain a balanced budget. A comprehensive system of taxes was initiated, culminating on January 1, 1993, when corporate and individual income taxes and a value added tax were introduced.

Government policy toward financing private firms constituted an important stimulus for their creation. Bank credit to private enterprises grew from virtually zero in mid-1990 to over 71 billion crowns at the end of 1991 and over 125 billion by mid-1992. Credit to private companies reached the equivalent of 12 percent of total credit extended by banks to state-owned enterprises at the end of 1991, and 22 percent by mid-1992, when large-scale privatization of state enterprises began.

The Czech economic success in the early years of transition was often presented as macroeconomic stabilization. Unlike most other economies in the region, Czechoslovakia enjoyed a considerable initial advantage of virtual price stability. Consumer prices rose from a rate of only 1.4 percent in 1989 to 9.7 percent in 1990 as the first policy measures took effect, then jumped to 56 percent in 1991 as prices were freed on a large scale. By 1994 consumer prices were back down to around 10 percent, the lowest of all the countries in the region. Likewise, inflation rates rose to 21 percent in 1993, in part because of the introduction of the value added tax, but then declined to 10 percent in 1994. Together with Slovakia and Hungary, the Czech Republic registered the lowest rate of inflation in the region.

The overall performance of the Czech GDP during the initial transition period offered a measure of relative economic success. While all countries in the egion registered negative GDP growth rates during 1990 and 1991, only Poland had turned the corner to record positive growth by 1992. Between 1990 and 1993 the Czech economy recorded negative growth rates ranging from 14 percent to 0.3 percent. Following the separation of the Czech and Slovak Republics in 1993, the Czech Republic succeeded in halting its GDP decline. By 1994 the economy was growing at a rate of 2.5 percent, compared with a robust 5 percent growth rate in neighboring Poland and zero growth in Bulgaria and Romania. The initial decline in the Czech GDP was to a large extent tied to a fall in industrial production, as was the case in most of the countries in the region. Not until 1994 did a turnaround in production occur.

After the quick fiscal stabilization and successful trade reorientation, the Czech economy began to grow at modest rates, while preserving low or moderate external indebtedness. Unemployment remained low, at around 3 percent, while inflation hovered at around 9 percent. Indeed, employment decline was much less pronounced during the period from 1990 to 1993 than that of the GDP, averaging 0.1 percent in 1990, 5.4 percent in 1991, and 1.5 percent in 1993.

In forestalling the rise of unemployment, the Czech Republic was a success, by both Eastern and Western European standards. Since 1990,

Czech unemployment has not exceeded 4.4 percent. In contrast, the Slovak unemployment rate reached 11 percent in 1991 and remained between 10 percent and 16 percent thereafter. Svejnar and associates advance the explanation that this was due in large part to the rapid growth of new, labor-intensive firms and the willingness of Czech workers to start their own private businesses or find work in Germany and Austria. At the same time, privatized enterprises struggled to find effective owners capable of rendering them internationally competitive. Banks and financial conglomerates had yet to become efficient intermediaries, and regulatory frameworks still needed to be strengthened and applied more rigorously.

While Hungary and Poland made the attraction of foreign investment a priority after the collapse of communism, the Czech Republic simply included it as one of its objectives in the first stage (Gray 1996). Although the government awarded the voucher scheme greater priority, it was sometimes difficult to reconcile with the needs of foreign investors. Furthermore, the Czech government phased out tax concessions to foreign investors in 1992. Some major investments were completed before the voucher system was launched. In the largest single investment, Volkswagen formed a joint venture with the Skoda car manufacturer. The cigarette industry was sold to Philip Morris, and most of the lime and cement industry was privatized and sold to foreign interests. However, after the first flurry of deals, few others were arranged that did not involve voucher privatized companies. In October 1995, American businessman Michael Dingman established Stratton Investments, a financing vehicle for buying significant stakes in eight Czech companies from voucher funds, the biggest deal of its kind.

Spring 1997: The Bloom Comes Off the Czech Economic Miracle

Six years after the reforms begun in Czechoslovakia, and four years after the birth of the Czech Republic, Czechs found that political and macroeconomic stability and fast privatization of state enterprises— while a necessary prerequisite for successful reforms—were only the first steps toward industrial restructuring and maintaining high economic growth rates.

Barring devaluation of the Czech crown in order to boost exports, by early 1997 it appeared that an economic slowdown might turn into a recession. Czech wages had become the highest in Central Europe *(The Prague Post* April 23-29, 1997). But the slowdown in export performance, modest productivity gains, and failure to bring down inflation further were indications that the easier part of restructuring might have come to an end. Since waste and inefficiencies had been so endemic under socialism, it had been relatively easy for Czech enterprises to take advantage of export markets close by when they were faced with hard budget constraints and rapid privatization at home—two key reforms applied more rigorously in the Czech Republic than in the other Central European countries.

There were several other signs of a weak economic performance (Hewer 1997):

- The GDP was expected to grow by less than 4 percent in 1997.

- The current account deficit reached 8 percent of the GDP in 1996. The foreign trade deficit more than doubled over a year to nearly $6 billion (160 billion crowns), followed by a 1997 first-quarter trade deficit of $1.3 billion (40.2 billion crowns).

- The budget deficit for the first quarter of 1997 reached some $330 million (10 billion crowns) and was growing. Between 1992 and 1996, the government maintained a balanced budget every year. There was a widening gap between planned budgetary income and lower-than-expected tax revenues, for several reasons. First, economic growth was slowing (the budget was calculated on the basis of 5.4 percent real GDP growth for 1997). Second, the debt owed to the state by many companies and banks had grown to around 40 billion crowns for taxes and 7 billion crowns for social and health care contributions. Third, "creative" accounting—a way of getting around tax payment—used by large companies and other corporate institutions was considerably reducing taxable income.

- Most larger enterprises were still struggling with over employment (official unemployment was only 4.1 percent), low labor productivity, and low profitability.

Micro economic transformation—streamlining, rationalizing, and increasing productivity at the enterprise level—was required to improve the country's economic performance.

Meanwhile, foreign investment slowed as well in the spring of 1997. As the Czech economic transformation had gained momentum, the official attitude toward investment took a negative turn. At first foreign investors were viewed as essential providers of capital and technology, as in neighboring Hungary. But with growing self-confidence, Czechs began to question the necessity of bringing in strategic investors. This attitude was fueled by unhappy experiences with certain foreign investors such as Air France, which had declared its interest in making Prague its hub for Eastern Europe. Discussions between the CSA, the Czech airline, and Air France fell through and the Czech government bought out foreign shareholders.

The Klaus government announced several economic measures, aimed at addressing these weaknesses and reluctantly regulating the heretofore so-called free market:

- As of April 17, 1997, 20 percent of the value of all food and consumer goods imports was to be deposited by importers interest-free in the banking system for 180 days. All local banks were to be allowed to participate in the scheme. Prices for imported consumer products could rise by 1 to 3 percent, as a net impact of the measure.

- Tax collection discipline was tightened: company management would have to declare bankruptcy if a firm was unable to pay its taxes or health and social security contributions. A new body to supervise tax collection and initiate relevant legislative changes was established.

- Efforts to strengthen capital markets supervision were intensified, through establishment of an independent securities commission.

- In the longer term, the government would step up the state's day-to-day control over enterprises in which it retained a significant stake; it would accelerate the privatization of banks and of regional electricity and gas companies; and it would continue to reduce tax rates—the corporate tax rate would be cut from 39 percent to 35 percent by 1998.

PRIVATIZATION AND ECONOMIC GROWTH

Together with former East Germany, privatization in the Czech Republic represents the largest transfer of state-owned property to private hands in modern economic history.

—Josef Kotrba, in Svejnar (1995), p. 159

In 1989 only 1.2 percent of the labor force, 2 percent of all the registered assets, and a negligible fraction of the Czechoslovak GDP belonged to the private sector (Svejnar 1995). Yet extensive privatization became the cornerstone of the Czechoslovak (later Czech) economic transformation. By the end of 1994, Czechoslovakia had carried out the most extensive privatization program in the CEE region. The two-wave voucher system that was the hallmark of Czech privatization had already been completed. The program consisted of restitution of property to previous owners or their heirs, privatization of small units in public auctions (small scale privatization), and privatization of large and medium-sized firms. The most important program was that of large scale privatizations. About four thousand firms out of a total of six thousand large firms had been privatized in two waves of large scale privatization by 1994.

By June 1996 the Czech government was preparing to close down the Ministry of Privatization, since its job was now finished (Gray 1996). The main assets remaining in the hands of the Czech state, such as the banks and the National Property Fund, were to be managed and sold on a case-by-case basis. There was no longer a need for a systematic approach to state assets since their share of the economy had been reduced from nearly 100 percent in 1990 to less than 20 percent. This was actually a smaller ratio than in some developed economies such as France and Italy. To all appearances, the Czech Republic was well ahead of the pack in the race toward privatization.

Until the end of the decade of the 1980s, the Czech economy had been highly centralized, consisting primarily of only a few thousand state-owned enterprises and cooperatives. Josef Kotrba, writing on the privatization process in a volume edited by Svejnar (1995), underscored the debt of the process, comparing it not just to the other countries in the region but to countries throughout history. Although the newly elected government introduced privatization as part of its program in July 1990, legislation on privatization took more than a year to complete. Eventually, over six million inhabitants received free shares in voucher privatization. From 1990 to 1993, tens of thousands of small and large businesses were auctioned, sold in tenders or directly to private entrepreneurs.

Since then, the Czech government has pursued three major programs of privatization: property restitutions as well as both small and large-scale privatization. The first two were begun in 1990 and were prominent during the early transition years. Restitutions legalized the return of certain property to its previous owners. In general, property confiscated before the communist takeover was excluded from all consideration. However, restitution was confined to Czech citizens and to some extent to churches. During the first two years, restitution had a significant impact in sectors such as retail trade in smaller cities, as well as housing and agriculture. Between 1991 and December 31, 1993, 742 pieces of property were sold to restitution claimants.

The second program, small-scale privatization, focused mainly on small state corporations involved in retail trade, catering, and services and sold at public auction. This privatization was infrequently used for entire companies; rather, some portion of property was separated from the state-owned firm and sold separately. Small-scale privatization got off to a very fast start in 1991, with over 14,000 units sold, and tapered off to only 855 in 1993.

The large-scale privatization program, launched in 1991, allowed combinations of several techniques. It applied to most state-owned assets in industry, agriculture, and services. Typically, the larger firms were transformed into joint stock companies, and shares were distributed within voucher privatization, sold for cash, or transferred for free to municipalities. The latter also benefitted from transfers of unused property within their territory. Large-scale privatization began rather slowly, with only 27 projects approved during the first eight months of the program.

By 1992 the first wave of voucher privatization had began. The idea of using vouchers was originated by the Poles in the late 1980s, but it was first implemented in the Czech and Slovak Republics and taken to its logical conclusion in the Czech Republic. Most of the joint-stock companies established within the privatization process were partly privatized through vouchers, the dominant method of shares. From the outset, this was the cornerstone of Czech privatization, although some companies, such as the Skoda car manufacturer, were sold to foreign investors. Most privatized firms had been transferred to new owners by the middle of 1993.

Kotrba concludes that while managers were the most successful players in the game, the program did involve a number of provisions to promote competition and the entry of noninsiders. This was somewhat unique in the region, where management and/or labor in state-owned firms have been the overwhelming winners of privatized assets. Voucher privatization succeeded in distributing ownership to the general public, although it failed as a simple method to reduce requirements on decision making capacities to a minimum. The scheme allowed several million Czech citizens to become shareholders and spawned the creation of voucher investment funds which would eventually become institutional investors, in turn paving the way to domestic capital market formation.

Since the mid-1990s, the private sector has accounted for the majority of the Czech GDP, in part the result of the Mass Privatization Program (MPP). In 1994, the private sector was already 56 percent of GDP and 47 percent of employment. By the end of 1996, only a few important large firms such as the railways, post, and national airlines remained fully state owned. Other enterprises such as telecommunications, utilities, and banking were partially privatized although the state remained a controlling shareholder.

It is not surprising that the question of how much enterprise restructuring actually took place in the Czech Republic has become a hotly debated issue, since the architects of the Czech mass privatization scheme had always emphasized that the new owners, rather than government bureaucrats, would be in charge of reorganizing enterprise activities. Czechs compare their experience with other countries such as Hungary or Poland, where more traditional privatization methods were applied.

The government

The role of the state has dramatically changed since the demise of communism. About 80 percent of output is now produced in the private sector, compared with less than 4 percent in the late 1980s. Nonetheless, the Czech government, as shareholder via the National Property Fund (NPF) in many enterprises and banks, is in a position to exert considerable influence, directly or indirectly, on economic developments.

A significant amount of state share holdings (estimated value: 230 billion crowns, or about $8.3 billion) is still held by the NPF, as unsold holdings (worth two billion dollars at the end of 1995) and as strategic enterprises (six billion dollars). The NPF has remained a largely passive owner: its small staff of 230 people could not even begin to exercise enterprise management control. It has been selling equity shares, mostly on the stock market and through tenders, and hopes to complete these sales by the end of 1997. In a few instances the state—through the NPF—has intervened directly to influence the restructuring and privatization of certain enterprises: for example, steel and aircraft manufacturers. The state has remained direct owner of some industries such as the railroads.

The Investment Privatization Funds (IPFs)

The investment funds acquired almost 60 percent of all enterprise assets that had been privatized via the coupon method. They emerged as the main industrial equity holders. Initially many analysts expected that these funds would take care of enterprise governance and make genuine restructuring efforts. But only the largest IPFs, those holding significant stakes in a few enterprises in selected sectors, met these expectations and demonstrated a strong interest and commitment to effective corporate governance. Most funds are passive investors and have not bothered to replace the managers of the companies they control. This passive behavior is explained by several factors:

- *Enterprise managers* continue to be considerably better informed about the operations and performance of their companies than fund managers. Close monitoring of enterprises is costly, and prohibitively so if investment funds have spread themselves thin by acquiring shares in too many enterprises.

- Many investment funds, owned by commercial banks, have allowed the banks to take charge of the companies.

- *Investment funds* find the trading of shares, transfer pricing, and non-transparent equity transactions far more lucrative than striving for profits and dividend payments through efficient governance. Indeed, profits and dividends have been an insignificant source of fund income so far.

The commercial banks

During the Mass Privatization Program, individuals sold their vouchers to proliferating investment funds, largely owned by the banks, which, in turn, are largely owned either by the government or by large investment funds. Banks, both as owners and lenders, have a twofold stake in enterprise governance and restructuring. As lenders, they find it more attractive to extend loans to their traditional clients, rather than getting involved in debt restructuring or reorganizing production, including bankrupting inviable enterprises.

Some analysts claim that the banks' dual role creates conflicts of interest, and that shareholders have to pay the price. This has contributed to the slow development of the Czech capital market. Other observers suggest that the performance of enterprises in which banks own significant equity is comparable with the performance of companies where banks do not have such a role. In any case, debt financing has not become an instrument of enterprise restructuring, and enterprise performance has not yet become a determining factor for obtaining credit.

Because competition in the banking sector is still relatively weak, banks can generate sizable profits through large spreads between deposit and lending rates, allowing them to set aside the necessary provisions and reserves. Furthermore, the partial removal of the banks' inherited bad portfolio, and their partial recapitalization, have tended to reinforce their passive behavior rather than bring about fundamental change.

The Enterprise Managers

The managers, with their clear advantage in controlling information and operating the available networks, have resisted outside influence, especially in mass-privatized enterprises, where dispersed ownership has tended to strengthen their position. Apart from those in foreign-owned enterprises, few managers seem to have been replaced. Although most Czech managers are highly skilled in their professional and technical abilities, they are still learning in such areas as finance management, product development, and marketing, skills very much required in a market economy.

Individual Shareholders

Citizens, having participated with great enthusiasm in mass privatization, seem to be less involved in the postprivatization phase. Having received their shares almost free, and making large returns on the money invested, they do not exert sufficient pressure on fund managers to improve enterprise performance. On the macroeconomic level there is plenty of evidence that the structure of the Czech economy has undergone substantial change over a brief period of time: more than one million jobs have been created in the services sector, and exports have been dramatically reoriented. The purchase of capital and equipment goods represents an important share in total imports, indicating that many enterprises are indeed in the midst of modernizing production facilities.

At the enterprise level, considerable "passive" restructuring of assets and liabilities took place initially, to maintain a certain cash flow or to improve cash management in general. But there was less evidence of successful physical restructuring. Except in sectors representing traditional strongholds of the Czech economy, such as glass and ceramics production, most products have not yet reached world-class levels.

Czech managers, with their entrepreneurial talents, took advantage of the initial transformation phase to quickly reorganize and expand production. They were aided by the large devaluation, low wages, and peaceful labor unions. But the situation had changed by the spring of 1997. Banks and investment funds were attracting the best minds of the Czech entrepreneurial class as sophisticated financial deals became extremely rewarding. By comparison, the second stage of enterprise restructuring—though more needed than ever—is less rewarding, more risky, and requires continuous hard work.

However, there have been examples of significant improvements in enterprise performance, especially involving strategic partnerships with foreign investors, such as the Skoda-Volkswagen enterprise. A study involving export performance, efficiency in applying labor and material inputs, and enterprise profits and losses as indicators—suggested that Czech companies in general have surpassed their counterparts in other transition countries in the region.

LOOKING TOWARD EUROPE

> By the time Europe decides to embrace the Czechs—which experts believe is likely to be seriously contemplated, as opposed to just blabbered about, around the year 2005—the Czechs will have surely flogged themselves into being more European than the Europeans.
>
> —Benjamin Kuras, *Czechs and Balances:*
> *A Nation's Survival Kit,* p. 18

Benjamin Kuras—a Czech-born journalist, broadcaster, and translator—would seem to have a rather jaundiced view of Czechs. His tongue-in-cheek style in fact belies a grudging pride in the Czechs. He reminds us that the Czechs see themselves as more Western than all the other Central and certainly Eastern European countries. The Czech

Republic, together with Hungary and Poland, has been among the leaders in the race to join NATO and the European Union.

In July 1997, NATO formally invited Poland, Hungary, and the Czech Republic to join this Western military alliance by the end of the century, taking a fateful step that would obliterate the last traces of the iron curtain and extend American security commitments to the former Soviet borders. The decision, made by leaders of the alliance's 16 governments, was hailed by President Clinton as "a giant stride in our efforts to create a Europe that is undivided, democratic and at peace literally for the first time since the rise of the nation-state on the European continent" (Droziak and Harris 1997). After enduring long, cold decades as satellites of the Soviet Union, the new NATO nations were expected to enjoy the protection of a Western alliance that vows to treat an attack on one member as an attack on all of them.

Czech President Vaclav Havel, Hungarian Prime Minister Gyula Horn, and Polish President Aleksander Kwasniewski held a joint news conference to voice their delight at NATO's offer. They expressed their deepest satisfaction for the invitation, calling it a historic decision paving the way to a more stable and secure Europe.

The U.S. Senate approved the candidature of the Czech Republic to NATO in April 1998. The two hundred-seat Czech lower house approved membership in NATO the same month by a vote of 154 to 38, with all parties except the Communist Party and the ultra-right Republican Party supporting it. They argued that it would be too costly and would lead to the stationing of foreign troops on Czech soil. President Havel, who had made NATO membership a top priority, fell critically ill while on holiday in Austria at the time of the vote. The opposition Social Democrats, who unanimously voted in favor of membership, decided to drop its demand for a referendum on the issue. Despite earlier ambivalence by many Czechs about joining NATO, polls at the time of the vote indicated that public opinion had come around to supporting NATO.

On December 13, 1997, the European Union invited the Czech Republic and five other nations (Poland, Hungary, Estonia, Slovenia and Cyprus) to become candidates for membership (Hockstader 1997). They were invited to begin membership negotiations in March 1998. Five additional Central and Eastern European nations were given precandidate status: Bulgaria, Romania, Latvia, Lithuania, and Slovakia. The invitation to join the EU was the first official step in a long process of negotiation and compromise. Membership for these countries is not expected before 2002, and likely later.

THE DEFINITION AND ROLE OF SMES IN THE CZECH ECONOMY

> The former Czechoslovak Republic, with the exception of the former East Germany and the Baltic States, had the most extensive restitution program of all post-communist countries.
>
> —Marie Bohata, "Small and Medium-Sized Enterprises
> in the Czech Manufacturing Industry" 1996

When the Czechoslovak parliament passed the Entrepreneurial Law in April 1990, legalizing the creation of private companies, only a handful of private firms existed (Webster and Swanson 1993, 18-25). Commercial codes were amended to provide for the incorporation of private firms as well as requirements for limited liability and joint stock companies and partnerships. In 1992, a new law required companies to obtain a business license before they could register with the Commercial Registry. Self employed persons were permitted unlimited access to foreign exchange for long-term financing and investment.

The number of registered private entrepreneurs in Czechoslovakia grew quickly from fewer than one hundred thousand at the end of 1989 to 488,000 at the end of 1990 (Webster and Swanson, 1993). By the end of 1991, 1175 million persons were already listed on official rosters as sole proprietorships, and by July 1992 this number had reached 1.4 million. The largest percentage of sole proprietors were engaged in industrial production and repair (26 percent), followed by construction (20 percent) and direct trade (20 percent). Also by the end of 1991, some forty thousand registered companies had been created in Czechoslovakia, although many were probably inactive. Registered companies included limited liability companies, joint-stock companies, and self-employed persons.

The growth of the private sector was impressive in the Czech Republic, as reflected in its contribution to the GDP during the early transition period. In fact, the private sector was virtually synonymous with SMEs (see description of SMEs below). Although the GDP declined by 16 percent in 1991, the private sector contribution rose by 28 percent (Bohata 1996). The share of the private sector in the GDP rose modestly from only 3 to 8 percent, while the share of private sector employment grew from about 1 to 16 percent. The share of SMEs in the total output of the manufacturing industry was still quite modest. Even so, the productivity of labor in SMEs was shown to be higher than in the state and cooperative enterprises. The development of the SME sector therefore became a stabilizing factor in the economy and contributed to a successful transformation even though its share of the GDP remained relatively small.

Perhaps the most important factor in the development of the Czech SME sector was the program of restitutions and small-scale privatization. These processes were unique in helping establish a foundation for an efficient market economy. Restitutions were not originally on the economic reform agenda, which instead focused on the privatization of large state-owned enterprises. In response to strong political pressure, however, several restitution laws were passed which provided for nationalized property to be restituted to original owners or their heirs. The former minister of privatization estimated the number of these restitutions at one hundred thousand, the majority of them in real estate.

The small-scale privatization program begun in the first half of 1990 enjoyed broad public consensus in Czechoslovak society. The process, which took place from 1990 to 1993, involved the sale of over twenty-two thousand units in public auctions. More than half of the small-scale privatizations involved shops, while others included restaurants and services. The reason for the success of this initiative in Czechoslovakia was that the employees were not favored as insiders in the auction process, as was the case in most other countries in the region. Thus, these two programs contributed substantially to the evolution of private retail and wholesale trade, services, and small-scale manufacturing.

According to the basic law governing small and medium-sized enterprises established in 1992, an SME is defined as a company that has no more than 500 employees. A medium enterprise has between 101 and 500 workers, a small enterprise from 10 to 100, and a micro-business fewer than 10 (UNIDO 1966).

FINANCING SMES: BANK AND NONBANK SOURCES

As in all the countries of the CEE region, the Czech Republic will be required to orient its banking system toward the private sector in order to obtain integration into the European Union. While the banking sector is showing increasing private sector shares of assets, loans, and deposits, substantial shares are still controlled on a stock basis by state-owned commercial banks (Borish et al. 1996). The transformation of the monobank system in the Czech Republic took place on January 1, 1990, when the Commercial Bank of Prague and the General Credit Bank of Bratislava were formed out of the National Bank of Czechoslovakia. The savings function was allocated to the separate Czech and Slovak savings banks, while Czechoslovak Trade Bank retained its monopoly role in foreign trade and exchange.

There were 31 banks operating in the Czech Republic at the end of 1991. In 1995, after four years of reform, there were 58 banks, of which four were majority or wholly state-owned and four were minority state-owned. Four large state-owned commercial banks still dominated the banking system, controlling 62 percent of assets, 58 percent of loans, and 77 percent of deposits, but only 38 percent of capital and reserves. However, as elsewhere in the region, these large banks were beginning to lose their dominant market position in the Czech Republic, facing stiff competition from the growing number of private banks in a range of banking activities. Foreign banks have been operating in the Czech Republic since 1990 when there were five banks with foreign capital. That number had grown to 30 by 1993, of which 19 were fully foreign owned. The average private bank is fairly small, with $425 million in assets, $231 million in loans, $151 million in deposits, and $68 million in capital. This is higher than the average for Central Europe, except for deposits, which are slightly lower.

In contrast to other countries in the region, privatization of the banking sector in the Czech Republic was treated as an important and urgent matter. Since the commercial banks created out of the monobank system inherited stocks of nonperforming loans to the large state-owned enterprises, the government devised a program to restructure and privatize the new banks. Bank privatization began early in 1992 with the partial sale of Zivnostenska Banka, one of the few independent banks to survive the communist era (Gray 1996). The other major banks were privatized at the same time through the voucher system. Reforms also meant that foreign banks could open branches and subsidiaries for the first time. Quite a few large banks did so, including Citibank, Creditanstalt, and Societe Generale.

The Czech Republic maintained an excellent record of allocating credit to the private sector during the early transition years. Domestic credit, as a share of GDP, has been fairly stable since 1992, at around

78 percent. Virtually all domestic credit has in fact been allocated to nongovernmental borrowers. As the private sector share of GDP and employment has grown, so has the allocation of credit. Already in 1992, the private sector accounted for 49 percent of total domestic credit, and by 1995 it had increased to 84 percent. Domestic credit has increased in all Central European countries except Hungary, a factor that has helped fuel economic recovery.

In dollar terms, lending to the enterprise sector has increased in the Czech Republic, although as a percentage of overall credit and GDP, it has declined. By 1996, lending to enterprises accounted for up to 70 percent of total credit in the Czech Republic, compared to only 50 percent in Poland and about thirty-three percent in Hungary. In the Czech Republic, lending to the private sector rose from 34 percent in 1992 to 52 percent in 1995, by far the highest percentage in the region. At the same time, lending to the state enterprise sector in the Czech Republic declined sharply from 36 percent of GDP in 1992 to a mere 12 percent in 1995.

In spite of the partial Czech success with privatization, banks have remained vulnerable because of poor credit management, reliance on good loans from blue chip businesses to subsidize bad loans, and insufficient restructuring of large enterprises that were the major debtors. Licensing conditions were initially quite liberal, prompting a large number of new, Czech-owned private banks to open. Some of them soon began running into problems in the mid-1990s, casting doubt on the country's economic reform. In several instances management was incapable of properly controlling the bank's lending policy, resulting in bad loans. The performance of the larger and more well-established banks also came into question. Czech banks generally failed to follow their counterparts in other countries in the region by tightening up lending procedures, resulting in high default rates.

GOVERNMENT AND DONOR ASSISTANCE TO CZECH SMES

The Czech government has begun to recognize the importance of the small business sector. Its vision of the development of the SME sector was put forth in the Act of State Support to Small and Medium-Sized Businesses in April 1992, recognizing SMEs as a key economic sector and justifying government support. The stated aim of the act was (UNIDO 1996):

To facilitate the establishment and to strengthen the economic position of small and medium-sized businesses that are active and have their seat in the territory of the Czech Republic. The supporting measures adopted hereunder shall promote the efficiency and competitiveness of small and medium businesses, thus counterbalancing their drawbacks due to low economic strength, assist the businesses in adapting to economic and technological changes, and guide them towards self-sufficiency.

Underlying this legislation was the political commitment to harmonization with European Union standards, and thus to the goal of joining the European Union in the near future. Government officials frequently cited Belgium and the Netherlands as the economies that the Czech Republic should aim toward emulating because they had similar populations and geographical areas. An example of this commitment was a focus on establishing the same databases for SMEs as were available in the EU. The legislation identified 10 key areas where support for SMEs was justified, focusing of themes such as undercapitalization and cooperation among businesses.

Under the provisions of a November 1994 law, the Czech Ministry of Economy was made responsible for state administration in matters concerning small and medium-sized enterprises. It approved the conditions for granting subsidies to SMEs through various initiatives designed to support their establishment and development. The basic principle of this assistance was to facilitate access to capital and the sharing of entrepreneurial risks by the state.

The ministry's SME-related activities were located within the business section, which was to provide consulting services to SMEs, prepare legislation in support of the sector, and act as an appeal body. Several other ministries, such as Agriculture, Industry and Trade, Finance and Labor and Social Affairs, have programs to promote small businesses in various ways. The Czech-Moravian Guarantee and Development Bank was designated as the delivery mechanism for the Ministry of Economy's major programs.

The Agency for Enterprise Development (ARP) was established within the Ministry of Economy as a new business support agency in May 1995. It serves as the focal point for several PHARE-funded projects and aims at becoming a self-supporting service agency for small business-support organizations. In addition to coordinating

PHARE activities, the agency seeks foreign SME assistance and collaborates with foreign institutions.

The Czech entrepreneurs interviewed in a World Bank survey in 1992 had little knowledge of or exposure to multilateral or bilateral aid programs (Webster and Swanson 1993, 49). Bilateral aid was negatively associated with the Czechoslovak-American Fund. Those who were aware of it were disappointed to learn that it was mainly limited to large loans and to firms with foreign guarantors, and that interest rates were comparable to those required by Czech banks. In this respect it should be recalled that Czech businesses had greater access to commercial banks than did those in other countries in the region. Other bilateral programs were virtually unknown, as were multilateral organization such as the International Fiinance Corporation (IFC) and European Bank for Reconstruction and Development (EBRD). Only later was the PHARE Program to come on stream.

EU PHARE funds are allotted by the recipient country within a general framework drafted by national governments, in cooperation with the European Commission. As PHARE represents an umbrella technical assistance program rather than a single-targeted initiative, there are several sectoral provisions that comprise PHARE funds. In the Czech Republic, the relevant sectors to management training and education are Private Sector Development and Enterprise Support and Education, Health Training and Research. With regard to management training and education in the private sector development category, it is the SME sector that EU-sponsored programs have focused upon (Jetton 1997).

Most significantly, a 1993 PHARE grant in the amount of 2 million ECU (1.6 million dollars) established the National Training Fund (NTF) as a quasi-independent organization based at the Czech Ministry of Labor and Social Affairs. The purpose of the NTF was to widen and subsidize the access of enterprises and ministries to ongoing relevant training. The PHARE program's purpose was for the NTF to encourage the development of the network of management training providers, support training providers, and assess and initiate the process of integration of the Training Fund's training activities within the formal Czech education system.

These ambitious goals distinguish the PHARE from the US Agency for International Development (USAID) program goals even further: Whereas the USAID programs establish an institution and build it up with exchange networks and foreign degree-granting possibilities,

NTF programs seek to promote the development of individual, private institutions that will not necessarily provide structured management training (as in courses which fit into a degree structure) but will develop short course offerings which can then be "sold" to existing firms and enterprises. One of the main activities of the NTF is to offer tuition subsidies of up to 60 percent (with ceilings) to firms who "buy" courses for their employees: this is thought not only to defray costs and encourage high participation rates but to develop the sector of independent training providers. There are efforts underway to establish an evaluative committee which will "grade" these providers, which will be used to promote services at the NTF level and will lead to the development of a quality rating for particular courses. USAID envisioned that such ratings would later be used to limit subsidies to those institutions which do not achieve high course ratings.

PROFILE OF CZECH ENTREPRENEURS

> Czechs consider themselves—not the Germans—the natural rightful business leaders of Central and Eastern Europe which they recall they have always fed, clad, housed, armed, machined, and vehicled.

> Czechs want to be left to themselves, to develop their talents and skills to their   best ability and marketability, let their long suppressed entrepreneurial drive explode.They have more registered private entrepreneurs, small companies, and small shareholders per capita than any other country in Europe.

> Benjamin Kuras, *Czechs and Balances,*1996, p. 43

A World Bank survey of private firms conducted by a team of researchers (Webster and Swanson 1993) in the former Czechoslovakia in January 1992 provides a useful profile of the first wave of Czech entrepreneurs. (A similar survey was conducted in Poland and Hungary.) The Czechoslovak survey included 121 businesses chosen randomly from registered, domestically owned manufacturers with seven or more employees. Excluded in the sample were self-employed persons engaged in trade and services. Those interviewed were generally well-educated, middle-aged, and predominantly male (there were only five women). Two-thirds had held posts as presidents or directors of state-owned enterprises or government agencies. Half had university diplomas, while the remainder were graduates of technical or commercial secondary schools. Most had chosen to manufacture products they had made in previous jobs. Few had received training abroad. In general, these entrepreneurs seemed well qualified for business success, except that they lacked experience in risk-taking.

Nearly all of those interviewed had registered their firms as private, limited liability companies since mid-1990. Fifty-five percent of them had fully private origins; most ran new start-ups and a few were prereform craftsmen. The remainder originated as former state enterprises or cooperatives. Two-thirds of the firms were engaged in five sectors in the sample: knitting, clothing, plastics, metalworking, and machinery. Bohemia and Moravia (in the present Czech Republic) accounted for 40 percent of each of the firms while Slovakia represented just over 20 percent. The average labor force was 42 workers per firm, with roughly equal representation of men and women. Half employed fewer than 20 employees. The men in the sample worked in nearly all sectors and positions but dominated completely in wood products, metalworking, and machinery, whereas women were more likely to be working in lower-paying sectors such as textiles and food processing (Webster and Swanson 1993, 27-35).

Nearly all the respondents said they purchased most of their intermediate inputs and raw materials from the state sector, and almost half of them reported having problems in obtaining domestic inputs. The research team was impressed with the high level of exports among sample firms, in light of the short period of operation. Forty-two percent were exporting some portion of their production, and one-third of the value of sales was accounted for by exports, all in hard currency. The major trading partners were neighboring Austria and Germany. Most respondents reported increasing production, sales, and profits since start-up, and few reported declines in output or sales.

Researchers were also surprised by the number of entrepreneurs who had received loans from banks. Unlike their counterparts in Poland in Hungary, most of whom started up with only personal savings, two-thirds of those in the Czechoslovak sample had received loans within six months of start-up. Three-quarters had received at least one bank loan, used to finance everything from land and buildings to equipment and stocks. Several had even obtained more than one loan, while few had been turned down.

Privatization seemed to be favorably affecting the entrepreneurs in the Czechoslovak sample. Nearly half of them had purchased their factory buildings from the state through direct purchase, competitive bidding in auctions, and buyouts associated with the restitution program. The level of property ownership among entrepreneurs in this survey was far higher than that in Hungary and Poland. This was attributable to the auctions which made real estate available to private buyers, and to banks that provided long-term loans.

Entrepreneurs interviewed sold 36 percent of their products to state enterprises, 27 percent to private traders and firms, and 28 percent directly from their factories to both private and state customers. While the advantage of selling to state enterprises was that contracts were typically large, the disadvantage was problems with delayed payment and declining orders. At the same time, most of those interviewed identified state enterprises as their chief competitors. In general, they faced far lower levels of competition than did their counterparts in Hungary and Poland. As might be expected, the smallest firms manufacturing the most homogeneous products, such as knitted goods and clothing, faced the largest number of competitors.

When asked to name their biggest problems, the entrepreneurs listed high taxes, delinquent payments by state enterprises, and high interest rates as the most important, followed by weak product demand, unstable business conditions, and problems with labor. They especially resented payroll taxes which totaled half of wages paid, claiming that these taxes eroded their profits. As a way of avoiding these taxes, many of them resorted to contract labor, which was exempted from payroll tax. Laws regarding taxes were constantly in a state of flux, making it difficult to plan. Delinquent payments, mostly by state enterprises, accounted for up to 70 percent of 1991 sales in some firms (Webster and Swanson 1993, 40-44).

Despite the fact that many had received loans, those interviewed described increasing problems in obtaining credit from banks. They said that interest rates were exorbitantly high, and collateral requirements excessive. Banks were claiming as much as 100 to 150 percent of the loan amount as security. Property judged acceptable by banks was limited to land and buildings, and excluded production equipment. The entrepreneurs also complained that financial services were poor, that domestic transactions within the same bank branch could take 10 days while international transactions could take up to two months. The World Bank team nevertheless discovered that many of the respondents had managed to obtain creative financing arrangements and a wide range of interest rates with their banks. On the other hand, banks resisted providing working capital loans. Meanwhile, state enterprises commonly demanded cash for purchases of raw materials, but took months to pay for goods delivered.

In addition to these major complaints, the respondents cited other factors affecting the business environment and the cost of doing business. These included excessive red tape, negative attitudes toward private enterprise, and weak product markets. Paper work and fees were considered excessive, especially the initial registration deposit. Entrepreneurs regularly had to confront social prejudice against profit making, which had of course been illegal under the socialist regime. Nearly half reported having problems obtaining domestic inputs, since many state managers were not inclined to cater to the needs of small private producers for small quantities. Concerning output, private producers enjoyed few alternatives for selling their products, most of them relying mainly upon state enterprises as their clients. Those who succeeded in selling to private sector clients preferred foreign markets due to the limited domestic marketing channels.

From its survey in the former Czechoslovakia, the World Bank team concluded that the policy environment in the transition process had been highly conducive to the successful formation of a private manufacturing sector. They cited five key factors: (1) a legal and regulatory framework that established equal rights for private business and abolished most restrictions on their operation; (2) a preannounced schedule for price liberalization; (3) opportunities to purchase factory buildings and production equipment through the small-scale privatization program; (4) provision of long-term financing from the banks; and (5) access to foreign markets.

In contrast to the experience in Poland, entrepreneurs in Czechoslovakia were spared the initial shock of price reforms since most of them started up after prices had stabilized in the second quarter of 1991. In Poland, the massive private sector start-up took place prior to price and trade liberalization. Although policies adopted under the transformation program were not necessarily intended to protect domestic producers, there were factors that slowed import penetration. But this slow import growth may in fact have retarded the growth of the private trading sector, an important source of inputs and markets for local producers.

Successful entrepreneurs in the former Czechoslovakia demonstrated technical skills and smart decision-making ability in the choice of products and markets. While hostility toward private business tended to be greater in Czechoslovakia than in neighboring countries, the entrepreneurs in the survey seemed to be resourceful enough to overcome these social attitudes as well as governmental red tape. It must be said that they were the beneficiaries of a generally favorable policy transformation, a banking system that opened its doors to them, and public confidence in the government.

THE POTENTIAL FOR SME GROWTH IN THE CZECH REPUBLIC

The Czech miracle of low inflation, low unemployment, and a growing economy was illusory. The fact is that in many ways they've never really begun to reform.

—Mark Sanders, American investment fund manager in Prague
(*The Washington Post*, December 7, 1997).

Not long ago, the Czech Republic could boast of robust performance on many measures: one of the highest GDP growth rates among post-communist countries, the lowest unemployment rate in Europe, a sharp increase in overall private income and personal purchasing power, and one of the few countries in transition with a stable and convertible currency. One hundred million incoming foreign tourists a year (to be sure, many of them Germans crossing the border for an evening beer) provided a host of opportunities for private entrepreneurs.

However, by early 1997 there were signs that the bloom was off the Czech "economic miracle." Once considered one of the more successful transition countries in the CEE region, the Czech Republic began to experience economic reversals. First quarter 1997 statistics indicated that industrial output continued to fall while wages skyrocketed. Consumption was growing faster than investment. Added to this was a drop in foreign investment and a worsening account deficit. Prime Minister Vaclav Klaus and his three member coalition government appeared to be unsure of how to handle the crisis. The government announced measures to cut public spending and restrain the trade deficit, which included curbs on public sector wages, possible quotas on some imports and help for exporters, as well as a crackdown on tax evasion and corruption (*Business Central Europe*, April 1997). It was too little too late.

"The Vaclav Klaus era of adherence to unfettered free-market capitalism came to an end with his resignation as Prime Minister." (Hockstader 1997).

By November 1997, Prime Minister Vaclav Klaus was forced to resign amid scandal and a slumping economy, two years after he had declared the transition to a free market complete. There had been bank failures, stock market scams, and political scandals. His resignation shattered the myth of his political genius along with any lingering belief in the Czech "economic miracle." His faith in the market's "invisible hand" was such that Klaus once suggested that to him there was no such thing as dirty money.

Klaus, head of the Civic Democrat Party (ODS), had come to be associated with one of Central Europe's most celebrated success stories. He had shown himself to be supremely confident of the rightness of his cause. Yet, even as he preached the gospel of the free market, Klaus presided over a government that did little to assure that it remain healthy. He eschewed anything that smacked of regulation or state interference in the market. Meanwhile, scandals engulfed his Civic Democratic Party, including reports that investors had channeled money into the party's Swiss bank accounts in return for favorable treatment in privatization arrangements.

At the heart of the malaise in the Czech Republic was the highly touted voucher system. Overnight the system turned four-fifths of the country's citizens into equity shareholders, among the highest in the world. But these vouchers were quickly bought up by investment funds, most of them owned by a handful of large banks still controlled by the state. The banks propped up failing state-owned enterprises with easy loans, refusing to cut off the flow of cash or to demand restructuring for fear of bankruptcy. The result was hundreds of companies operating much as they did during the communist era, with bloated payrolls, incompetent management, and poor production facilities.

The jury is still out on the ultimate effect of the vaunted Czech large-scale privatization scheme (Gray 1996). From an economic point of view, the question is whether the voucher-privatized companies produce more profits and restructure more quickly than their counterparts in other countries where other approaches prevailed. There is some evidence to indicate that Czech companies are restructuring more slowly because their largest shareholders—voucher funds controlled by domestic banks—are not pressing management enough to effect change.

Nor did the Klaus government do much to attract foreign direct investment, which it tended to dismiss as an unnecessary interference with market forces. It relied instead upon its head start in the transition process, a strong industrial base, and skilled labor to attract investors. But investors went elsewhere, mainly to neighboring Poland and Hungary, because of the sagging Czech economy. Many Western investors who did come into the Czech market got burned and vowed not to return. Investors such as Mark Sanders, an investment fund manager living in Prague since 1989, found little to attract them to the Czech Republic. With a portfolio of $32 million to invest in the region, Sanders chose to invest no more than $1 million in the Czech Republic:

"If the Czech Republic wants its share of global funds, it has to compete for them and create an attractive environment. You don't see that here. In fact, you see a lot of arrogance." (Hockstader 1997).

President Havel named Josef Tosovsky to serve as caretaker Prime Minister until the June 1998 election. The center-right Freedom Union party began to chip away at the Social Democrats' lead in the run-up to the election. The unaffiliated Tosovsky quickly won high approval ratings in the polls. No matter who succeeded in forming a new government, he would have to reflect on the pros and cons of the Klaus approach and determine how to revive the economy.

As in all economies in transition, the Czech small business sector is vulnerable to macro-economic trends. Even without the recent economic downturn, the SME sector would have had to face two critical hurdles: large-scale privatization and import competition. The further privatization of the large state companies will likely reduce overall economic demand as the nonperforming ones are mothballed, while the newly privatized ones provide increased competition for the SMEs. Nor is it clear whether privatization will lead to improved practices of state enterprises as suppliers and customers to SMEs. Many of the advantages small businesses enjoyed in the beginning, when the private sector was being created, are disappearing. They were able to exploit the classic advantages of small firms in an economy dominated by large firms such as responsiveness to consumer tastes and innovation. When import competition begins in earnest, it is the smaller firms producing low-tech goods such as clothing and plastics that will be at risk. It is a well-known phenomenon that consumers offered a choice between cheap local products and name brand foreign products will opt for the imported ones.

As in every economy, Czech entrepreneurs interviewed in surveys expressed frustration with government impediments, regulations, and policies. They felt that continued domination by state enterprises was impeding the growth of the private sector, and they urged privatization as quickly as possible. They viewed taxes as onerous, accounting to a large extent for the widespread tendency toward evading payment, especially on labor taxes. Collection of payments on overdue accounts with state-owned enterprises was seen as a particularly serious problem. Czech entrepreneurs were more preoccupied with reducing government red tape than were their counterparts in Hungary and Poland. The number of permits and licenses required and the time and money needed to obtain them were deemed excessive. Most of the respondents felt the need for improved commercial information on products, markets, and technology in order to make optimal decisions affecting their company operations.

A second order of concerns among Czech entrepreneurs had to do with the long-term competitiveness of private firms such as expanded outward orientation and banking reforms. Promotion of exports and private investment, with continued emphasis on joint ventures, was seen as important in responding to import competition. Even though banks in the Czech Republic have been relatively active in lending to private entrepreneurs, the nature of the loans and the banking services could use improvement.

Also from a social and cultural perspective, it would appear that Czech entrepreneurs must overcome public prejudice against private enterprises and profitmaking. Those interviewed in the World Bank study tended to characterize their fellow Czechs as a jealous lot who resented others' gains. They complained that the pro-business government policy had not trickled down to the typical bureaucrat, who was inclined to be unhelpful at best. This type of prejudice is hard to address through government policy. At best, business owners need to develop support institutions such as chambers of commerce, business and civic clubs, and policy research centers.

However, there is a beginning of an entrepreneurial culture among the stronger firms in the Czech Republic. A common strategy among those interviewed in the World Bank study was product differentiation of sophisticated, high value-added goods. They had chosen their markets carefully, concentrating on local and export markets and avoiding national markets dominated by state enterprises. The strongest firms were those with exceptional managers who had a firm grasp of their financial status and their competitors. Often they were innovative, introducing new products with modern technology and custom design. They were risk-takers eager to explore new markets in which they had little experience. If the observation of Benjamin Kuras is correct, it may well be that Czechs have a long suppressed entrepreneurial drive that is still waiting to explode.

REFERENCES

Bohata, Marie 1996 "Small and Medium-Sized Enterprises in the Czech Manufacturing Industry" Working Paper No. 94 Prague: CERGE-EI, March.

Borish, Michael, Wei Ding, and Michel Noel 1996 *On the Road to EU Accession: Financial Sector Development in Central Europe*, World Bank Discussion Paper No. 345.

Business Central Europe "The Czech Bubble Bursts" April 1997.

CERGE-EI 1997 *Czech Republic 1996: Basic Socio-Economic Indicators* Prague: Center for Economic Research and Graduate Education (Charles University) and Economics Institute (Academy of Sciences).

Drozdiak, William, and John F. Harris "NATO Invites 3 Former Foes to Join," *The Washington Post*, July 9, 1997.

Gray, Gavin 1996 "The Czech Republic" *Eastern Europe: Investing for the 21st Century,* London: Euromoney Books.

Havel, Vaclac 1995 *Toward a Civil Society: Selected Speeches and Writings 1990- 1994* Prague: Lidove Noviny Publishing House.

Hewer, Ulrich 1997 "Czech Enterprises Seeking True Owners" *Transition: The Newsletter about Reforming Economies* Vol. 8, No. 3, World Bank, June.

Hockstader, Lee "Czech's Downfall Shatters Hope for Economic Miracle" *The Washington Post* December 7, 1997.

Jetton, Michael 1997 *Management Training in Central and Eastern Europe* masters thesis paper submitted to London School of Economics, June.

Kotrba, Josef 1995 "Privatization Process in Czech Republic: Players and Winners, in Svejnar ed. *The Czech Republic and Economic Transition in Eastern Europe*, San Diego, CA: Academic Press, pp. 159-198.

Kuras, Benjamin 1996 *Czechs and Balances: A Nation's Survival Kit* Prague: Baronet.

Pehe, Jiri, and Jolyon Naegele 1997 "Inside the Czech Stabilization Package: Another Package" World Bank *Transition Newsletter* Vol. 8, No. 3, June.

The Prague Post, April 23-29, 1997.

Spolar, Christine "Czechs' Post-Communist Boom Running Dry," *The Washington Post,* June 29.

Svejnar, Jan et al. 1995 *The Czech Republic and Economic Transition in Eastern Europe*, San Diego, CA: Academic Press.

UNIDO 1996 *A Comparative Analysis of SME Strategies, Policies and Programmes in Central European Initiative Countries: Part III Czech Republic*. Vienna: UNIDO.

Webster, Leila, and Dan Swanson 1993 "The Emergence of Private Sector Manufacturing in the Former Czech and Slovak Federal Republic" World Bank, Technical Paper Number 230.

CHAPTER 4
Hungary

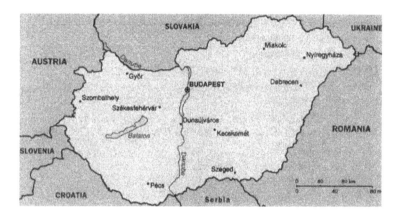

HUNGARY

Hungary Profile

Area: 93,030 square kilometers, slightly smaller than Indiana

Bordering countries: Austria, Croatia, Romania, Serbia and Montenegro, Slovakia, Slovenia, and Ukraine

National capital: Budapest

Population: 10,232,404 (July 1997 est.)

Population growth rate: -0.25% (1997 est.)

Ethnic groups: Hungarian 89.9%, Gypsy 4%, German 2.6%, Serb 2%, Slovak 0.8%, Romanian 0.7%

Religions: Roman Catholic 67.5%, Calvinist 20%, Lutheran 5%, atheist and other 7.5%

Languages: Hungarian 98.2%, other 1.8%

GDP real growth rate: 0.5% (1996 est.)

GDP per capita: purchasing power parity ($7,500 1996 est.)

Inflation rate—consumer price index: 20% (1996 est.)

Unemployment rate: 11% (1996 est.)

Administrative divisions: 19 counties

Natural resources: bauxite, coal, natural gas, fertile soils

Independence: 1001 (unification by King Stephen I)

National holiday: St. Stephen's Day (National Day), 20 August (commemorates the coronation of King Stephen in 1000 AD)

Chief of state: President Arpad Goncz (since August 3, 1990; previously interim president since May 2, 1990)

Head of government : Prime Minister Viktor Urban (since 15 July 1994)

Source: U.S. State Department

Hungary

THE HISTORIC AND ECONOMIC SETTING IN HUNGARY

Rise Hungarians, your country calls!
The time is now, now or never!
Shall we be slaves or free?
This is the question, choose!
To the God of the Hungarians,
We swear,
We swear we shall slaves
No longer be!

> —Opening lines from Sandor Petofi's "National Song," March 15,
> 1848 (quoted in Lazar, *Hungary: A Brief History* 1997, p. 147)

Hungary was among the most Western-oriented economies in Central
and Eastern Europe before the transition to a market system began in
1990, and is often considered a success story in the region. Today
Hungary is the second smallest country in the CEE region, with an area
of just over 35,000 square miles (roughly the size of Indiana), and a
population of 10.3 million. Bordered by Serbia, Croatia, Slovenia,
Austria, Slovakia, and Russia, Hungary is located at the crossroads
between Eastern and Western Europe. Taking into account those who
have left the country or who are minorities in neighboring countries,
there are perhaps 16 to 18 million Hungarians in the world today.
Hungary is ethnically very homogeneous, with Magyars (Hungarians)
accounting for over 90 percent of the population. The largest minority
is composed of Roma (gypsies). One-fifth of the population lives in the

capital city of Budapest, which has a history reaching back over a thousand years.

Hungary is at once a modernizing country in transition and an ancient nation, recently celebrating 1,100 years of recorded history. The House of Arpad sprang from nomadic warlike tribes that originated somewhere along the Volga River above the Sea of Azov in Russia in the middle of the first millennium a.d. Speaking a unique language belonging to the Finno-Ugric group, the Hungarian nomads found their way into the Carpathian basin under the leadership of Arpad the Conqueror in a.d. 895 where they encountered and subdued the local Slavic peoples, eventually taking up a more sedentary life-style. At the dawn of the second millennium the Hungarian nation was led into the Christian era by King Stephen. At its zenith in the fourteenth and fifteenth centuries, three seas—the Adriatic, the Black, and the Baltic—were said to have washed the borders of the Hungarian empire. King Mattias Hunyadi Cornivus presided over the flowering of a Renaissance culture and the introduction of modern managerial practices in the collection of taxes.

Hungary did not escape the social upheavals that swept across Europe in the middle of the 1800s. It was a feudalistic system characterized by the domination of the noble class on the one hand and embittered and impoverished serfs on the other hand. The conflict of interest between noblemen and serfs led to a cry for freedom by the oppressed classes in 1848, captured in Sandor Petrofi's National Song, which was to echo through time to the revolution of 1956. In both cases, the prevailing system was oppressive and in decline and new rights were being asserted.

As with other countries that came under Soviet domination, Hungary experienced a Stalinist period from 1948 to 1953, when economic planning emphasized central decision-making and heavy industry. All enterprises employing more than 10 workers were nationalized, and a program for the collectivization of agriculture was initiated. Lacking in raw materials, Hungary had historically never placed much stress on heavy industry, but had concentrated on the development of agriculture-based products and the manufacture of consumer goods. Initially the Stalinist plan produced spectacular results: heavy industrial production increased fivefold and the engineering industry increased seven times since 1938. By 1953, however, serious shortages began to appear in raw materials and fuel supplies. Agriculture began to stagnate under the combination of collectivization and a decline in investment. Consumer prices rose faster than wages and salaries, resulting in a decline in the standard of living during the five year plan period from 1948 to 1953.

Political and economic discontent eventually led to the uprising of 1956, one of the most defining events in Hungarian history. Janos Kadar, who was installed in power by Soviet forces, took measures of the most forceful kind against resistors, using mass terror. During the days of the October 1956 revolution, more than three thousand people fell victim to street fighting and armed reprisals. Although Soviet troops put down the largely unarmed resistance, the uprising of 1956 demonstrated the fundamental dissatisfaction of the Hungarian people with the Soviet puppet rule. As a result some two hundred thousand people fled to the West. During the next five years there were signs that the government was willing to relax its tight political and economic control of the country. By 1962, however, it was proudly reported to the Communist Party Congress that 90 percent of all farmland had been collectivized and that nearly all industrial products were from fellow socialist countries. Hungary had achieved a largely socialized economy.

After nearly 20 years of suppression, private enterprise had already begun to re-emerge in Hungary by 1968 (Seleny 1991). An informal sector took shape alongside the official economy. While the 1968 reforms failed to improve the efficiency of state enterprises, some measures succeeded in setting the stage for more sustained private sector initiatives later on. The rural private sector was stimulated when farmers were encouraged to sell their produce directly to consumers through agricultural cooperatives. Already by 1972, half of all Hungarians were engaged on a full or part-time basis in private farming with private plots. State employees were also allowed to work legally part-time in small private enterprises. A variety of illegal and quasi-legal activities laid the groundwork for the official recognition of private enterprise in the late 1980s.

Following the severe economic reversals in the late 1970s and early 1980s, a new set of reforms in 1982 marked the turning point for private sector development. A decision was taken to legalize new quasi-private enterprise forms such as household plots related to industrial production. The government's objective was to mobilize private investment, reduce the shortage of consumer goods, and maintain the standard of living among workers in the state sector. This enabled hundreds of thousands of industrial workers to participate in various forms of private activities and left Hungary better prepared than other CEE countries for the transition.

Political Winds of Change: The Revolution of 1989 and Its Aftermath

The winds of change began to blow strongly throughout the CEE region in 1989, including Hungary. In that year Janos Kadar died, only weeks after being divested of his remaining political powers. Thus did one political era end and a new one begin. The Communist Party changed its name to the Hungarian Socialist Party. Kadar's successors surprised the world with their preparations for democratic changes and peaceful handover of power. In March 1990, in the first free elections since 1945, Hungarian voters repudiated both the Socialist Party and the communist United Workers' Party. Although no single party received a majority, it was a coalition of parties known as the Democratic Forum that came out ahead, thus winning the right to form a new government. A coalition government was formed, headed by Jozsef Antall, chairman of the Hungarian Democratic Forum. Arpad Gonz became president of the republic and has remained in that position since.

Meanwhile, the Socialist Party was reduced to minority status. The new government focused on establishing policies that would move Hungary toward a market economy, including privatization. This task was less difficult in Hungary than in most other countries in the region because the communist government itself had already gone further in that direction than elsewhere. Still, state-owned enterprises constituted 90 percent of the productive sector of the economy. The deliberately gradual approach to privatization brought about criticism from those who thought the country's wealth was being sold out. This in turn gave rise to right-wing nationalism, which undermined the ruling Democratic Forum.

In the elections of 1994 the Socialist Party was returned to office, having received more than half of the votes in the parliament. The Socialists chose to form a coalition government with the Alliance of Free Democrats, with Gyula Horn as Prime Minister. Both of the first two coalition governments served out their full terms.

The first round of elections in May of 1998 pitted Horn's ruling Socialists against the opposition right-wing parties under the umbrella of the Young Democrats (Fidesz) led by charismatic Viktor Urban.

Opinion polls indicated that the Socialists had a slight edge over Fidesz. Pundits were suggesting that although Fidesz would lose this election, Urban would be ripe for power in the 2002 elections. Prime Minister Horn himself became a campaign issue when it was revealed in the press that he had taken up arms in 1956 against his own people to assist Soviet invaders in crushing the revolution (*Budapest Sun*, April 9-15, 1998). It was further revealed that Defense Minister Gyorgy Keleti had voiced his opposition to NATO in 1988 in a textbook, claiming it was a threat to world peace. It was even suggested that the U.S. Senate's decision to postpone final debate on NATO expansion was linked to these revelations. But the center-right coalition forces of Fidesz were divided. While some sought to exploit the matter, others said they supported speedy approval by the Senate before opponents of ratification could launch a new campaign.

Macroeconomic Reform

The macroeconomic reform process in Hungary accelerated between 1988 and 1991 with the introduction of ambitious market-oriented reforms that are now largely in place. Comprehensive liberalization was introduced for prices and foreign trade, the tax system was revised, the currency made convertible, and interest rates were liberalized. During the same period the legal and institutional framework necessary to develop the private sector and encourage foreign capital into Hungary was put into place. Most consumer prices were freed of administrative controls and reforms begun in the energy sector aimed at setting prices to cover costs. An indication of how politically charged this issue would become was the key decision taken by Prime Minister Horn in October 1996 not to raise energy prices as he had promised to the foreign companies who had invested two billion dollars in the sector. Trade liberalization had been phased in gradually, with licensing requirements and quotas eliminated from many imports.

On the positive side of the economic ledger, the austerity measures and general improvement in the macroeconomic picture increased Hungary's access to international capital markets since March 1995 (EBRD, 1996). A standby loan agreement was signed with the International Monetary Fund in March 1996 and Hungary's membership in the Organization for Economic Cooperation and Development was granted in May, confirming the country's achievements in economic, legal and institutional reforms. Hungary became a member of the World Trade Organization in December 1994 and some import tariffs have since been phased out. Between 1990 and 1995, Hungary received more than $11 billion in cash contributions associated with foreign direct investment, the highest amount of any country in the region. By 1998, fully 40 percent of the region's total foreign investment was going to Hungary.

Change has not come without a price, however. Not until 1994 did real GDP increase by a modest 2.9 percent—following several years of steep decline. In 1995 it fell to 1.5 percent and to 1 percent in 1996. Unemployment reached 14 percent in early 1993 before gradually falling back to 10 percent in 1995. Inflation oscillated, reaching 40 percent in mid-1991, dropping to 17 percent in early 1994, and then jumping back to 31 percent by mid-1995. Following the introduction of the austerity program, living standards dropped markedly in Hungary with a 12 percent decline in real income for 1995. The general effect of the structural reforms that were introduced from 1989 onward was to widen the gap between rich and poor and between the developed and underdeveloped regions of the country, in particular in the northeast, which was previously the center of heavy industry. The government's policy of devaluing the currency also had negative effects on the population. As Hungary wooed foreign investors, the gap between foreign- and locally-owned firms grew ever wider. In spite of the generally improving macroeconomic trends, the average Hungarian still did not feel tangible benefits.

The 1990s have been characterized by an overall decrease in employment and a corresponding increase in unemployment in Hungary. Although unemployment has tended to decrease slightly in recent years, it varies geographically and among minority groups. In Budapest unemployment has been in the range of 5 to 6 percent, compared with 20 percent in the northeast and over 75 percent in some Gypsy communities. While the national level of unemployment has hovered around 11 percent, certain areas of the country have reached 25 percent. However, the growing share of the private sector within the economy has served to counterbalance the decline in employment within large state-owned firms. In several areas unemployment has provided impetus for start-up efforts in business.

PRIVATIZATION AND ECONOMIC GROWTH IN HUNGARY

Within the CEE region, Hungary is considered to be further along in the privatization process than many other countries even though privatization has been more gradual. The Act on Economic Associations enacted on January 1, 1989, set forth the requirement for establishing and operating commercial firms in Hungary. This covered both the creation of new domestic and foreign companies and the transformation of previous enterprise forms, including state-owned enterprises. Spontaneous privatization, where managers in state enterprises moved assets out of the firm into their own private companies, was common for the first two years (Webster 1993). This practice occasioned public outcry, and the privatization process stalled by September 1991. Of the 10,000 retail outlets singled out in 1990 for auction to private bidders, only 680 had been sold by 1992. A State Property Agency was created to regulate the transfer of assets from state to private hands.

The privatization process in Hungary was deliberate and slow, the gradualist approach as opposed to the shock therapy applied in Poland. In one of its first steps, the Democratic Forum coalition government drew up a list of laws and regulations needed to foster private initiative, encourage investment, and develop capital markets. The government committed itself to reducing the state enterprise sector to less than 50 percent by 1995. As a strategy for privatization, the government opted for a company by company policy, based on finding Western companies that would either take over the company entirely or come in as a partner. As a result, foreign investment increased rapidly and a good many companies were able to find foreign partners or purchasers. Small and medium-sized companies were privatized locally, some to groups of employees. Many companies found it difficult to compete and salaries remained low. Unemployment grew significantly. The government came under criticism from both sides: those who felt it was moving too slowly toward privatization and those who feared that it was giving away the country's wealth.

Despite these contentious issues, both the privatization process and the creation of new enterprises by domestic and foreign entities have continued steadily since the late 1980s (EBRD 1996). Foreign participation in the private sector has become substantial, largely a result of the positive international image of Hungary as a country with a favorable investment climate. This foreign investment has been accompanied by technology transfer from Western strategic investors that has been applied in restructuring the privatized companies. Hungary has pursued a privatization model of individual corporate sale, generally through tenders, in which cash price was the key factor. The government has not implemented a voucher or other popular privatization scheme, so the process has been slower and more difficult than anticipated. Although Hungary made good progress in the initial years of transition, the reform process slowed in 1993-1994, in part because of the May 1994 elections, which brought the Socialists to power. In that year the privatization of state firms ground to a halt.

Hungary has been relatively successful in generating private sector growth with a government program of concessional financing that has facilitated the transfer of state activities to the private sector. Loans on preferential terms have been made available to finance management/employee buyouts. The legal privatization framework has been modified several times since 1990 in attempts to speed up the process and to provide for management of those state-owned companies not yet privatized.

By 1995, already more than 60 percent of the Hungarian GDP was estimated to have been generated by the private sector, thus exceeding the government's stated objective of reducing the share of the state enterprise sector to less than 50 percent. The situation improved sharply as a renewed privatization effort resulted in over 80 percent of the state companies being sold, with only 364 companies still in state ownership and scheduled for sale. Privatization proceeds reached a total of $8.3 billion, including $3.8 billion in 1995 alone. The selling of the largest flagship enterprises was virtually completed, including all regional electricity distributors, two power generating firms, and six gas distributors. These sales would be used to reduce Hungary's large foreign debt. Only 36 major firms remained fully state-owned, including the postal service and railways.

The sale of small enterprises to the private sector has also been comprehensive. The Hungarian private sector is characterized by small and medium-sized companies with sales of less than $20 million. Out of approximately eleven thousand shops in state ownership in 1990, more than nine thousand have been transferred to private hands. However, privatization of agricultural enterprises has been less successful. Although most of the small and medium-sized state-owned farms have been privatized through a compensation scheme, the privatization of large state-owned farms has not begun because of legal limitations on foreign ownership of agricultural land, a politically sensitive issue.

The privatization and restructuring process in Hungary has had two types of results: unsuccessful companies that were resold or closed down, and successful ones poised for expansion. Privatization has remained very much in the news. In the fall of 1996 a new board for the state privatization agency was appointed after the previous board was sacked in the wake of a major scandal over unusually high payments made to a consultant.

LOOKING TOWARD EUROPE

> Hungary should interpret the NATO vote in the U.S. Senate as a sign that the country has met international requirements of freedom, democracy, and a market economy.
>
> —Prime Minister Gyula Horn,
> following the favorable vote of April 1998

Hungary is looking increasingly toward Europe, and Hungarians are very much preoccupied with joining NATO and the European Union. Membership in NATO could well pave the way for Hungary into Western European institutions. In 1995, Hungary began hosting logistics bases for four thousand United States troops in support of NATO forces under the Dayton Peace Accords. Political-military cooperation between the United States government and Hungary has been excellent. The United States has already provided material and technical assistance to help Hungary restructure its armed forces and promote professionalization of the military. Hungary continues to provide a vital staging and support base for NATO troops serving in Bosnia, including Hungarian support troops.

Russia and the United States joined other NATO leaders in signing a Founding Act of mutual cooperation and security between the alliance and its former principal adversary on May 27,1997. The effect of the accord was to improve the possibility for three countries in the CEE region—Hungary, the Czech Republic, and Poland—to join NATO by 1999. Then, meeting in Madrid on July 8, 1997, NATO formally invited Poland, Hungary and the Czech Republic to join by the end of the century. Hungarian Prime Minister Gyula Horn, Czech President Vaclav Havel, and Polish President Aleksander Kwasniewski held a joint news conference to voice their delight at NATO's offer (Drozdiak and Harris 1997).

On November 16, 1997, Hungarian voters put a stamp of approval on the government's intention to join NATO by a margin that pleased their political leaders (Spolar 1997). They had agreed to the referendum largely as a way to ease internal political squabbles over NATO membership. Half of all eligible voters cast ballots in a nationwide referendum to gauge public support for the eastward expansion of the Western military alliance. Of those who voted, more than 85 percent said yes to the single question on the ballot: "Do you want Hungary to ensure its safety by joining NATO?" Of major concern to the Hungarian government was the potential economic impact of NATO membership. If, as the Ministry of Finance projected for 1997, the GDP grew at 4 percent or better, NATO membership would cause no undue economic burden. If growth were only between 2 and 4 percent, membership would be a substantial burden to the economy, and under two percent GDP growth would cause major problems.

Hungary's political elite was eager to show this high-profile measure of public support in the most positive light in the referendum. Prime Minister Gyula Horn called the vote a "fantastic result" (Spolar, 1997). He said the fact that the vote was a success "provides a lesson" in public participation to Hungary's neighbors and sends "an important message to Washington." Foreign Minister Laszlo Kovacs, whose ministry had undertaken an unprecedented, well-financed campaign to draw out voters, said the vote went well beyond his expectations. Both played down the low turnout, which fell below the government's last internal forecast and would have invalidated the results but for a change in election laws.

Coming five months after NATO extended invitations to Hungary, Poland, and the Czech Republic to join NATO talks, the vote essentially changed nothing. The Hungarian government had in fact supported NATO membership for years. But the referendum helped strengthen the public relations campaign, which still faced scrutiny by NATO's 16 members, including the United States.

Attaining membership in the European Union also remains a major objective of the Hungarian government, which presented its national program for harmonizing internal markets as a strategy for accession to the EU at the July 1997 Madrid Summit. The period since 1994 has been characterized by the establishment of democratic institutions such as the court system and by bringing Hungarian legislation into closer harmony with the international norms of organizations such as the European Union and the Council of Europe.

In 1995, a five-year program to bring 470 Hungarian laws into harmony with EU standards was initiated and is proceeding on schedule. A sound legal and regulatory framework is in place which reflects international corporate accounting standards as well as bankruptcy and liquidation laws. Foreign investment is encouraged by a liberal foreign investment code. Tariffs and import restrictions have been significantly reduced and two-thirds of Hungarian trade is now with the countries of the EU. The transition to a market economy has created an environment conducive to foreign investment but less so to the creation of new businesses. Debate over the issue of integration with the EU is likely to continue to define the economic and political agenda in Hungary for the foreseeable future.

Some issues that tend to condition Hungary's aspirations for membership in the European Union have to do with relations with neighboring countries. The signing of treaties with the governments of Slovakia and Romania in 1996 stipulating the rights of the Hungarian ethnic minorities in those two countries should improve relations with Hungary's neighbors.

On December 13, 1997, the European Union invited Hungary and five other nations—Poland, the Czech Republic, Estonia, Slovenia and Cyprus—to become candidates for membership (*The Washington Post* December 14, 1997). They were invited to begin membership negotiations in March 1998. Five additional Central and East European nations were given pre-candidate status: Bulgaria, Romania, Latvia, Lithuania and Slovakia. The invitation to join Europe's 15 wealthiest nations is the first official step in what promises to be a long process of negotiation and compromise. Membership is not expected before 2002 and likely later.

Hungary's industrial policy, which aims at creating conditions favorable to the development of private enterprise, clearly has integration into the European Union in view. It sees modernization as necessary to enhance competitiveness and to increase value added. To attain membership in the EU, it will be necessary to achieve its prerequisite regulations. Harmonization of the legal and regulatory environment must be introduced into the areas of quality control and environmental protection. International product quality and standards control will have to be complied with in order for Hungarian exports to reach European markets. Cooperation with the EU in research and development in management training must be pursued, especially for small and medium-sized enterprises. Administrative burdens for enterprises will have to be reduced. The banking system must be made more responsive to the needs of enterprises. And more effective measures will be required to reduce the informal (black market) economy.

THE ROLE OF SMES IN ECONOMIC GROWTH IN HUNGARY

> The contribution of small enterprises to the Gross Domestic Product cannot grow unlimited and yet be declared less and less on tax returns.
>
> —State of Small and Medium Sized Businesses in Hungary,
> 1997 Annual Report

Hungary has had a relatively long history of experimentation with private enterprise initiatives; there was already a substantial informal sector in place by the time the government formally embraced the market economy in 1989. Two years later, fully one-third of total employment and of GDP was already accounted for by the private sector, similar to the figures for Poland. This was in striking contrast to the Czech and Slovak Republics, where comparable figures were about 16 percent and 8 percent respectively.

At the beginning of the transition period the structure of the Hungarian economy was somewhat advanced in the CEE region to the extent that quasi-private entities were recognized under the socialist system. There were three categories of enterprises: state-owned large enterprises, small to medium-sized cooperatives managed by their members, and the "privates." The last category consisted of the self-employed, or micro-entrepreneurs, responsible to and for themselves. As a class they were maligned but envied, tolerated despite going against communist principles. In the early 1980s the government began gradually to ease the economic centralization and suspend the repression of this nonstate sector.

From 1982 onward many semi private or fully private entities in the informal sector actually out-performed the official state sector (Fulop and Hisrich 1995). New economic formations developed rapidly under the name of civil law associations. One form of such associations, "the economic working community," was codified and subject to a 3 percent corporate tax. Another form was the small cooperative, grassroots-based and voluntary, whose members felt a strong loyalty to the association. They functioned as legal entities as opposed to other forms which were also recognized. Yet another type of association concerned catering facilities operated by private individuals on a contract basis. In 1985, the majority of state-owned companies were put under the control of local authorities, thus easing their hierarchic dependence and allowing discretion with respect to central control.

These changes opened up an unprecedented movement toward private enterprise. By the end of the 1980s, even before the regime change, there were 24,000 business associations, 19,000 company business associations, and 3,000 small cooperatives. The number of full-time small craftsmen grew from 75,000 in 1980 to 120,000 in 1989. This process was accelerated after the regime change by the elimination of legal constraints on cooperatives and by the privatization of state-owned companies which entailed massive layoffs of workers. Thanks to the Company Act of 1988, the number of registered enterprises grew by the tens of thousands every month, the vast majority of them small start-ups, although some were the product of privatization.

The Institute for Small Business Development in Hungary (ISBD), which was established to monitor and analyze the small business sector, has begun publishing a yearly report on the SME sector. The institute draws upon and analyzes data provided by the Central Statistics Office (CSO). In its first Annual Report (1996) the institute explained that the term *small business* would be used to include the full range from micro- and small to medium-sized enterprises. The sector gathered momentum at the beginning of the 1990s. But within the sector the proportion of micro-businesses—including many that were registered but for whatever reasons were not operational—have increased faster than small and medium-sized firms. Small businesses have taken over in many sectors that had been dominated by big state-owned enterprises before 1990. They have often provided the supplier and sales networks for growing Hungarian firms and to a much lesser extent for foreign companies moving into the country.

Two reasons were offered by the institute for the relatively high proportion of small business failures in Hungary. First, many Hungarian entrepreneurs got their start in the 1980s at a time when there was not yet a market economy and therefore little competition.

But those who started later without any experience have faced greater risks in a market environment. The second factor has had to do with a growing and changing regulatory environment which poses a hindrance to small business development. On balance, however, the changes in such areas as accounting methods, certain taxation measures, and foreign currency management from 1995 to 1996 were found to be favorable to the growth of small enterprises.

Although no uniform and generally recognized definition exists for small enterprises, the European Union uses a working definition based on the number of employees. In Hungary, the Ministry of Industry and Trade, together with the Institute for Small Enterprise Promotion, elaborated a draft proposing a modified classification which included the number of workers as well as net sales. The micro-enterprise category remains the same as that of the EU but the small and medium-size categories for Hungary are slightly different (Institute for Small Business Development *1997 Annual Report*): See Table 1.1 below:

Table 1.1: Definition of Enterprise Size: European Union and Hungary

Size of Enterprise	European Union	Hungary
Micro-enterprise	fewer than 10 employees	fewer than 10 employees
Small enterprise	10—99 employees	10—49 employees Net annual income of HUF 1,000 million or previous annual balance of no more than HUF 600 million.
Medium-sized enterprise	100—249 employees	50—249 employees Net annual income of HUF 5,000 million or previous annual balance of no more than HUF 3.750 million
Large enterprise	250 employees	250 and over

Source: Institute for Small Business Development, *1997 Annual Report*, p. 59.

In its first *Annual Report 1996,* the Institute noted that there are numerous caveats with regard to these categories. For example, It is difficult to obtain reliable data in general, but it is important to define how figures are being used. For example, information about enterprises in the agricultural sector in Hungary are treated separately from the industrial sector. Current statistics in Hungary do not allow for a distinction between enterprises in direct or indirect state ownership. And it is a mistake to assume that all registered enterprises are also commercially active since many, possibly over half, that are registered do not function.

The *1996 Annual Report* emphasized that the number of registered and commercially active enterprises is not one and the same thing. In the first place, many of those registered are dormant and do not operate at all (not unlike those in more developed capitalist economies). Furthermore, some commercially active entities that are not registered are also included in the records. The difference between the number of registered companies and those paying taxes is substantial, a situation that is true in many developing economies. The CSO does not provide a clear distinction between these types of enterprises. But the gap between the number of registered enterprises and those sending in tax returns is substantial, corresponding roughly to the number of commercially inactive enterprises. Forty percent of all enterprises are located in Budapest and County Pest, and the capital city also has the highest ratio of enterprise to population.

The *1997 Annual Report* of the institute notes that the CSO introduced a new specification for labeling economic organizations in 1995. By the end of 1996 there were just over one million registered companies in Hungary. Of these, more than 75 percent were sole proprietorships, 19 percent were partnerships, and 12 percent limited liability companies. The number of sole proprietorships increased as compared with registered companies. However, more than a third of sole proprietorships and cooperatives were categorized as nonoperational. The overwhelming majority of firms (97 percent) that filled out tax returns in 1995 in Hungary were micro-enterprises. Small enterprises made up 2.4 percent of the total, medium-sized firms 0.7 percent and large firms 0.1 percent.

Small Business Contribution to GDP and Employment Creation

Small businesses in Hungary are making an increasingly significant contribution to the Gross Domestic Product and the generation of employment. However, the share of the contribution of small and medium scale enterprises in the Hungarian GDP is subject to interpretation. According to the institute's *1997 Annual Report*, when giving information on the GDP, the CSO neglects to break down data by size of enterprise. At the same time an assessment is made about the contribution of small enterprises to the GDP, taking into consideration the unreliability of data. Data gleaned from tax returns are presented and then compared with "corrected figures." Thus, based on tax return data, the contribution of the small business sector to GDP remained fairly constant at around 27 percent from 1992 to 1995. The contribution of the medium-sized sector increased from 16 to 23 percent, while that of large businesses fell from 57 to 51 percent during the same period.

The discrepancy between tax return data and reality is striking, however. Undeclared or "invisible" income accounts for a large portion of the actual contribution of small business to the GDP. In practical terms, this phenomenon is characteristic mainly of the small business sector where the tendency not to report earnings is fairly common. When the data is "corrected" to account for this informal sector contribution, the figures look quite different; the share of small business contribution to to GDP increases from 41 percent in 1992 to 44 percent in 1995. That of the medium-sized sector increases from 14 to 18 percent, while that of large businesses declines from 45 to 40 percent during the same period. When taken together, the small and medium sectors accounted for fully 62 percent of the GDP in 1995.

Net turnover of Hungarian enterprises doubled between 1992 and 1995. While large enterprises increased their turnover by 50 percent during this period, the turnover for micro- and small enterprises increased two and a half times. The share of large firms in turnover decreased while that of small and medium-sized firms grew. By 1995, the share of large companies stood at just 37 percent, compared to 20 percent for medium-sized companies, 17 percent for small, and 27 percent for micro-enterprises. The share of micro- and small enterprises in turnover is preponderant in such areas as education, health care, real estate, commerce, and social services. Medium-sized firms dominate in agriculture and forestry, and large firms in mining, processing, gas, heating, and water supply.

Small and medium-sized enterprises are beginning to make their contribution to export growth as well, even though large firms still account for the lion's share of exports. In 1992, small businesses accounted for 25 percent of all Hungarian exports, and medium-sized businesses, 19 percent. The following year, their combined contribution exceeded half of total exports, although export growth came to a standstill in 1994. Within the SME sector, export activity was concentrated in the hands of no more than a thousand companies. Export growth was particularly pronounced in the agriculture and forestry sectors, where the percentage of small businesses grew as the contribution of large exporters declined. The transport and telecommunications sector was likewise dominated by large companies, although the contribution of medium-sized exporters was significant.

Equally important is the contribution of SMEs to the creation of employment. As the process of privatization has made headway, more and more people who previously worked for state enterprises are now employed in the private sector. In 1980, only 3 percent of the working population were self-employed in Hungary; by 1996, that figure had reached 15 percent. However, nearly half a million claimed to be unemployed, largely a result of the restructuring and downsizing of state enterprises. Between 1992 and 1995, large Hungarian firms dismissed more than half a million workers, while the corresponding increase in employment in the small business sector during that period was 430,000.

There was also a decline of some sixty thousand employees among medium-sized firms. Unemployment increased by 9 percent since 1990. By the end of 1995, only one-third of the employed worked for large companies, down from nearly half in 1992. The share of employment in the micro-enterprise sector rose from 22 percent in 1992 to 37 percent in 1995, that of small enterprises from 10% to 13%. The share of medium-sized firms declined slightly from 21 to 19 percent during the same period. Thus, by 1995 fully two thirds of all those employed in Hungary worked in the small and medium-enterprise sector.

The Case of Northern Hungary

Under the socialist economy northeastern Hungary, and particularly the town of Miskolc, was known for its heavy industrial production (Fulop 1994). With the transition, the large state-owned enterprises were privatized and thousands of workers lost their jobs. By 1994 large enterprises accounted for only 8 percent of the total in the region, while medium-sized enterprises represented 17 percent and small enterprises fully 67 percent. Even so, 75 percent of all employment remained in the larger companies. Smaller enterprises have begun to play an important role by absorbing some of the unemployment and satisfying customer demand. Professor Gyula Fulop of Miskolc University has been studying the informal and small business sector for several years. His research indicates that the competitiveness of medium-sized enterprises in the region falls far behind the rest of the country, and small businesses have not been able to employ as many workers as those in other parts of the country.

He cites numerous problems facing small businesses in the region. Not surprisingly, one of the major difficulties they perceive is financing. Reform of the banking system began in 1987 with the establishment of five large commercial banks, later expanded to 20. Ten specialized financial institutions and a savings bank network are also functioning. However, these banks are very much in their formative stage. Like most banks, they tend to require collateral guarantees from their clients rather than looking at their business plans, so credit is hard to come by. Loans that are available require at least 35 to 40 percent interest rates and default is common. Inflation, also amounting to between 35 and 40 percent in 1991, compounds the problem. Insolvency is frequent, although bankruptcy is generally not declared. Fulop reports that debts among businesses in the region amount to 200 billion HUF.

Small Business in Agriculture

The agricultural sector of the Hungary economy is proportionately more important to economic development than it is in more industrialized economies. As has been noted earlier, during the socialist era agricultural land was virtually all under state control. Therefore, the trends toward privatization since the early 1990s are having an especially important impact on this sector. The expansion of agricultural small enterprises since 1990 is due to the break up of state farms and cooperatives into smaller units, as well as the transformation of household and supplementary economies into agricultural enterprises.

By the end of the 1980s the Hungarian food processing sector experienced a crisis brought on by the process of privatization. There were three types of farms: state farms, cooperatives, and private farms. Most of the land under cultivation was in the hands of the cooperatives. Privatization involved transforming the farm system and ownership of factories and property in order to assign a greater role to private initiative. The Compensations Act provided for the distribution of cooperative estates and property assets. Nearly half of the former cooperative assets were transferred to the ownership of active cooperative members and employees. The privatization of state farms has progressed rather slowly. By 1995, 34 state farms had gone bankrupt, 39 had been privatized, and 23 were being privatized. Nearly half of all property assets of state farms had been sold.

Although land ownership remained with the state, farms were leased for periods of 10 to 15 years. Land ownership relations began to change radically after 1990. In that year 27 percent of agricultural land area was under state farms, 64 percent under cooperatives, and only 7 percent under private farms. By 1995 the ratio was reversed: private farms accounted for 43 percent of agricultural cultivation, cooperatives 38 percent and state farms only 19 percent. The average farm size declined rather substantially, as did the number of farm workers. By 1995, over 70 percent of all legal-entity farm enterprises employed fewer than 20 workers. This reflects the fact that large farms frequently broke up into smaller ones. Activities other than basic agricultural production such as agro-processing were separated into independent companies as were subsidiaries.

The agricultural sector in Hungary has undergone a significant decline during this period, including a reduction in the agricultural workforce. Because of the collapse of markets in the former Soviet Union and the shrinking of internal demand, profitability in the agricultural sector has diminished. Large farms suffered the greatest reversals with the loss of state subsidies. The agricultural utilization of credit schemes elaborated for small enterprises in the agricultural sector was restricted because of strict terms of credit. A new program of state assistance to small farmers was established under the Credit Guarantee Foundation for Agrarian Enterprises, but generally speaking the transformation of the agro-processing sector has occurred in a very unfavorable economic context.

FINANCING FOR SMES IN HUNGARY: BANK AND NON-BANK SOURCES

Access to formal banking institutions is essential to the growth of small businesses, although many start out with personal savings or informal loans. Traditionally the banking system in Hungary catered to the large state-owned enterprises. The Hungarian banking system prior to 1987 resided in the National Bank of Hungary, which carried out central bank as well as all commercial functions, including savings, local cooperatives, and foreign trade. One of the first banking sector reforms implemented by the transition countries of the CEE was the break up of the monobank system into two tiers: a central bank responsible for the conduct of monetary affairs, and state-owned commercial and specialized banks responsible for deposit mobilization, lending, and other commercial banking activities. Slovenia was the first to break up its monobank as early as 1971, and Hungary was second in 1987 (Borish et al. 1996).

While the first tier was a fairly straight forward matter, implementation of the second tier was complicated by the fact that the banking reforms were not accompanied by changes in the legal and regulatory framework. The commercial activities of the monobank were taken over by three banks: Hungarian Credit Bank, Commercial and Credit Bank, and Budapest Bank. Two other banks, the Hungarian Savings Bank and the Hungarian Foreign Trade Bank, were also allowed to carry out a full range of banking activities. The state-owned banks were characterized by special functions: savings, foreign trade, and cooperatives. Then, in 1991, a regulatory framework was put in place. Although there has been some movement away from specialization, the largest state banks continue to focus on their original core business activities.

In addition to the state-owned banks, there were ten smaller banks and specialized financial institutions in Hungary in 1989. By the end of 1992 there were 32 banks operating in the country and by 1995 the number had risen to 44 (of which 26 were private). Another 255 cooperatives focused primarily on rural banking. Of the 44 banks, 17 remained majority state-owned, and another five had minority state ownership. Even though private banks have grown rapidly, state banks still accounted for 56 percent of banking sector assets, 45 percent of loans, and 67 percent of deposits in 1995. Hungary has had a relatively open banking environment compared with other countries in the region. This has served to stimulate investment and development among private and foreign banks.

Hungary has allowed new private, joint venture and wholly owned foreign banks to establish themselves freely since 1987. Of the 26 private banks operating in Hungary, 22 are majority foreign-controlled. The private banks are generally smaller, but better capitalized than are the state banks. In fact, the latter have been losing ground because of their high levels of nonperforming loans.

Whatever small-scale enterprises existed under the socialist regime were dependent upon informal capital markets or their own savings for capital investment. In fact, the financial situation of small businesses is influenced by numerous factors other than their relationship to banks. Traditionally, they have obtained credit from other enterprises for the provision of raw materials and advances on delivery of goods. These factors in turn may have effected the firm's relationship with banking institutions. In any case, contacts with banks eventually play an important role in determining the ability of a small business to grow. In Hungary, many smaller enterprises emerged beside or in place of companies with substantial assets. In anticipation of their future success, banks initially tended to give these new enterprises the benefit of the doubt. However, their enthusiasm had begun to give way to caution by the mid-1990s as a result of high nonrepayment of loans and problems of mortgage foreclosures.

Since then, there has been a decline in small enterprise credits, which must be seen in the context of the overall business sector. Overall lending to SMEs has decreased at the same time small business bank deposits increased. In fact, the share of small business loans actually fell from a modest 11 percent in 1993 to only 7 percent in 1995. The decline in credit to small businesses was due in large part to strong austerity measures taken by the government of Hungary and the Central Bank in 1995. The banking environment for small businesses is very competitive. Foreign banks have become very active while Hungarian banks have become increasingly wary about lending to small businesses because of poor repayment rates. Local banks themselves were lacking in capabilities to manage risk and credit. Typically, banks in Hungary require collateral of 150 percent or more on business loans, which small businesses consider a major deterrent to securing credit. It is interesting to note the importance of foreign currency credits taken abroad in the financing of Hungarian enterprises in recent years, although this is less true of small businesses than of larger ones.

There are a number of programs of financial support and preferential credits now available to SMEs in Hungary. In recent years the government of Hungary has initiated programs of subsidized credit to small businesses. The start-credit program is aimed at those businesses that have been in operation for no more than three years, whether they are sole proprietorships or limited liability companies. The loan is for 15 years in the building industry, 10 years for procuring equipment or machinery, and eight years for other assets such as opening stock. The interest rate is 75 percent of the basic interest of the day, although the bank may add another 2 percent margin for profit.

Micro-credit loans are available through the offices of the Hungarian Fund for Enterprise Development and Local Enterprise Agencies. These loans, which do not exceed one million HUF, are for enterprises that employ no more than 10 people and have a yearly turnover of no more than eight million HUF. Repayment is due in three years, with a six-month grace period.

The PHARE Program of the European Union has provided funds to improve the competitiveness of SMEs employing fewer than 60 people and in business for less than a year. The credit—up to 10 million HUF—is primarily for investment, including the purchase of land or buildings. The loans are for a period of two to seven years with a two-year grace period. The part of the loans guaranteed by the PHARE Program and the National Bank carries an interest that is 75 percent of basic interest, plus an added 2 percent margin.

GOVERNMENT AND DONOR ASSISTANCE TO SMES IN HUNGARY

The industrial policy elaborated by the government in 1995 aimed at the creation of an environment favorable to enterprise. This entailed maintaining programs that increase competitiveness and added value. The policy aimed at reducing administrative burdens and combating the black (informal) economy. Domestic plants of multinationals—car manufacturing, spare parts, pharmaceuticals, household machinery and consumer electronics—were seen as being of strategic importance to Hungary. Preparation for the EU is all the more crucial since industrial exports have been completely free as of the end of 1997. Legal harmonization is to be introduced into areas of quality control and environmental protection. EU market guidelines for quality and standard controls, product responsibility, and competition policy are to be adopted. Likewise, cooperation with the EU in research and development is to be promoted and linked to the modernization of management.

Hungarian Government SME Policies and Agencies

Hungary did not have a clearly articulated small business development policy in the early years of the transition. In 1994 a government decree set forth the outline of a program for the development of small and medium-sized businesses under the Ministry of Industry, Trade, and Tourism. But owing to the changes in the macroeconomic environment and their impact on small businesses, there was a need for reassessment. In particular, it became increasingly important to locate Hungary's SME development in the context of tenets of the European Council. Membership in the European Union would require harmonization with European standards. Two basic and related concerns emerged. In light of the trend toward integration within the EU, there was a need for Hungarian small businesses to improve their competitiveness. In order for this to occur, there was a need to develop a nationwide network of business support services, especially in regions of the country where unemployment was highest. In the industrial field it was deemed of paramount importance that the multinationals in Hungary should have a healthy circle of domestic suppliers (subcontractors).

To achieve these objectives the government sought to enhance the performance of small businesses through a variety of measures (Institute for Small Business Development, *1997 Annual Report*). They addressed such issues as reliable statistics, measures for improvement of the financial situations of SMEs, and the simplification of start-up conditions. A system for gleaning data on small and medium- sized enterprises was established. The Central Statistical Office conducted a full-scale survey of companies in the first half of 1997. This was to lead to a new registry of companies that would be less cumbersome and onerous for them. The tax system was to be revised to alleviate the burden on SMEs, encouraging them to reinvest profits by reducing taxes and decreasing the ratio between health and retirement contribution and the GDP. Increased access to credit was to be promoted through a system of guarantees and loans through banks and venture capital. Financial institutions specializing in development were to be encouraged by broadening the sphere of credit financing and preferential credit in investments. As a partner to the PHARE Programs, the Hungarian government proposed providing more resources for small business advisory and information services.

The Hungarian Foundation for Enterprise Promotion

One of the most prominent efforts to promote entrepreneurship in Hungary, the Hungarian Foundation for Enterprise Promotion, was established under the initiative of the government in 1990, with an initial capital of 4.2 billion HUF. Its purpose is to promote professional and entrepreneurial development by strengthening capital assets of small businesses, whether they are officially registered or not. The action program of the foundation aims at the deployment of an institutional system of enterprise support and the promotion of an "enterprise culture." Foundation assistance includes financing on preferential terms, guarantees, and the giving of nonrefundable grants. Support is also given to educational and research projects promoting small businesses. In 1990, its first year of operation, the Foundation extended investment credit to over two thousand entrepreneurs in the range of 500,000 to 20 million HUF.

After a series of negotiations, the foundation began to implement the PHARE Program in early 1991. There followed the launching of a micro-credit scheme and the first steps toward implementation of a regional enterprise support program, which included the establishment of enterprise centers located in the county seat in six counties. By 1994 there were 14 such centers in as many counties providing training for entrepreneurs. Training programs for entrepreneurial trainers and bank managers administering the Phare credit were organized. By 1995, the foundation was operating more than 100 Local Enterprise Centers throughout the country. Some thirty-six thousand persons had received counseling or taken part in the foundation's training programs. Nearly three thousand entrepreneurs were granted preferential credits totaling more than 1.7 billion HUF through the various credit schemes.

The Institute for Small Business Development

The institute monitors the small business sector in Hungary and publishes an annual report which provides data on the sector and identifies major trends. The Institute provides a very useful service by reporting data comparable to the contents and subject matter of the European Observatory for SMEs, which reports on this sector for the EU.

In 1988, legislation was enacted in Hungary which recognized noneconomic associations, making it possible for small-scale producers to develop medium-sized enterprises by raising the quota required from

30 to 500 members. A small venture section was also established in the Chamber of Economics, which was eventually transformed into an independent organization known as the National Association of Entrepreneurs (VOSZ). This was Hungary's first independent economic interest federation. Although there are now several such organizations, they have remained relatively weak in the absence of an infrastructure supporting the development and growth of enterprises.

There now exists a wide range of organizations engaged in providing support to small enterprises. These include a network of local business centers, special financial programs, and guarantee institutions. The country has yet to develop export promotion programs or training for business promotion professionals.

On June 13, 1996, the Hungarian government approved the SME development concept submitted by the Ministry of Industry and Trade (*European Council for Small Business* 1997). The Entrepreneurship/ SME/Development Council of the Ministry of Industry and Trade assisted in the drafting of the development concept. A working group of the Council prepared a draft SME law for submission to the parliament. In response to frequent critical comment on its figures for the number of economic units in Hungary, the Central Statistics Office began to publish two series of data to distinguish between dormant and active firms.

European Union PHARE Program

In 1991 Hungary concluded a Europe Agreement with the European Union, and in April 1994 formally submitted its application for full membership with the EU. During the period preceding membership, PHARE Program support is extended by the EU as a tool to facilitate Hungary's participation in the process of European integration. This relates particularly to certain political, economic, and legal reforms and to sustainable economic growth. Total EU-PHARE commitments to Hungary during 1990-1995 amounted to 582.8 million ECU and were focused on private enterprise support in training, education, and research. The PHARE Multi-annual Indicative Program (1995-1999) is geared to helping Hungary tackle the main issues which the country must overcome before becoming fully integrated into the EU.

The PHARE credit scheme provides credit on preferential terms for development projects to be implemented by SMEs. The credit can be drawn for the purchase of machinery, equipment,and other fixed assets. Up to 25 percent of it can be allocated to the financing of working capital with a state or foreign investor share of less than half. The maximum loan is 10 million HUF for two to seven years, with a repayment holiday of two years and an interest rate of 28 percent. The applicant's own contribution must be at least 15 percent, and the bank can require collateral of up to 150 percent.

European Bank for Reconstruction and Development (EBRD)

Since its creation in 1991, the EBRD has approved 44 projects in Hungary (European Bank for Reconstruction and Development, 1996). As of July 1996, this amounted to 998 million ECU and represented 12 percent of the EBRD portfolio. Over 90 percent of the investments have been in the private sector and roughly 13 percent of the Hungarian portfolio has been in the form of equity. In its early projects, EBRD sought to promote the participation of foreign strategic investors in Hungary. In recent years, however, the EBRD has put increasing emphasis on local companies without strategic partners. The capacity of the market to provide funding to SMEs, which is riskier and requires more effort, is limited both for debt and equity. Due to its size and resource constraints, the Bank is dealing with the SME target group via investment funds, credit lines, and other wholesale products. EBRD is cooperating with EU-PHARE in several areas, including a joint initiative to seek efficient ways of promoting and financing SMEs.

The EBRD has a program for financing agricultural restructuring aimed at companies in agriculture and the food processing industry. Financing can be used for the purchase of second hand equipment from agricultural firms under transformation. Loans may not exceed more than $5 million. Loans are for 10 years and the interest rate varies depending upon tax qualifications, business risk, and financial status.

British Know-How Fund

Britain's Department for International Development manages an annual budget of nearly two billion dollars. Through its British Know-How Fund, the department plans to support a new program. In 1998 the fund began helping to pay for consultancy firms such as Price Waterhouse and McMillan & Baneth to teach Hungarian companies to succeed in the European Union. The Change Management Project (CHAMP) is designed to enable Hungarian firms to adapt to the demands of an increasingly competitive environment in the context of the European market. The three-year program aims at making it possible for senior and mid-level managers of small firms to implement major changes within their organizations in order to become more competitive. CHAMP makes consultant services available to SMEs at a fraction of the cost on the market. In the first phase of CHAMP, it is expected that 20 change management consultants will be trained in Budapest, who will in turn train another 80 consultants.

PROFILE OF HUNGARIAN ENTREPRENEURS

Behind the fragmentary statistics that describe the growing small business sector in Hungary are the real-life entrepreneurs who have risked life and limb to succeed in the transition economy. What constitutes success in the new private sector in Hungary?

Several recent surveys of SMEs in Hungary have helped to flesh out the picture of the performance of this sector. One of the earliest was a study conducted by Leila Webster of the World Bank in September 1991 (Webster 1993). The World Bank study was drawn from a sample of 106 firms with the objective of developing a profile of entrepreneurs and assessing the impact of reform on firm-level operations. The profile that emerged from the Webster survey on Hungary was similar to that in Poland and Czechoslovakia: these firms were owned by overwhelmingly middle-aged men with technical educations and previous employment in large state firms. It was different from other countries in that many of those interviewed had had substantial experience in private business before 1989. One third of them had owned another private firm. Ties to the West were substantial, developed through frequent travel in Western countries and by investors and trading partners. They were more sophisticated than their counterparts in other CEE countries in their ability to analyze foreign markets and negotiate foreign contracts.

Nearly all the firms in the Webster study were limited liability companies, generally lacking in finances and collateral. Half were in Budapest and the other half in communities throughout the country. The sample was chosen with a focus on five productive sectors: plastics, clothing, knitting, metalworking, and machine manufacturing. Nearly half of the firms employed fewer than 20 workers, while 22 percent employed more than 50. Only 25 percent of the sample firms were new start-ups. The rest predated the 1989 reforms, having begun as traditional craftsmen, small cooperatives, or as industrial divisions of agricultural cooperatives. Nearly half of the Webster sample of firms had received short-term loans, and a few had received long- term loans. However, they had obtained the loans after having been in business for years, in contrast to those in other CEE countries, where most received loans within a month of going into business.

The average firm size in the Webster survey was 44 employees, and the largest had 437 workers. Fifty-five percent reported 20 or fewer workers, of which the smallest were in clothing and machine shops. Producers of plastics and metal goods were the largest. The main concentration of small firms (with 11 to 20 workers) was in small and medium-sized towns where many new start-ups were found.

Professor Marjorie Lyles of Indiana University's School of Business has conducted a longitudinal survey of 129 owners/managers of small Hungarian enterprises. The baseline study was undertaken in 1993 and a second follow-up survey was done in 1995 (Lyles, 1997). A primary selection criterion was that the firm be Hungarian-owned, although it could have some minority foreign interests. Many of the findings were similar to those of the Webster survey, although the Lyles study aimed at determining the rate of survival of the firms initially interviewed and ascertaining the factors involved in their growth (or demise).

Lyles verified that of the 135 firms that had participated in the 1993 survey, 103 had survived and 32 were out of business. There did not seem to be any systematic differences by industry type between the survivors and those that had gone out of business. Nor did they show any major differences in terms of experience with banks or in the number of loans obtained. Both groups had few loans and poor access to capital, although the survivors were capitalized at four times the amount of the others. Survivors were more likely to have been in business longer, an average of six years. Firms with higher levels of exports were actually less likely to survive.

The profile of the typical owner/manager in the Lyles surveys was a 45-year-old male with either a university or technical college degree. Manufacturers were more likely to have a university degree while those in commerce were least likely. Most of the firms were owned by partners in which at least half of the equity was held by a Hungarian, although many reported a change in ownership. The average firm was a limited liability company whose operations were initiated between 1989 and 1993, although one had been in business since 1935!

Larger firms (with an average of 63 employees) tended to be in manufacturing and smaller ones in commerce and services. Manufacturing firms reported the highest growth in net earnings after taxes adjusted for inflation (200 percent), compared with 60 percent in service, 22 percent in commerce, and 49 percent in agriculture. Growth in sales was fairly even across the sectors, averaging 24 percent. The average sales growth of the Lyles sample was 25 percent for one year, adjusted for inflation. The firms' earnings increased on average by 92 percent while earnings as a percentage of sales averaged 5.3 percent.

The average growth in the number of employees from 1994 to 1995 was -10.1 percent. For manufacturing it was a decline of 20 percent, compared with increases of 43 percent in agriculture, 7.4 percent in commerce, and 0.5 percent in service. While manufacturing firms tended to record the highest growth in earnings, they also registered the sharpest decline in employment, a trend common among state-owned enterprises as well.

Three-quarters of the firms in the Lyles survey had never obtained credit from a bank, and only 15 percent had even received one loan, although several had obtained multiple loans. High interest rates were cited as the most serious concern of the firms in the Lyles survey. Lack of access to credit, diminished demand for their products and services, and delinquent payment by state enterprises were also concerns of the owners/managers.

The following are profiles of real-life Hungarian entrepreneurs, some drawn from the author's personal interviews and others from various reports.

PEKO Steel Works, Ozd

The small town of Ozd is an industrial center where the PEKO Steel Works is today one of several thriving enterprises run by the Janos Petrenko family (cited in Hisrich and Fulop 1995). It is a complex network of enterprises which are the result of over 20 years of effort of the head of the family, Janos Petrenko. His story is evidence that the Hungarian situation may have been somewhat different from other countries in the region in the extent to which small-scale entrepreneurs were tolerated under the socialist regime. Mr. Petrenko was working as an electrical locksmith in a foundry works in Ozd in 1971 when he traveled to Switzerland, where he was introduced to advanced metallurgy. Upon his return to Ozd he began a second job as a small-scale craftsman with financing from family and friends. By 1978 this operation was sufficiently established for him to quit his other day job and go into business full time. He eventually hired seven workers and by 1989 there were 27. Mr. Petrenko persevered in his business and won prizes for his inventions at industrial fairs.

In 1990 Mr. Petrenko founded the PEKO Steel Works by renovating a previously closed steel rolling mill with start-up capital of 90 million HUF ($600,000 at 1996 exchange rate). As the first factory owner in Hungary after the regime change, Petrenko would eventually enjoy wide acclaim. His first contact was with his former employer. In its first year of operation PEKO Steel achieved sales of 1.5 billion HUF, nearly all of it from exports. However, in the second year contracts for his product dried up as prices on the export market declined. Cheap steel from other socialist countries was beginning to flood the Hungarian market. In the third year the pendulum swung the other way again, as demand from both domestic and foreign customers increased. PEKO Steel Works developed a specialty item—quarter-circle steel—which was in demand around the world. PEKO Trade House was incorporated in 1991 as a retail and wholesale venture, trading in appliances, textiles, pharmacy and delicatessen goods. The company has been represented in numerous trade fairs throughout Europe and new items are regularly introduced into the PEKO inventory.

Pick Salami Factory, Szeged

The town of Szeged in southeastern Hungary near the Yugoslavia border is one of the more picturesque in the country. Located at the point where the Maros river flows into the Tisza, Szeged has a population of just under two hundred thousand. It is a town of rich historical significance as reflected in the fine architecture. It is also the home of one of the most well-known industries in Hungary, the Pick Salami Factory. Established in 1869 by Mark Pick, the company remained a family affair for many years, passing from father to son. Pick began making salami and paprika, two products for which Hungary is known throughout the world. By the early 1900s, Pick Salami was a well established medium-sized company and was winning prizes in fairs in Europe. In 1948, Pick Salami was nationalized and the Pick family lost control of the firm. The name was changed several times and operations merged with local butcheries. By the 1950s there were over four hundred workers and by the 1970s exports represented an important part of the company's market. Today, after many internal changes and a program of privatization in the early 1990s, Pick Salami ranks as the twelfth largest firm in Hungary.

One of the significant features of Pick Salami's operations is its reliance upon small-scale subcontractors in the region as suppliers for its pork and cattle used in the production of salami. That is to say, the the company has a strong multiplier effect on the local economy. For its part, Pick is concerned that its suppliers maintain the product quality it requires. The company entered into an agreement with the local college of Food Industry to provide training in for its staff and for its suppliers. The training of highly qualified food specialists began at the College in the 1960s, and today it operates as a Faculty of Budapest University of Horticulture. Courses in food quality and hygiene assurance are being provided in collaboration with veterinarians, and another course in food regulations is being offered to small producers. The new Hungary is thus being transformed in numerous ways and at various levels in its march toward a market economy.

Advanced Motion Control Europe, Budapest

Laszlo Konrad is an electrical engineer with a masters degree from the Technical University of Budapest who was working in the service division of a machine tool manufacturing company when he was selected to participate in a four week training program in New York where he was also able to visit several businesses. There he was exposed to the principles of total quality management. He also visited an old friend in California and began to explore with him ideas for starting a business. Upon his return to Hungary, Konrad resolved to put his plans into action, entering into a partnership with the friend in California and establishing a joint venture machine tool software company they called Advanced Motion Control Europe. The research and product development was done in California for the European market. The company is ISO 9000 certified, employs seven engineers, and exhibits its software at professional shows in Hungary in English.

Hangasci Print Company, Eger

Eger is a historical city in northeastern Hungary in the center of wine country famous for it bull's blood wine. Mr. Hangasci, owner of the firm, produces and sells customized brochures, cards, and stationary using a laser printer, and employs 15 workers. His clients represent a wide range of interests. He secured a contract to print the tickets for a regional soccer tournament using watermarked paper with bar coding and a hologram. He attended a seminar on marketing communication in Eger in which the presenter discussed the importance of attractive and inexpensive product packaging, which is a concept not well-known in Hungary. The consultant described a modern technology using a laser printer to pre- print paper, cards, and folders with. Pictures, borders, and colors are all pre-printed on the paper stock and then the customer's text is added on a template with the laser printer. The customer gets a high quality brochure at a lower cost. Hangasci has made his own line of pre-printed template design forms and is preparing to launch the new product.

THE POTENTIAL FOR SME GROWTH IN HUNGARY

> Hungary has become a two-tier economy, and the bulk of people are feeling trapped at the bottom.
>
> —*Business Central Europe*, 'Two Track Hungary" April 1998

> The Socialists are perceived in the West as a business-friendly government because the macroeconomic figures aren't bad. But if you ask local entrepreneurs, many of them will say the government is very anti-business.
>
> —Viktor Urban, leader of Fidesz, during electoral campaign of 1998

Overall trends in Hungary would appear to be favorable for economic growth and development, but the small business sector has yet to achieve its potential.

The Hungarian economy is generally doing well.

By 1997 much of Hungary's macroeconomic news was good, meeting or exceeding the projections made earlier in the year. Projections by the Hungarian Finance Ministry indicated an expected growth in the GDP of over 4 percent for 1997. The current account deficit was projected to be around $1 billion, compared to $1.7 billion in 1996. Inflation was expected to fall to around 18.2 percent from 23.6 percent in 1996, although this would still be higher than Slovakia (6 percent), the Czech Republic (9.3 percent), and Poland (15 percent). The budget deficit was predicted to be in the range of 4.9 percent, higher than both the Czech Republic and Poland, and about equal to that of Slovakia.

According to a 1997 Organization of Economic Cooperation and Development (OECD) study of Hungary, the Hungarian economic boom was expected to accelerate until the turn of the century (World Bank 1997). OECD analysts predicted a slightly more modest GDP growth rate of 3.9 percent in 1998, and 4.2 percent in 1999. The export increase was predicted to compensate for the expected boom in imports. The OECD forecast inflation of 14.4 percent in 1998, in light of an agreement with employer organizations on a wage increase. The decline in inflation in 1997 was slowed by wage increases, potentially jeopardizing the 1998 inflation and exchange rate targets. The main monetary policy target for 1998 was to ensure that the decline in inflation be sustained in the next few years as Hungary prepared for EU and Monetary Union membership.

The chief reason the EU put Hungary at the top of its list of aspirants was Hungary's success in attracting foreign investors. Hungary had the highest per capita foreign direct investment in the region by 1996: approximately $1,300, compared to $586 in the Czech Republic and $265 in Poland. Hungary leaped from fifth to first place on the list of Central European countries ranked by their investment worthiness, published annually in the *Central European Economic Review*. Poland ranked second, followed by Slovenia, the Czech Republic, and Estonia. The OECD report also projected that the country would continue to attract large amounts of foreign capital because the return on investment ratio and market competition were improving. Hungary received high grades for international integration, legal system, accessibility to investment, productivity, political stability, and fighting corruption, and lower grades in economic growth, price stability, and current account balance. The list was based on assessments by economic analysts from PlanEcon, Deutsche Morgan Grenfell, Daiwa Research Institute, and the Vienna Institute.

Despite the fact that economists were giving Hungary thumbs up as the region's success story, many ordinary Hungarians were not sharing in the success.

A special survey on Hungarian industry in *Business Central Europe* (April 1998) provided a troubling picture of a two-tiered economy in which a handful of foreign companies accounted for the boom in exports but a majority of the population was trapped at the bottom. Growth was coming mainly from just one sector: engineering, which contributed 70 percent of the export increase. Foreign companies employed 20 percent of the workforce to produce 40 percent of output and 80 percent of Hungarian exports.

Even the engineering boom was being driven by a few multinational greenfields such as Audi, the German car manufacturer, not by restructured Hungarian companies. Audi and other multinationals were refusing to use any local suppliers, claiming they produced poor quality goods. The foreign companies in industrial parks were attracted by government tax breaks and cheap labor but remained unintegrated into the local economy, despite the government's stated policy to promote subcontracts with local suppliers. Multinationals were shipping in finished components, bolting them together using cheap labor, and shipping them out. Reliance upon foreign cash was resulting in a few islands of excellence detached from the rest of the Hungarian economy.

Meanwhile, many local companies saw their output and sales declining. While the economy surged ahead on the back of buoyant exports, real wages fell and much of industry was stagnant, as was consumer spending. Two-thirds of the work force in Hungary was employed as low-paid bureaucrats or worked for small businesses, which *Business Central Europe* characterized as "a motley group of tiny companies, some of them split off from state companies, many of them set up by sacked workers." Most of them, the survey concluded rather pompously, "aren't much good." *(Business Central Europe* April 1998).

There were only a few local firms that managed to turn themselves around without the help of a foreign partner. Those that did, such as the home improvements group Graboplast, did so by expanding beyond the troubled Hungarian market to the rest of the CEE region. This was partly because of the lack of local demand and also because they faced stiff competition breaking into the Western European market. Graboplast, which specializes in plastic flooring and carpets, set up a factory in Romania and was successful in reaching regional markets because of competitive prices.

Meanwhile, small business interests seemed to be finding their way onto the domestic political agenda in Hungary.

The Spring 1998 elections brought a change of government to Hungary as the center-right Fidesz-Hungarian Civic Party celebrated a stunning election victory over the ruling Socialists (Reuters News Agency, 1998). Final results gave Fidesz, led by Viktor Urban, a youthful 35-year-old, the most seats with 148 members in the 386-seat parliament. In fact, Urban would become the youngest freely prime minister in the twentieth century. The Socialists, led by former communist incumbent Prime Minister Gyula Horn, won 134 seats. The Democratic Forum, a Fidesz ally, won 17 seats. All three parties supported membership in NATO and the European Union.

Fidesz had achieved its victory by embracing most of Hungary's rightist forces which had been disunited in a humiliating defeat by the Socialists four years before. Urban was reported to have been told by ailing former conservative Prime Minister Jozsef Antall in December 1993 that he was the man to take up Antall's center-right mantle. Urban, who had made the fight against corruption and rising crime a theme of his campaign, said he would ask tax authorities to screen himself and his family and then his entire administration. He declared Fidesz in favor of foreign investment, although he wanted to see more money going to the country's poorer eastern half. Urban assured investors that while Hungary would reevaluate some social priorities, a Fidesz-led government would not alter major economic goals. He was quick to allay fears that Hungary would jump the tracks of reform.

During the campaign Fidesz had played to the rural communities, young middle-class couples and small town tradesmen and business owners *(Central European Economic Review* 1998). Urban pointed out that small firms faced interest rates of 20 percent, which required a return on investment that was impossible to achieve without breaking the law. Foreign companies had access to cheaper credit. His solution was more government guarantees for Hungarian businesses via the state export promotion banks and a policy to fight inflation. Support for the party among small entrepreneurs had increased markedly in the polls as the election drew near.

*While small business has accounted for much of the growth in GDP
and employment creation, the Hungarian government has not been in
the forefront of SME promotion.*

Experiments with liberalization in Hungary since the early 1980s
allowed small businesses to expand more rapidly than in many other
countries in the region. Already by 1989 there was a sizeable informal
sector that was the seedbed for private sector growth. Unlike other CEE
countries, the private sector was initially well integrated with (and
dependent upon) the state sector. It was not a particularly adversarial
relationship, with both sectors realizing their interdependency. There
were many personal relationships with managers of state enterprises
dating from previous employment. In Hungary there was a culture
much more supportive of private initiative and conducive to
collaboration with the public sector than elsewhere. All of these factors
seem to bode well for the future of SME development in Hungary.

Surveys have indicated that firms that were privatized before 1989
performed better than those begun after that year, if only because they
had more experience. Many of these entrepreneurs were among the
most highly technically skilled workers and managers in Hungarian
state enterprises, as well as skilled craftsmen. But we have also seen
from the surveys that Hungarian firms formed in the early years of
privatization have demonstrated a strong ability to survive and grow. It
is unlikely that the rapid rate of expansion of new enterprises in the
early 1990s will be maintained, because competition has become keen.

Small enterprises have already begun to make a difference in the
economic transition of Hungary. They are creating jobs while large
firms are eliminating them. They are growing at a faster pace than are
large firms and are responding to the latent demand for consumer
goods. They are providing an outlet for the pent-up entrepreneurial
skills of ordinary Hungarians. And a few of them have managed to
reach export markets with their products, thus bringing in hard currency
and helping the country's balance of trade.

Surveys of small business owners, however, indicate that they
continue to face numerous problems, many of them related to the slow
pace of change in government regulations to promote the private sector.
For example, the initial opening of the banking system to small
borrowers resulted in a high loan default rate, partly due to the lack of
experience in dealing with credit. Bankers understandably became more
cautious in handing out small loans. Anecdotal evidence indicates that

many more start-up businesses fail than succeed in Hungary, but perhaps no more than elsewhere in the world.

While access to research and development has been readily available to foreign firms, little has gone to small local firms. They have remained starved for credit and are often poorly managed and lacking in new technology. Privatized banks have shown few signs of recognizing the small business sector as a profitable market. Interest rates for small-scale borrowers remain 7 percent higher than for large ones. Nor has the government provided more than a few subsidized loan schemes for small businesses. Although the need for a strategy of promoting the integration of local firms into the supplier networks of the multinationals has been recognized, funds available for this have been meager. If the Ministry of Industry's strategy hinges on encouragement of local firms to become suppliers to multinationals—helping out in such areas as quality certification—it must be judged to have failed thus far.

The size of the informal sector in Hungary is coming to be seen as a problem in Hungary, even though it may not be any more substantial than in some Western European countries. From the point of view of the tax authorities it is disconcerting that the share of unreported income has grown. And with respect to economic growth, the decline in the number of small businesses and the corresponding increase in micro-enterprises is not an especially encouraging trend. It may in fact be interpreted as an unhealthy sign in the transition process when small enterprises fail to grow. As the Institute for Small Business Development points out in its *1997 Annual Report* , the contribution of small enterprise to the GDP cannot grow unlimited and be declared less and less on tax returns.

The development of medium-sized firms in Hungary warrants particular attention, since growth of this sector would indicate a maturing of the private sector.

Although medium-sized firms experienced rapid growth in the early part of the 1990s as did the small enterprises, they registered a sharp decline in growth in 1995. Since then they have recovered only slowly. The transformation process from socialist to market economy in Hungary has already seen some start-up enterprises grow into medium-sized ones capable of attracting foreign partners and capital. Yet the portion of those who have been successful at making a living and adjusting to changes in markets and legislation is small. In fact, from 1993 onward there were signs of some initially successful enterprises beginning to stumble. Productivity among smaller enterprises increased more slowly than among larger firms. Many small businesses began to shrink into micro-enterprises, retaining some employees but laying off the rest. There are still numerous constraints to smaller businesses attaining medium-size status which the government is only beginning to address.

Small businesses in Hungary have been little helped by macroeconomic policies aimed at stabilizing the overall economy. Measures to encourage exports and discourage imports, improve balance of payments, and limit domestic consumption may have resulted in a stabilized economy without improving the lot of small firms. Most small businesses sell their products and services in the domestic market and thus depend upon consumption rather than growth. Only in recent years has there been a specific focus on the needs of small business. The transition to a market economy in Hungary is well on the way, but the small-scale entrepreneur should be essential to its eventual success.

REFERENCES

Borish, Michael, Wei Ding, and Michel Noel 1996 *On the Road to EU Accession: Financial Sector Development in Central Europe*, World Bank Discussion Paper No. 345.

Budapest Sun "Government Will Lose Out on NATO Ratification Delay," April 9-15, 1998.

Business Central Europe "Two Track Hungary: Hungarian Industry Survey" Vol. 6, No. 50 April, 1998.

Central European Economic Review "Third Time Lucky?", Vol. VI, Number 3, April 1998.

Drozdiak, William, and John F. Harris "NATO Invites 3, Strengthens Ties to Ukraine," *The Washington Post*, July 9, 1997.

European Bank for Reconstruction and Development 1996 S*trategy for Hungary* (BDS/HU96-1) October 29.

European Council for Small Business 1997 *Newsletter: SMEs in the Transition Economies* Zoetermeer The Netherlands January 1997 No. 4.

Fulop, Gyula 1994a "Entrepreneurship, Small and Medium-sized Enterprises in Northern Hungary," *Entrepreneurship & Regional Development* Vol. 6, 1994 pp. 15-28 Budapest.

Fulop, Gyula 1994b *Small Business Management* Budapest: Aula Press.

Flop, Gyula, and Robert Hisrich 1995 "Hungarian Entrepreneurs and Their Enterprises" in the *Journal of Small Business Development* Vol. 33, No. 3 July.

Institute for Small Business Development *State of Small and Medium-Sized Business In Hungary, 1996 Annual Report* Budapest: published in cooperation with the Hungarian Foundation for Enterprise Promotion.

Institute for Small Business Development *State of Small and Medium-Sized Business in Hungary: 1997 Annual Report* 1997 Budapest.

Lazar, Istvan 1997 *Hungary: A Brief History* Budapest: Corvina Books.

Reuters News Service "Champagne Flows as Hungary's FIDESZ Party Toasts Win," May 25, 1998, .

Seleny, Anna 1991 "Hidden Enterprise, Property Rights Reform and Political Transformation in Hungary Harvard University Center for European Studies Program on Central and Eastern Europe Working Paper No. 11 November.

Spolar, Christine "Hungarians Vote for NATO" *The Washington Post*, November 17, 1997.

Webster, Leila 1993 *The Emergence of Private Sector Manufacturing in Hungary: A Survey of Firms* World Bank Technical Paper Number 229 Washington, DC: World Bank.

World Bank, 1997 "Milestones of Transition" *Transition* December.

CHAPTER 5

Poland

POLAND

Poland Profile

Area: 312,683 square kilometers, slightly smaller than New Mexico

Bordering countries: Belarus, Czech Republic, Germany, Lithuania, Russia (Kaliningrad *oblast*), Slovakia, and Ukraine

National capital: Warsaw

Population: 38,615,239 (July 1997 est.)

Population growth rate: 0% (1997 est.)

Ethnic groups: Polish 97.6%, German 1.3%, Ukrainian 0.6%, Byelorussian 0.5% (1990 est.)

Religions: Roman Catholic 95% (about 75% practicing), Eastern Orthodox, Protestant, and other 5%

Languages: Polish

GDP real growth rate: 6% (1996 est.)

GDP per capita: purchasing power parity ($6,400 1996 est.)

Inflation rate consumer price index: (18.8% 1996 est.)

Unemployment rate: 13.3% (year-end 1996)

Administrative divisions: 49 provinces (*wojewodztwa*, singular— *wojewodztwo*)

Natural resources: coal, sulfur, copper, natural gas, silver, lead, salt

Independence: November 11, 1918 (independent republic proclaimed)

National holiday: Constitution Day, May 3 (1791)

Chief of state : President Aleksander Kwasniewski (since 23 December 1995)

Head of government: Prime Minister Jerzy Buzek (since 1997)

Source: U.S. State Department

Poland

THE HISTORIC AND ECONOMIC SETTING IN POLAND

Geographically, Poland belongs and always has belonged to the East.
In every other sense, its strongest links have been with the West.

Norman Davies, *Heart of Europe: A Short History of Poland,*
1984. p. 343

The Republic of Poland is among the leaders in the Central and Eastern
European region in sustained economic growth and in attracting
Western European investors and partners. It is the largest country in the
region, covering about the same area as the state of New Mexico. With
a GDP of nearly $100 billion, the Polish economy is also the largest in
the region. Its population of 39 million is overwhelmingly Polish (97
percent) and Catholic (95 percent). During the pre-World-War-II
period there were significant ethnic minorities—4.5 million Ukrainians,
3 million Jews, 1 million Belorussians, and 800,000 Germans. The
majority of the Jews were killed during the German occupation in
World War II, and many others subsequently emigrated. Many
Germans left Poland at the end of the war, while most of the Ukrainians
and Belorussians lived in territories incorporated into the Soviet Union.
Small Ukrainian, Belorussian, Slovakian, and Lithuanian minorities
still live along the borders, and a German minority is concentrated in
the southwest.

The history of Poland begins with the legendary Piast, a peasant
boy who probably lived in the middle of the ninth century a.d. and
came to rule as the tribal chief of the Polanians. The House of Piast

emerged from the mists of prehistory in 965 a.d. when Prince Mieszko I accepted Catholic baptism for himself and his kingdom and married a Czech princess. In Mieszko's time, the "Poles" were just one tribe among many. Today, the Republic of Poland is overwhelmingly Polish, the result of wars and social engineering. Norman Davies suggests that a wholly Polish Poland has lost the need to worry about its ethnic roots.

The Polish state reached its zenith under the Jagiellonian dynasty in the years following the union with Lithuania in 1386. Indeed, the link with Lithuania was to prove one of the formative experiences of Polish history. The monarchy survived many upheavals but eventually went into a decline which ended with the final partition of Poland by Prussia, Russia, and Austria in 1795. A period of Polish Enlightenment leading up to the partition was directly linked to France. The Polish parliament (*sejm*) crafted a liberal constitution on May 3, 1791, only two years after the American constitution. The *sejm* was shortly forced to renounce the new constitution and submit the country to partition, after eight hundred years as a nation. While many of the institutions of the old republic died, others such as the Polish church, schools, universities, and the city charters were left alone. Among these was the Jagiellonian University founded in 1364, second oldest seat of higher learning in central Europe after Charles University in Prague. These would form the living bridge between Poland's glorious past and its uncertain future.

Poland's claim to be the most Catholic country in Europe is hard to refute. Invasions of the country by Protestant Swedes, Orthodox Cossacks, and Russians in the wars of the seventeenth century greatly reinforced the country's Catholicity. The Bishop of Krakow, Cardinal Karol Wojtyla, became Pope John Paul II, head of the Roman Catholic Church in October 1978. Polish Catholics rejoiced at the elevation of a Pole to the papacy and greeted his June 1979 visit to Poland with an outpouring of emotion.

Among the 14 points enunciated by President Woodrow Wilson during World War I was independence for Poland, which it achieved in 1918. Then, on August 23, 1939, Germany and the Soviet Union signed the Ribbentrop-Molotov nonaggression pact, once again providing for the dismemberment of Poland into Nazi and Soviet-controlled zones. On September 1, 1939, Hitler ordered his troops into Poland; two weeks later Soviet troops invaded and occupied eastern Poland under the terms of the agreement.

After Germany invaded the Soviet Union in June 1941, Poland was completely occupied by German troops. The Poles formed an underground resistance movement and a government-in-exile, first in Paris and later in London, which was recognized by the Soviet Union. During World War II, four hundred thousand Poles fought under Soviet command, and two hundred thousand went into combat on western fronts in units loyal to the Polish government- in-exile. In July 1944, the Soviet Red Army entered Poland and established a communist-controlled Polish Committee of National Liberation. Resistance against the Nazis in Warsaw, including uprisings by Jews in the Warsaw ghetto and by the Polish underground, was brutally suppressed. The Germans leveled the city as they retreated in January 1945. About 6 million Poles had been killed during the war, and 2.5 million were deported to Germany for forced labor. More than three million Jews (all but about one hundred thousand of the Jewish population) were killed in death camps such as those at Auschwitz.

Following the Yalta Conference of early 1945, a Polish Provisional Government of National Unity was formed in June 1945. Although the Yalta agreement called for free elections, those held in January 1947 were controlled by the Communist Party. The Communists then established a regime entirely under their domination. In October 1956, after the twentieth ("de-Stalinization") Soviet Party Congress at Moscow and riots by workers in Poznan, there was a shake-up in the communist regime. While retaining most traditional communist economic and social aims, the government of Wladyslaw Gomulka liberalized Polish internal life. In December 1970, strikes in the port cities such as Gdansk, triggered by a price increase for essential consumer goods, reflected deep dissatisfaction with living and working conditions in the country. Edward Gierek replaced Gomulka as first secretary.

Fueled by large infusions of Western credit, Poland's economic growth rate was one of the world's highest during the first half of the 1970s. But much of the borrowed capital was misspent, and the centrally planned economy was unable to use the new resources effectively. The growing debt burden became insupportable in the late 1970s, and economic growth had become negative by 1979.

In July 1980, with the Polish foreign debt at more than $20 billion, the government made another attempt to increase meat prices. The resulting chain reaction of strikes virtually paralyzed the Baltic coast by the end of August and, for the first time, closed most coal mines in

Silesia. Poland was entering into an extended crisis which would change the course of its future development. In August, workers at the Lenin Shipyard in Gdansk, led by an unemployed electrician named Lech Walesa, signed a 21-point agreement with the government which ended their strike. The key provision of these agreements was the guarantee of the workers' right to form independent trade unions and the right to strike. After the Gdansk agreement was signed, a new national union movement—Solidarity—swept Poland. The discontent underlying the strikes was intensified by revelations of widespread corruption and mismanagement within the Polish government and party leadership.

Alarmed by the rapid deterioration of the Polish government's authority following the Gdansk agreement, the Soviet Union proceeded with a massive military buildup along Poland's border in December 1980. In February 1981, Defense Minister Wojciech Jaruzelski assumed the position of prime minister as well, and in October 1981, he also was named party first secretary. Meanwhile, at the first Solidarity national congress in September 1981, Walesa was elected national chairman of the national union. In December the regime declared martial law and used the army and special riot police to crush the union. Virtually all Solidarity leaders and many affiliated intellectuals were arrested or detained.

Western countries responded to martial law by imposing economic sanctions against the Polish regime and the Soviet Union. Unrest in Poland continued for several years. In a series of slow, uneven steps, the Polish regime rescinded martial law until December 1982, when it was suspended. A few political prisoners were released. Although martial law formally ended in July 1983 and a general amnesty was enacted, several hundred political prisoners remained in jail. In July 1984, another general amnesty was declared, and two years later, the government had released nearly all political prisoners. However, dissidents and Solidarity activists continued to be harassed. Solidarity remained proscribed and its publications banned. Independent publications were censored.

As in other countries of the Central and Eastern European region, 1989 was to be a watershed year in the transition process in Poland. The government's inability to stem the country's economic decline led to waves of strikes across the country in 1988. The government gave de facto recognition to Solidarity in an attempt to take control of the situation, and talks began with Solidarity leader Walesa in August.

These talks broke off in October, but a new series—the round table talks—began in February 1989, producing an agreement in April for partly open National Assembly elections. The June election produced a *sejm* (lower house) in which one-third of the seats went to communists and one-third went to the two parties which had previously been their coalition partners. The remaining one-third of the seats in the *sejm* and all those in the Senate were freely contested, and virtually all were won by Solidarity candidates.

The failure of the Communist Party at the polls produced a political crisis. The roundtable agreement called for a communist president, but on July 19, the National Assembly, with the support of some Solidarity deputies, elected a military figure, Jaruzelski, to that office. Two attempts by the communists to form governments failed, however. On August 19, President Jaruzelski asked Solidarity activist Tadeusz Mazowiecki to form a government. The *sejm* subsequently voted Mazowiecki prime minister. For the first time in more than 40 years, Poland had a government led by noncommunists.

In December 1989, the *sejm* considered the government's reform program to rapidly transform the Polish economy from centrally planned to free market, amended the constitution to eliminate references to the leading role of the Communist Party, and renamed the country the Republic of Poland. The Polish United Workers' (Communist) Party dissolved itself in January 1990, creating in its place a new party, Social Democracy of the Republic of Poland. Most of the property of the former Communist Party was turned over to the state.

Since the early 1990s Poland has made great progress in many respects toward achieving a fully democratic government. The May 1990 local elections were entirely free. Candidates supported by Solidarity's Citizens Committees won most of the races they contested, although voter turnout was only a little over 40 percent. In the cabinet reshuffle of July 1990, the national defense and interior affairs ministers—holdovers from the previous communist government—were among those replaced. In October 1990, the constitution was amended to curtail the term of President Jaruzelski. Free elections were held for the presidency in November 1990 and for parliament in October 1991 and September 1993. Freedom of speech, religion, assembly, and the press were instituted. A wide range of political parties representing the full spectrum of political views was created.

In November 1990, Solidarity's Walesa was elected president for a five-year term, becoming the first popularly elected president of Poland. From 1991 to 1993, three parliamentary coalitions of post-Solidarity origin parties governed in quick succession, none longer than 14 months. At Walesa's request, Jan Krzysztof Bielecki formed a government and served as its prime minister until October 1991. His government continued the Mazowiecki government's "big bang" package of economic reform, which introduced world prices and greatly expanded the scope of private enterprise. The first free and fair parliamentary elections were held in October 1991. Although more than 100 parties participated, no single party received more than 13 percent of the total vote. President Walesa then asked Jan Olszewski—the candidate of a minority coalition of five parties—to form a government. He succeeded in putting together a coalition government that was ratified by parliament. After a vote of no-confidence in June 1992, however, Olszewski and his cabinet were forced to resign over their efforts to purge alleged former secret police informers from political life.

"Shock Therapy": The Balcerowicz Plan and Its Effect

The Balcerowicz Plan was successful and appropriate not only because it laid the foundation for restructuring large state enterprises, but also because its sudden stabilization and liberalization measures quickly created conditions conducive to private business development in every part of the economy.

—Johnson and Loveman, *Starting Over in Eastern Europe*, 1995, p. 13

Meanwhile, Poland embarked upon a bold but risky program of economic reform. As a party in opposition, Solidarity had had no coherent set of economic policies. After the elections the economic situation was desperate, with inflation spiraling out of control. It was clear that strong measures were necessary to bring the country out of the crisis. To undertake this task, Solidarity chose Leszek Balcerowicz, an economist who had been working on a comprehensive plan with colleagues since the beginning of the 1980s. As deputy prime minister, on January 1, 1990, Balcerowicz initiated a program which was to carry his name and become associated with the "shock therapy" approach to economic reform. Convinced that gradualism would not be successful, Balcerowicz and his associates believed that the conditions for long-term stabilization could be established only at the cost of a short-term recession and declining living standards. The cornerstone of the stabilization package was the devaluation of the Polish currency, the *zloty*.

The stated goals of the Balcerowicz Plan were to limit inflation within a year to less than 100 percent and to achieve a monthly inflation rate of around 1 percent in the second half of the year. The plan had five main elements that together came to be popularly known as "shock therapy." The first was a unified exchange rate tying the *zloty*, to the U.S. dollar. The second was a very restrictive income policy which provided for tax penalties on wage increases. The third element was a state budget deficit of less than one percent of GDP from a deficit of more than 8 percent. Fourth was an increase in the refinance rate of the National Bank of Poland to 3 percent a month from only 7 percent in order to maintain positive interest rates. Fifth was a substantial liberalization of trade, liquidating nearly all foreign trade monopolies and ending quotas for most goods.

This shock therapy was apparently appropriate for Poland. Already in the first quarter of 1990 there was a remarkable change in economic conditions. The budget showed a surplus, real credit from the banking system fell sharply, the exchange rate remained stable, exports rose, and inflation declined quickly. By eliminating excess demand in the economy, it began to pick up. Shops were soon full of goods and queuing up as a way of life began to disappear as hyperinflation came to an end. There was a down side to the shock therapy. State sector industrial output fell sharply as unemployment rose. The GDP fell the first year by 12 percent and inflation continued to be higher than targeted. But blame for this was placed on the failure of state enterprises to adjust sufficiently to the new economic realities.

Simon Johnson and Gary Loveman point out in their book *Starting Over in Eastern Europe* (1995) why the Balcerowicz Plan was a success. It was precisely the stabilization and liberalization of the Polish economy that allowed the private sector to take off. And it is the private sector that has been the source of Poland's economic growth ever since. In their view, the macroeconomic changes involved in the Balcerowicz Plan were well designed in terms of their effect on the micro-economy. They conclude that Polish success has had little to do with privatization of state enterprises, which has proven to be slow and difficult. Rather, the emergence of small private businesses has played by far the more important role in the necessary allocation of labor and capital from activities driven by plans for productive employment created by markets.

Contemporary Political and Economic Trends in Poland

On September 22, 1997, 59 percent of eligible voters went to the polls in Poland's third fully free parliamentary election since the collapse of communist rule in 1989. A revitalized Solidarity, offspring of the labor movement that overturned communist rule in the 1980s, ousted Poland's governing coalition of former communists from power with a surprisingly strong showing (Spolar 1997). Solidarity Election Action, the most cohesive alliance to rise from the conservative groups that had failed to win any seats in the Parliament in 1993, won a third of the vote. The Democratic Left Alliance, the ruling coalition of communists-turned-social democrats, took a quarter of the vote while its coalition partner, the Peasant Party, saw its electoral support drop sharply. Under Poland's formula of proportional representation, the vote gave Solidarity 189 seats in the *sejm*; the Democratic Left, 158; Freedom Union, 70; and the Peasant Party, 32.

The Solidarity trade union formed the core of the Solidarity Action coalition that emerged victorious in the election. Marian Krzaklewski, head of Solidarity Action, had been at the helm of the trade union since its founder, Lech Walesa, was elected president in 1990. After Walesa lost that office, Krzaklewski proved relentless in his efforts to shore up right-wing opposition to the government and to end infighting that weakened its political appeal. Krzaklewski was able to convince like-minded politicians that this election was a critical test of maturity and strength for Poland's fledgling democracy, tapping into voter frustration over how democracy had evolved over the past eight years. A mild-mannered academic, Jerzy Buzek, was chosen to serve as prime minister, and Leszek Balcerowicz was made minister of finance.

The new government promised it would continue Poland's free market reforms but would begin to "repair all the errors" of the past few years. Krzaklewski pledged to give power and money to local governments and to revamp large state-owned enterprises such as coal, steel and telecommunications that have yet to be modernized. A devout Catholic, he quoted Pope John Paul II in a television appearance, saying that the new coalition would focus on "pro-family and social issues" and "defend those who suffer most." The year before, parliament had overturned a ban on abortion instituted shortly after communist rule, a move that Poland's high court later challenged on constitutional grounds. The centrist Freedom Union, a group led by Solidarity intellectuals who broke with the mainstream movement in 1990, was a coalition partner. Freedom Union was headed by Balcerowicz, architect of the reform program that has made Poland's economy the most successful in the former eastern bloc.

Solidarity has positioned itself in favor of privatization but in opposition to the former Communist *nomenklatura* (party operatives), which many see as the free market's main beneficiary. This appeals to those voters who believe that the heirs of the despised communist regime should not hold power. Quietly supported by the Catholic Church, Solidarity also holds up family values and the principle of social justice, though its election platform on how to achieve them has tended to be vague. The party's rather protectionist bent appealed to the unemployed, even if it contradicted Solidarity's strong commitment to Poland's future membership in the European Union.

With the collapse of the Soviet bloc, Poland has successfully reoriented its trade toward the West. Since 1990, its exports to OECD countries have more than doubled. In 1996, Germany was Poland's largest trade partner, accounting for a third of total exports and a fourth of total imports. Other leading export markets included Russia (6.8 percent), Italy (5.3 percent), the Netherlands (4.8 percent), France (4.4 percent), and Great Britain (3.8 percent). In fact, Poland managed to develop an over- reliance on exports as the primary growth factor in 1994 and 1995. Exports in 1996 declined, in part because of real *zloty* appreciation, resulting in a "soft landing" to more reliance on domestic demand to sustain GDP growth.

PRIVATIZATION AND ECONOMIC GROWTH IN POLAND

Four years of experience have shown that the restructuring, privatization, and revitalization of large Polish state enterprises have not been the central mechanism for reform at the enterprise level. Instead, and much to the surprise of many policy makers, the emergence and growth of small private businesses have played by far the more important role.

—Johnson and Loveman, *Starting Over in Eastern Europe,* p. 2

For over 40 years state-owned enterprises in Poland operated as virtual monopolies, were generously subsidized by the central government, and were never faced with competition. A central plan determined inputs, managers were rewarded for achieving production targets, and full employment was the principal goal of industrial policy. Labor was continually in short supply. The result under the communist system was low worker motivation and poor output quality. State enterprises tended to be highly vertically integrated, manufacturing many of their own inputs required for assembly of final products. They tended to hoard intermediate goods to protect against supply shortages as well employees to protect against labor shortages. During the early years of transition the state enterprises accumulated enormous debt, thus finding it increasingly difficult to secure outside financing.

The extent to which the productive capacity of the countries of Central and Eastern Europe was in the hands of state-owned enterprises at the beginning of the 1990s is reflected in figures for Poland. At the beginning of the reform program there were over eighty-five hundred state-owned enterprises representing 90 percent of industrial output as well as employment. Big firms predominated: there were more than two thousand with more than five hundred workers, accounting for 80 percent of employment in industry. Those with more than one thousand workers numbered about 1,000 and accounted for 66 percent of employment. This illustrates the marginal role that even medium-sized enterprises with fewer than five hundred workers played in employment and production, not to mention the negligible role of smaller enterprises.

The first noncommunist government in Poland assigned the highest priority to laying the rules for a British-style privatization program. A law passed in July 1990 envisaged privatization of large firms mainly through case-by-case sales. But the ambitious initial goal of 150 privatized enterprises was first scaled down to 50 and finally to only five by January 1991. By the end of 1991, a grand total of 26 firms, valued by specialist consulting firms, had been sold through public offerings. Even though some 2,813 of the 8,500 state enterprises had begun some form of privatization by 1994, only 121 had actually involved the sale of equity to those who did not work in the company (Johnson and Loveman, 1995). Public reaction was against alleged sweetheart deals in which managers would agree with workers to sell their own firms directly to foreign investors. The perception was that only former *nomenklatura,* black marketeers, and foreigners would benefit from these deals.

The privatization process was revitalized during 1995, due mostly to the implementation of the Mass Privatization Program after three years of delays. Under this program, groups of large enterprises were to be packaged for allocation in phased intervals. Shares in one hundred of the largest enterprises were to be allocated as follows: 60 percent free distribution, 10 percent to workers, and 30 percent to government. Although this program was ready to be put into effect in 1991, it was delayed due to political problems. Some 627 state enterprises had been converted into joint stock companies wholly owned by the Polish treasury, of which half were to be included in the Mass Privatization Program. Over five hundred enterprises—about 12 percent of state-owned assets in manufacturing—were transferred to national investment funds. Revenues from other methods of privatization rose sharply from about $600 million in 1994 to over $1 billion in 1995.

Privatization of small and medium-sized firms was more successful than that of large-scale firms (Berg and Blanchard 1994). Once new local governments were in place by the spring of 1990, privatization of retail shops began steadily, most of it through leasing. By the end of 1991 it was largely achieved. About 150 Polish medium- sized enterprises had been privatized, most of them through leveraged worker buyouts. In these arrangements, there were no direct loans from the government, although lease agreements specified that workers initially put up the equivalent of 5 percent of equity followed by another 15 percent over two years.

The process of privatization of Polish small-scale retail and service outlets was quite rapid, in contrast to large-scale privatizations (Thomas 1993). A wide variety of mechanisms was employed, including outright sale, protected so-called liquidation, and formation of new companies. Leasing of assets by small firms to large companies was also permitted. Once the new local governments were in place in the spring of 1990, privatization of retail shops proceeded steadily and had been largely achieved by the end of 1991. Seventy percent of small scale activities had already been divested that year, accompanied by an explosion in the registration of new enterprises. Through August 1994, some 990 small and medium enterprises (with fewer than seven hundred employees) had been privatized through "liquidation." In most cases, however, this meant that the company was leased to its previous managers and employees. In another 1,197 cases, the assets of state enterprises were sold following bankruptcy.

Berg and Blanchard (1994, 51-91) described the initial results of the privatization process in Poland as "gloomy" for the large state-owned firms but successful for the nascent private sector. Both 1990 and 1991 saw a spectacular increase in the size of the private sector. Growth had been strongest in those sectors that had been suppressed during the Soviet period, namely trade, services, and construction. And, given the concentration of private sector activity in trade and services, most of the jobs created in those early years were in very small businesses. The problem was that even though more jobs were being created in the smaller firms, the large state-owned enterprises continued to extract resources from the government and the banking system that might otherwise have been channeled to the new enterprises.

There were a few celebrated examples of privatized firms that would make their way into case study literature (Harvard Business School 1993). Professor Loveman and his colleagues at Harvard developed the case study of Prochnik, a clothing manufacturer in the industrial city of Lodz. Prochnik was established shortly after World War II to produce uniforms for the Polish military and eventually became the country's largest manufacturer of men's overcoats. With four factories and over two thousand workers, Prochnik became the most established clothing manufacturer in Lodz. Most of the high-quality coats were exported to the West, generating much-needed hard currency. Shortly after the new government took over in 1989, Prochnik was one of the first five firms chosen to participate in an experimental privatization program. In a public offering, Prochnik was sold out to Polish investors and in 1991 became one of the first firms traded on the Warsaw Stock Exchange. Despite international acclaim for its pioneering privatization initiative, Prochnik began to experience serious difficulties during its first year as a publicly traded company.

The slowness of privatization in Poland does not imply that state firms were under the effective control of the state, however. With the fall of the communist government in 1989, workers' councils began to take on a progressively more important role. Thus, the stalling of privatization did not preserve the strong role of the state in running firms. Rather, it led to an increase in the power of insiders, in particular workers, in companies while making their stake in the ultimately privatized firm very uncertain.

Not only did most policy makers view privatization as a necessary condition for enterprise restructuring, they tended to see it as sufficient as well. Initially, attention thus focused on methods of privatizing large-scale enterprises as quickly as possible. It was thought that private ownership would create the incentives to liquidate the nonperforming companies and revitalize those with prospects for success. But this notion was to run into the political realities of the privatization process. While the large firms continued to suffer from poor management, the best of their workers and managers were finding their way into the private sector.

Poland has privatized proportionately fewer of its large state enterprises than other countries in transition that have done less well economically. Even so, by the end of 1996, over 5,000 of Poland's 8,400 state-owned enterprises were in some stage of privatization. Of those eligible to claim privatization vouchers, 95 percent had done so.

By November 22, 1996, more than 25 million Poles claimed privatization vouchers offered by the government. The privatization process was expected to receive an additional boost with the privatization of KGHM Polska Miedz (Polish Copper) which holds one-fourth of the world's copper market.

Although a plan to privatize 512 state enterprises was launched in July 1995, all of the companies and the 15 funds set up to manage them are still owned by the government. The funds and their companies will become private only when they enter the Warsaw Stock Exchange. Prospectuses for the 15 funds, which are managed by a consortium of Polish and international financiers and consultants, were approved by the Treasury Ministry and passed along to the securities commission.

While more extensive privatization would no doubt contribute to greater growth, the fact remains that Poland's economic success has not been dependent upon it. As we shall see in the following pages, the source of Poland's impressive growth has been the new private sector, comprised primarily of SMEs.

LOOKING TOWARD EUROPE

Only 16 years ago, martial law was imposed in Poland. As of today, the 13th of December (1997) shall be associated with a day of great opportunity, a chance to link ourselves with a great European tradition.

—Polish Prime Minister Jerzy Buzek,
on Poland's accession to the EU candidature

Poland's adaptation to EU requirements is not only a road strewn with complexities and the need to do some hard homework. It is an opportunity to support a high rate of economic and social reform.

—Polish President Aleksander Kwasniewski, 1998

Poland has been among the most ardent seekers of membership in the European Union (EU) and the North Atlantic Treaty Organization (NATO). Together with Hungary and the Czech Republic, Poland has emerged as one of the top candidates for admission to NATO. All three countries have freely elected their governments at least twice since the end of communist rule in 1989. All have fledgling but solid free markets. All have struggled to winnow their militaries while maintaining economic equilibrium (Spolar 1997).

Public opinion polls in Poland and Hungary show strong public support for NATO membership, while apathy in the Czech Republic illustrates what may be a lingering weakness of the new democracies: relatively little public discussion or debate, even on crucial issues of national security. Poland's enthusiasm for NATO is unparalleled in the region. Opinion polls conducted in March 1997 in each country on whether that country should join the alliance showed Poland with the highest percentage voting yes (88 percent), as compared with 47 percent in Hungary and 40 percent in the Czech Republic. Newspapers and television zeroed in on NATO preparation with intense coverage.

But when NATO expands into the former Soviet bloc, its new members will have few military assets to offer and a multitude of logistical obstacles to overcome. As the countries vie for membership in the world's most sophisticated military alliance, their military is working to overcome tremendous logistical and technological obstacles (Spolar 1997).

Invitations to join the alliance, issued at the NATO summit conference in July 1997 in Madrid, were seen as a first step toward a historic expansion that, in time, could stretch from Estonia to Romania. A majority of NATO nations favored the entry of two additional countries—Slovenia and Romania—but President Clinton made it clear that the United States wanted only three. Poland, the largest and most eager aspirant, represents the seminal argument for NATO expansion. Its history, marked by periodic invasions by neighboring Germany and Russia, illustrates its security fears. Its determination is evinced by the millions of Poles who mocked communism for decades and then survived market reforms.

But even Poland attended the Madrid summit with a mixed portfolio. A contender adept at political maneuvering and persuasion, Poland offered a proud military heritage but few military assets to the alliance. With the biggest army in Central and Eastern Europe, Poland maintained a large force but of low quality, in both readiness and modernity. Poland would have to come up with at least $10 to $13 billion over the next 12 years to finance its NATO membership. An independent research center in Poland considered that a bargain. Poland had slashed the number of troops under arms, but this had not produced the savings anticipated. Even as it enjoyed the highest economic growth rate in the CEE region, Poland was fighting to maintain current levels of military readiness. The cost of manufacturing tanks and helicopters at state-run plants had more than doubled.

NATO's criteria for admission of new nations are largely political. Candidates must foster a stable democracy, adhere to market reforms, create military commands that fall under civilian control, and respect their neighbors and minorities at home. Poland, the Czech Republic, and Hungary were resolute in living up to those demands during the stormy years after the fall of their communist governments, and have become the region's strongest democracies.

Poland lobbied the United States the most, taking its case to Washington in addition to lobbying other capitals across Europe. Its lobbyists, seeding goodwill and playing to the millions of Americans with Polish roots, persuaded a dozen state legislatures to back Poland's entry. Even Pope John Paul II's visit to Poland in June 1997 was given a NATO twist; the Foreign Ministry passed out pamphlets promoting Poland's case for entry to reporters covering the papal visit.

Strong support for NATO in Poland exists mainly because the country has been a fault line between Russia and Germany, and no generation in this century has escaped its terrible tremors. Poles also take great pride in their military, and the army remains one of Poland's most respected institutions. This contrasts with Czechs and Hungarians, who do not grant their armed forces such respect.

Poland is actively pursuing membership in the European Union, as are the other countries in the CEE region. Poland was among the five countries invited to begin negotiations regarding its admission to the European Union in March 1998. The Polish cabinet has accepted a document outlining the principles for integration into the European Union. This National Integration Strategy provides for the gradual elimination of trade barriers and protectionism.

One of the most sensitive issues that Poland has to face in pursuit of this objective has to do with agriculture, a sector which still employs a large portion of the Polish population (*New Europe* 1997). In April 1997, Poland and the European Union managed to settle a potentially damaging trade dispute following a meeting of ambassadors from 15 nations. Poland agree to lower a value added tax on imported citrus fruits, a decision which the government said would cost it $65 million in revenues. In return, Poland expected the European Union to make concessions on its demands for more access of Polish food products to European Union markets in order to reduce the country's large trade deficit.

The issue of accession to the European Union in Poland became a source of public disillusionment. By early 1998 opinion polls began to register frustration with the slowness of the process. Over half of those interviewed were convinced that Poland would be treated as a second class member in the EU. Angry workers from a Warsaw tractor factory demonstrated their discontent with the company's insolvency by burning the blue and gold EU flag on the streets. Some two thousand farmers marched through Warsaw carrying banners declaring Poland's accession to EU would take place over their dead bodies. Meanwhile, the European Commission was insisting that Poland submit a plan to trim its declining steel and coal industries as well as hasten the privatization of the banking system and improve customs controls. Much was at stake since, depending upon its progress toward these and other targets, from the year 2000 Poland stood to receive $650 million a year in preaccession funds to speed its transformation. But the Polish honeymoon with the EU appeared to be over.

Polish President Aleksander Kwasniewski called for a deadline to be set in negotiations for joining the EU, reflecting the popular fear that they would otherwise "become bogged down in a mire of eternally prolonged negotiations" (*New Europe* April 5-11, 1998). He noted that Poland had earned the right to join because it had taken steps to prevent the economy from overheating and had no financial crisis as did certain neighboring countries. Kwasniewski aligned himself with the political opposition, telling his cabinet to review readiness for Poland's membership by 2002. He questioned the center-right government's progress in preparing key documents required by the European Union for the formal talks.

Nevertheless, entry into the European Union continued to be high on the domestic political agenda. In May 1998, in an unprecedented move the European Union cut $37.4 million from its 1998 aid budget for Poland under the PHARE program (Reuters News Agency, May 27, 1998). The executive European Commission said that some 140 projects submitted by Poland to use the money were irrelevant to entry preparations, or else were not ready for implementation. This was a slap in the face to Poland, which considered itself the leader among the six states negotiating for membership in the EU. Prime minister Buzek's government came under attack from all sides. He was obliged to dismiss the deputy director of his European Integration Committee, who he claimed was responsible for the fiasco. The question was which ministry should control funds coming from the European Union. Following this episode, it appeared likely that Finance Minister Balcerowicz would have that authority, rather than the European Integration Committee.

THE ROLE OF SMES IN THE POLISH ECONOMY

Private sector growth (in Poland) has been impressive. . .Most of the jobs have been created in very small businesses. . .More than 80 percent of the growth of employment over 1990-91 was in individual businesses . . . averaging one or two employees.

—Andrew Berg and Olivier Jean Blanchard, 1994, p. 76

The important challenge is to use Poland's enormous potential. We have a lot of educated people with a lot of entrepreneurial dynamism. For the first time in 200 years—except for the interwar period—we have the chance to bridge the gap between Poland and the West. . .

—Leszek Balcerowicz, architect of Poland's
"shock therapy," and Minister of Finance, 1998

The private sector in Poland operated in very cyclical fashion from the period after World War II until 1989. Extended periods of repression, with exorbitant taxes and restrictions on types of activities and number of employees, were followed by brief steps toward liberalization. While private entrepreneurs were tolerated to the extent that they filled gaps in the state enterprise sector, the accumulation of profit was nevertheless considered illegal. Shortly after the war medium and large scale firms were nationalized and restrictions were placed on smaller enterprises. The Stalinist period from 1949 to 1953 witnessed the nearly complete dismantling of the private sector. Following intermittent periods of liberalization, private industry was banned in 1972 and all small-scale activities were classified as handicrafts and limited to six employees. In 1981 martial law once again imposed tight restrictions on private businesses (Webster 1993).

The Law on Economic Activity, passed in January 1989, set the stage for the rapid expansion of the private sector by removing the restrictions on the activities and numbers of employees permitted in private firms. The response was remarkable. Over eight hundred thousand sole proprietorships and sixteen thousand new companies had been registered by the end of that year. The share of private sector in the GDP, excluding agriculture and cooperatives, rose from 11 percent in 1989 to 19 percent in 1990. (Agriculture had remained mainly private under communism). By the end of 1992, private sector share of the GDP had reached 35 percent.

While there was little progress toward the privatization of large state-owned firms following the privatization law passed in 1990, the nascent private sector was booming, (Berg and Blanchard 1994). Although privatization of small firms proceeded more quickly than did large firms, the number of new privately owned small enterprises still far exceeded the number of privatized firms. Of the two hundred thousand or so small firms in Poland by November 1990, at least 80 percent were newly created rather than already existing privatized firms.

The private sector played a crucial role in the early transition in the creation of employment. In 1980 the nonagricultural private sector employed no more than six hundred thousand workers, representing less than 5 percent of urban employment and perhaps as much as 3 percent of the total GDP (Johnson and Loveman, 1995). By 1988, that figure had already climbed to 1.3 million, representing 10 percent of urban employment, rising to 1.8 million (13.2 percent) in 1989, and 4.5 million (40 percent) in 1994.

Between the end of 1990 and the end of 1991, total employment in Poland, excluding agriculture, dropped by 2.8 percent, a decline of 7.4 percent in the state sector and an increase of 6.5 percent in the private sector. By the end of 1991, private employment outside of agriculture had reached 3 million compared with 1.8 million at the start of stabilization in 1989, a cumulative increase of 67 percent over a two-year period. Private sector share of total nonagricultural employment doubled from 13 to 26 percent. The share of private sector employment including agriculture—already mostly private—reached 45 percent of total employment by the end of 1991 and has since climbed well above 50 percent.

As might be expected, the growth of the private sector in Poland was stronger in those sectors that had traditionally been off-limits during the Soviet period, namely trade, services, and construction (Berg and Blanchard 1994). Given the concentration of private sector activity in trade and services, most of the jobs created in the early transition years were in micro-enterprises. Because individual businesses represented more than 80 percent of employment at the start, more than 8 percent of the growth of employment over 1990-1991 was in individual businesses, with an average employment of 1.7 workers. By the end of 1991, the private sector accounted for 75 percent of sales in trade, compared with only 10 percent at the end of 1989. This was due both to small-scale privatization and the high rates of new enterprise creation. The private sector quickly became dominant in the construction sector as well. Private sales in construction accounted for half of total sales in the sector by the end of 1991, an increase of 22 percent over in 1989.

The manufacturing sector was where the private sector progressed least. The private sector accounted for scarcely 5 percent of industrial production in 1981. Firms with fewer than 100 employees represented only 1.4 percent of total manufacturing employment in 1989. The problem was that the large state-owned enterprises that continued to dominate manufacturing were extracting resources from the government and the banking system that might otherwise have been channeled to the new enterprises. However, by the end of 1991 the private sector contribution to industrial production had grown to 25 percent, and by 1994 it was 35 percent. By 1994 Poland had a GDP per capita income of $5,200 and a growth rate that reached 6.5 percent in 1995, the highest in the region.

In September 1993, when the reformed successors of the socialist and peasant parties that had been in power in 1989 won the absolute majority in the parliamentary elections, there was widespread concern with the continued transformation of the Polish economy. However, these fears have been put to rest by the impressive performance of the Polish economy, the best among the transition economies. Since 1993 under the three governments in Poland, economic growth, which only began to revive in 1992, had already reached 7 percent in 1995 and stayed at 6 percent in 1996.

In the Polish recovery process, the private sector has served, and continues to serve, as the key stimulus for economic growth (World Bank 1997). By 1997, it accounted for 52 percent of total industrial output: over 90 percent of retail trade, agriculture, road transportation, and construction; 62 percent of exports; and 75 percent of imports. More than 65 percent of Poland's workforce (totaling 22 million people, or 57 percent of the population) is now employed in the private sector. By December 1996, the private sector was represented by over two million private enterprises. One hundred firms were listed on the Warsaw Stock Exchange, considered to be the most dynamic exchange in Central Europe, with capitalization of eight billion dollars.

The last few years have witnessed a significant restructuring of the productive capacity of the Polish economy. Despite such restructuring, unemployment continued to fall, from 17 percent in 1993 to 14.6 percent in 1995, and to 13 percent in 1996. Manufacturing registered a particularly rapid growth, with a 12 percent increase of output in 1994, 10 percent in 1995, and 8 percent in 1996. At the same time, these developments have been accompanied by a sharp rise in productivity.

In terms of attracting foreign investment, Poland has an investment grade from the top rating agencies such as Moody's and Standard and Poor's. These ratings have boosted the demand for Poland's Eurobond issues well beyond the original expectations. Foreign investment in Poland is becoming increasingly more desirable due to access to government credit guarantees by developed Western countries, including the U.S. Export-Import Bank (EximBank) and credit lines for large Polish projects. This positive investment climate has developed because of the high level of Poland's political stability, reflected in the fact that all major political parties in Poland support development of a functioning market economy and opening of the economy to foreign investment and competition. The desired speed of the transformation may be debated, but the basic direction is no longer questioned.

Definition and Role of SMEs in the Polish Economy

There is no official definition of the term *small and medium enterprises* (SMEs) in Poland, although institutions that support them have applied various definitions for their own purposes (UNIDO 1996). The Central Statistical Office has for reporting purposes defined the term small enterprise as one employing fewer than six workers and medium-sized enterprise as employing between six and 50 employees. Eligibility criteria have been established by banks, guarantee funds, and foreign assistance programs. For example, Bank Gospodarstwa Krajowego offers credit guarantees to companies employing up to 250 employees and having an annual income of less than 20 million ECU. CARESBAC, a venture capital company, defines its clients as firms employing 15 to 100 workers with an annual turnover of less than 1.5 million ECU.

A private company in Poland is officially defined as having at least 51 percent of its shares privately owned (Johnson and Loveman, 1995). It is necessary, however, to distinguish between trade law companies and individuals who operate as firms. Both limited liability and joint-stock companies are trade law companies, known collectively in Polish as *spolka* (singular) or *spolki* (plural). Polish law defines a *spolka* as private when at least 51 percent is owned by private individuals. During most of the communist era, it was not possible to create new *spolki*. This changed in 1987 when modest steps were taken by the authorities to encourage private businesses. Some people actually registered several *spolki* during the late 1980s since the capital required was minimal.

The number of incorporated *spolki* grew from 1,275 in 1988 to 11,693 at the end of 1989 and to 38,516 by mid-1991. A portion of these were joint ventures formed between Polish and foreign partners, which required a minimum investment of $50,000 in hard currency. The number of joint ventures rose from only 32 in 1988 to 1,645 by the end of 1990. Many private entrepreneurs, however, chose to operate as individuals even though they may have had substantial resources. It takes only a few days to register as an individual business, in contrast to registering a *spolki*, which is relatively complicated. There is no minimum capital required for individual businesses and fewer taxes than for *spolki*. Official statistics recorded a total of 357,000 unincorporated firms by the end of 1980. This figure had risen to 1136 million by the end of 1989. Activities of these firms typically included handcrafts and trade. By the end of 1991 there were already 2.5 million employed as individual entrepreneurs in Poland.

FINANCING SMES: BANK AND NON-BANK SOURCES

Banking in Poland has not kept up with the explosive development of the private sector. Major reforms in the banking industry were already under way by the time Poland elected the Solidarity government in mid-1989 (Johnson and Loveman, 1995). During the 1980s, the National Bank of Poland (NBP) served as the country's central bank and conducted nationwide commercial activities in nine regional branches. Under the communist government in Poland private banks were not permitted and the NBP functioned as a monopoly. In 1982, the NBP was separated from the Ministry of Finance and allowed to operate as an independent commercial bank.

In January 1989, the New Banking Law and Act for the National Bank of Poland provided for the break up of the NBP monopoly and the creation of nine independent commercial banks from its regional offices. While the NBP retained central banking functions, it was obliged to withdraw from all but a few commercial operations. Meanwhile, the requirements for establishing new private banks were liberalized. By the end of 1991, over 100 licenses had been granted for the establishment of new commercial banks, most of which were private, although some were cooperatives. Despite the proliferation of new private banks, the nine state-owned banks still held over 80 percent of the economy's entire loan portfolio. Those banks that began to loan to private entrepreneurs focused mainly on the trade sector rather than on manufacturing. Banks preferred to lend to trading companies because of their greater likelihood of repaying the loan.

By 1992 there were several private banks that had become more oriented toward private sector lending, especially in the Gdansk region, charging high nominal interest rates. Some private banks, such as the Sopot Bank, demonstrated in the early years of the Balcerowicz Plan that there was money to be made by lending to consumers, whereas it was difficult to justify lending to entrepreneurs because they lacked a track record and because of the uncertainty of the overall business environment. According to most Polish entrepreneurs, the greatest financial constraint since 1989 has been the high level of nominal interest rates rather than the reluctance of commercial banks to extend loans. It will likely take several years for a market-oriented banking system to evolve since new banks must raise capital and develop expertise in lending to businesses.

The largest single government financial initiative in support of SMEs in Poland is the Loan Guarantee Fund of the Ministry of Finance. Managed by the Bank Gospodarstwa Krajowego (BGK), the program involves 11 participating banks throughout the country. The fund guarantee covers up to 60 percent of principal and interest for a maximum term of five years. The collateral required on the guaranteed position of the loan is no less than 50 percent. Firms with no more than 250 employees and annual sales no higher than 20 million ECU are eligible.

GOVERNMENT AND DONOR AGENCY ASSISTANCE TO SMES IN POLAND

Polish Government SME Policies and Agencies

The Polish Ministry of Industry and Trade has the prime responsibility for policies regarding small enterprises, (UNIDO 1996). The ministry's activities in policy formulation include the preparation of government documents on policy toward SMEs, the drafting of relevant laws, and the development of the business environment. From 1990 to 1994, an SME department existed within the ministry but was then replaced by a new Department of Economic Strategy and Policy. In 1995, the SME department was reestablished. But the Ministry of Industry and Trade itself is slated to be replaced by a Ministry of Economy, which is to inherit responsibilities for SME development.

The Ministry of Privatization also plays a role in small business development, since it is responsible for privatization of all Polish state-owned enterprises, including smaller ones. Within this ministry there is also an SME department which employs two basic techniques for privatizing state enterprises: capital or indirect and direct privatization. Organizations eligible for direct privatization are enterprises with fewer than five hundred employees and sales of less than eight million ECU.

During the early stage of the transition, the Polish government lacked a clear policy on the SME sector (Krajewska and Piasecki 1997). Preoccupied with many urgent problems, the new government did not perceive small businesses as a priority. There were frequent changes of government officials and policies. Those institutions that were responsible for SME development were too weak to ensure formulation of such a policy. The entrepreneurs themselves did not have a strong political lobby or institution to support their interests. There was no tradition of private sector pressure groups articulating their concerns. There were, however, numerous foreign organizations that regarded the SME sector as a priority. To coordinate these various initiatives, a group for small and medium-sized companies was set up in 1993 which included representatives of the Polish government, foreign assistance organizations and institutions (such as the World Bank and European Community), and bilateral governments. The group began by compiling a list of actions to be taken to promote SMEs.

Then, in June 1994, the Polish government issued a strategy for socio-economic development consisting of several programs indirectly influencing SMEs (UNIDO 1996). One of the key programs of this strategy for Poland was international competitiveness of the economy. The successful implementation of the industrial policy program would entail maintaining economic growth at a minimum of 5 percent per annum. Repeatedly referring to the development of SMEs, the policy program committed the government to providing exporting SMEs with advisory services, access to new technologies, and reviewing laws and regulations affecting SMEs. The government's policy aimed at an increase in rate of sales of the SME sector greater than the overall economy as well as a significant growth of employment. The Central Planning Office prepared a document on regional policy to promote decentralization and to reduce unemployment in poorer regions.

In April 1995, the Ministry of Industry and Trade prepared a document entitled "SMEs in the National Economy: Policy Toward SMEs." The policy it articulated was the creation of an environment conducive to SME development and reduction of the risks involved in running a small business. Constraints to SME growth addressed in the document included the system of taxation, high interest rates, unclear legal system, and insufficient competitiveness of SMEs due to low demand and lack of skilled labor.

Donor Support Programs

European Union PHARE Program

In Poland the PHARE program is the most important source of outside assistance to SMEs (UNIDO, 1996). It includes two basic initiatives: the SME Support Program (eight million ECU) and the Private Sector Development Program (six million ECU). Both are implemented by the Cooperation Fund and directed toward intermediary organizations involved in supporting SMEs at the national and regional levels (chambers of commerce, regional development agencies, and management training centers). To qualify for assistance, these organizations must have the status of legal entity, be nongovernmental, noncommercial, and have separate financial statements. Support takes the form of advice and consultancy, business management training, and financial assistance.

The SME program supports the activities of over 30 Business Support Centers (BSCs) and three Business Information Centers (BICs) located in various regions of Poland. The BSCs provide services in business plan development, loan applications, marketing, financial and trade matters, information and training courses. BICs are located in Lodz, Gdansk, and Gliwice. From the end of 1991 to 1996, these centers reached a total of fourteen thousand clients with some twenty thousand services.

The Private Sector Development Program implemented through the Ministry of Industry and Trade encompasses support in legal, fiscal, and regulatory areas as well as information dissemination and institutional development. Initiatives under this program have included a pilot mutual guarantee scheme, a national business register, a business development training program for accounting consultants, and strengthening regional development agencies. In 1996 the Polish Foundation for SME Promotion and Development was established to handle new activities resulting from these programs.

The EU PHARE-funded Local Initiatives Program aimed at developing the capacity of local communities to independently take advantage of the opportunities created by economic reform. A two-year initiative begun in 1994, the program selected nine communities for participation in 60 separate projects. Support to SMEs consisted of business support centers, incubators, and credit and guarantee funds. Regional Development Agencies were responsible for the supervision of the implementation plan.

Also implemented locally through the Regional Development Agencies is the EU PHARE-funded Structural Development in Selected Regions (STRUDER) with a budget of 76.7 million ECU. The STRUDER program is intended to assist in the restructuring of the economies of regions dominated by obsolete industries and agriculture to better function in a market economy. Program resources include direct financial support for SMEs, training, consultancy, and strengthening regional institutions.

The Grant Fund is the primary tool for supporting investment by the private sector. Grants are provided to start-up and existing firms employing no more than 100 workers. Firms may apply for grants not to exceed 25 percent of the value of an investment up to 450,000 ECU. Grants are available to enterprises involved in production as well as services. The firm must contribute at least 20 percent of the total value of the investment. By January 1995, six hundred projects had been supported by the scheme.

Polish-American Enterprise Fund

This fund, established in 1990 by the U.S. Congress, aims at the development of the Polish private sector. There are three specialized branches in the fund. The first, the Enterprise Credit Corporation, works through a series of windows in eight banks which provide loans to SMEs. The participating banks receive 25 percent of the interest. Initially the maximum loan available was $20,000, increased to $500,000, at 11 percent interest. While most loans are on investment, some are made for working capital. The corporation has made some 2,700 loans and has a repayment rate of 97 percent. The second, the Polish Private Equity Fund, works with both private firms and state enterprises in the process of privatization. Of the 30 companies in which the Fund has invested, only five have been state enterprises under privatization. The third, the Educational Enterprise Foundation established in Lodz, has as its goal the promotion of business knowledge. It finances training programs and supports business schools and has promoted the establishment of a network of 13 Polish American Enterprise Clubs.

CARESBAC Polska

The CARE Small Business Assistance Corporation (CARESBAC) began operations in Poland in 1992 as a development venture capital fund. With funding from a variety of sources, including USAID and the European Bank for Reconstruction and Development, CARESBAC seeks to promote economic development and encourage entrepreneurship in Poland. Long-term risk capital financing and technical assistance is provided to Polish SMEs. By 1996, CARESBAC had made 20 investments and disbursed $4.5 million. Priority sectors have included agribusiness, nontraditional exports, and light manufacturing.

Polish-British Enterprise Program

The British Foreign and Commonwealth Office agreed to assist the depressed eastern region of Poland in 1994. The program provides support for networks of business service organizations and incubators, and a marketing development program aims at enhancing the SME presence in new markets through consultancy service and trade links in the United Kingdom. A loan guarantee fund provides funding for SMEs through banks.

Microenterprise Development Project (TOR 10)

Known as the TOR 10 Project, this program is implemented by the Polish Ministry of Labor and Social Policy and financed from a World Bank loan and Polish public resources. The program consists of three components. The goal of the Enterprise Development Fund has as its goal to establish a network of local credit funds that provide credit to entrepreneurs. Some 27 Small Business Support Centers have been established since 1994 which provide clients with counseling and consulting services as well as training and market information. Under TOR 10 Project, 30 business incubators have also been set up for start-ups.

PROFILE OF POLISH ENTREPRENEURS

Without question, the manufacturing firms surveyed in this (World Bank) project had benefitted enormously from many aspects of the reform program. Legal and regulatory reforms cleared the way for massive entry into the private sector and set out the terms under which firms would operate.

—Leila Webster, et al., *The Emergence of Private Sector Manufacturing in Poland,* 1993

A team of World Bank researchers conducted one of the first surveys of the private sector in Poland in May 1991. Ninety-three manufacturing firms, randomly drawn from registered firms with seven or more employees, were interviewed (Webster 1993). The firms were selected from five sectors: knitting, clothing, plastics, metal working and machinery. The profile that emerged from this study was similar in many respects to other countries of the region but dissimilar in other respects. The typical Polish entrepreneur was a middle-aged, well-educated man with strong technical skills, usually in engineering. Many of those interviewed had been managers in state enterprises and were quite inexperienced in the operation of private business. It was the first business for most of them, and many were manufacturing products different from those produced by their previous firms.

Most of the firms in the 1991 World Bank Poland survey were limited liability companies (*spolki*) owned by groups of three to six individuals. More than half of them had fewer than 20 workers and three-fourths of them reported monthly sales of less than $50,000. Ninety percent had originated as private firms as opposed to state enterprises, thus reflecting the minimal contribution of the state sector to the formation of the private industrial sector in Poland. Three-quarters were start-ups, while a handful were previously private sector craftsmen who had registered as corporations. This was in contrast to firms interviewed former Czechoslovakia and Hungary, where half of the firms interviewed by World Bank researchers during the same period had originated in the state and cooperative sectors. Nearly all of the Polish entrepreneurs relied on used equipment from state enterprises through personal contacts and purchased at reduced prices.

Well over half of those interviewed in the World Bank Polish survey had received short term loans from banks since 1988. Surprisingly, there was general agreement that it was fairly easy to obtain a bank loan if one were prepared to pay high interest rates. Loans were distributed equally across weak and strong firms, a possible reflection of the inability of Polish banks to appraise loan applications. Interestingly enough, most of the respondents had managed to secure factory space with relative ease—even when ownership questions were unresolved—with long-term leases. Very few of them owned their own buildings, in contrast to Czechs and Slovaks interviewed at the same time.

When asked about the major problems confronting them, the Polish entrepreneurs cited lack of demand, financing, and changing government regulations. They had lost markets to competition, mainly imports, as a result of liberalization. This was no doubt due in part to the pent-up demand for Western goods among Polish consumers, as well as the relatively inferior quality and higher prices of Polish goods. Those who cited financing as one of their main problems generally mentioned high interest rates, lack of working capital, and slow payment by state enterprises for goods delivered. In fact, shortages of working capital were directly linked with slow payment by state enterprises.

The Polish entrepreneurs interviewed in the World Bank study verified both positive and negative consequences of the government's reforms. On the one hand, most of them had little or no difficulty in obtaining the necessary licences and permits at start-up. On the other hand, they complained about frequent and unpredictable changes in tax regulations which made it difficult to plan. Likewise, they reflected a certain ambivalence toward private enterprise and accumulation of personal wealth in Polish society. Half of those interviewed felt that attitudes of public officials and average citizens toward them was negative.

Johnson and Loveman also began their survey work for *Starting Over* in 1991 and continued into 1993. They interviewed nearly a thousand entrepreneurs in four cities and towns: Warsaw, Monki, Krakow, and Lodz. They found that many businesses registered were not in operation, while some in operation were not registered. Still others were registered to conduct one type of business activity and yet were actually doing another. In contrast to those individuals in the World Bank survey, most of those interviewed by Johnson and Loveman (1995, 103-132) had left the state sector and were employed in private business before the Balcerowicz Plan came into effect. Johnson and Loveman concluded from their sample that the private sector was already well-established in Poland before the implementation of the Balcerowicz Plan in 1990. In this respect, among the countries of the CEE region only Hungary could claim a comparable private sector.

One-third of those interviewed actually had a private sector job before starting their own firms, although 85 percent had worked in the state sector at some point. Johnson and Loveman noted that the private sector in Poland was fairly easy to enter in the 1980s, since barriers to entry were quite low; half of those interviewed had started their business before 1990. With the exception of Hungary, this was in contrast to all other countries in the region, where the private sector had scarcely begun to emerge until the reforms unleashed in 1989.

The average age of those interviewed by Johnson and Loveman was 40, although there was a wide range of ages, from 19 to 80 years old. (There is no reference to gender distinctions in the sample.) Many of the entrepreneurs interviewed had been part of the Solidarity movement from the beginning and had already become disillusioned by socialism and state sector employment by the early 1980s. Those who had started their firms before 1980 tended to be considerably older than those who had started them after that date. Overall, the respondents had an average work experience of twenty years, although fewer than half of them had worked in the sector in which they established their own enterprise.

In the Johnson and Loveman survey, one-third of those who answered the question regarding education indicated that they had completed a university degree. University-educated entrepreneurs were more highly represented in the firms that were started in the 1980s than after 1990. The proportion of university education was smaller among those businesses begun before 1980. Advanced education tended to be more common in some sectors than in others. For example, those in modern services, transport, and production were the most well represented. Education was lowest in traditional services such as restaurants and wholesale trade. Of those who started their enterprises in Poland before 1980, 37 percent said their business was a family tradition, while only 5 percent of those who started their business after 1990 gave the same answer.

Financing of start-up operations is always a critical issue. The Johnson and Loveman survey suggested that Polish entrepreneurs began their operations with very small amounts of capital. Remarkably, one-third of the firms in their survey began their businesses with less than $100, and more than half began with less than $500. As might be expected, the proportion of firms starting with smaller amounts of capital declined after 1990. When asked about the sources of initial capital, nearly all said they used their own funds, earned exclusively inside Poland. Johnson and Loveman concluded that until 1991 there was little need for large amounts of capital in order to enter the Polish private sector.

In contrast to the respondents in the World Bank survey who reportedly had little difficulty in obtaining bank loans, those in the Johnson and Loveman survey were clearly deterred from borrowing by high nominal interest rates after 1990, even though real interest rates were quite low. This was a reflection of the high inflation rates during this period. The new private businesses lacked sufficient collateral to be able to borrow. Most of them had small amounts of their own fixed capital and most of their money tied up in working capital. The following are profiles of a few of the Polish entrepreneurs who typify the growing small and medium enterprise sector.

PROMAX, Lodz

Lodz is the second city of Poland, the traditional textile manufacturing center of the country. Today the economy is diversifying into a range of high-tech industries. In 1987, Marek Sokolowski and four partners founded PROMAX, a computer hard and software company. They began servicing such clients as the post office, banks, and manufacturing firms. For the first two years they worked only with industrial automation and micro-processing. Then operations were expanded to include computer assembly of IBM PCS and systems information, and eventually encompassed network installation. PROMAX provided the post office with a complete information system for the entire region of Lodz.

But the computer business did not grow as rapidly as Sokolowski and his partners had hoped. They did what any entrepreneurial firm might have done: they launched a completely unrelated operation: selling electric batteries for radios, cameras, and industrial uses. Some of the products PROMAX handles are produced in Poland, including such brands as Duracell, Phillips, and Matsushita. The new line took off, and by 1997 PROMAX had three thousand customers and controlled 55 percent of the market in batteries in Lodz and the surrounding region. PROMAX now employs 40 workers full time, including four in accounting. Sales growth eventually brought problems of cost control and the need for personnel training. UNESCO provided training for ISO 9000 certification which PROMAX believes will help in dealing with the foreign investors they anticipate will be coming to Lodz.

Ab Ovo, Morag

As its Latin name would imply, Ab Ovo, located in the small agricultural town of Morag northwest of Olsztyn in northern Poland, is a chicken hatchery owned and operated by Arkadiusz Tomaszewski and his two partners. In 1991, the three partners bought a hatchery from a state-owned firm that was doing poorly and began to renovate it. They invested their own money rather than rely upon bank financing. Tomaszewski, who had received a university degree in agriculture and had worked all his life for a state-owned hatchery, noted that the old system allowed for "arranging things on the side." He characterizes the market as ruthless: if you don't work hard and produce, you don't stay in business. He now works long hours and leaves nothing to chance.

The Ab Ovo partners own three hundred hectares of land and operate fully modern computerized equipment imported from Belgium. The click of a button either raises or lowers the temperature and light in the large metal containers that house the chicks. With 30 employees, Ab Ovo produces one hundred twenty thousand chicks a week. Plans are to add a slaughterhouse that will complement the hatchery. All operations are conducted according to strict government health regulations. Ab Ovo products are already reaching the populous markets of Gdansk and Warsaw. But Tomaszewski has his sights set on Western European markets and is keenly aware of the necessity of measuring up to EU standards.

EKO-Mysiadlo

EKO-Mysiadlo, one of the largest private greenhouse complexes in Europe with three locations in Poland, is an example of the growing number of partnerships between Poland and Holland *(The Warsaw Voice,* April 26, 1998). Whether it is large agribusiness firms or small private farmers, Poland has much to tempt Dutch investors in terms of its market size, location, and low production costs. Dutch agriculturalists offer their skills and knowledge of modern technology to their Polish partners. A combination of Polish entrepreneurship and Dutch technology has placed EKO-Mysiadlo at the top of its field in the production of tomatoes and cut roses. Tomasz Maj, the Polish partner, took over the greenhouses in 1992 when the industry was being privatized and started modernizing. Using Dutch technology, the company was able to increase productivity and product quality dramatically. In 1997, EKO-Mysiadlo began cooperating with a Dutch trading company in the distribution and selling of imported plants in addition to its own. The company also expanded its production to include cut chrysanthemums and potted plants.

POTENTIAL FOR SME DEVELOPMENT IN POLAND

> I think values are at stake (in this election), not the economy and not politics. People who are in power and who rule the country should be people of honor. They should be making decisions based on principle. I don't want people who can change their convictions based on circumstances.

> —Katarzyna Czolnik, an advertising saleswoman,
> casting her vote in Warsaw for Solidarity, September 1997

> In our laws, too much depends upon interpretation by state officials, which often invites corruption. This must be changed to create an environment for economic growth.

> —Henryka Bochniarz, head of the Polish
> Business Roundtable in Warsaw, April 1998

Several trends in Poland bode well for its future growth and development, and that of its small business Sector.

Democratic institutions are alive and well in Poland.

Political stability and free public discourse have afforded Poles the choice of determining the type of economic system they prefer. Political change has come by way of the ballot box. After Solidarity led the way in opposing communist rule and eventually bringing it down, in 1993 Poles voted former Communists of the democratic left back into power. In 1995 voters picked Aleksander Kwasniewski rather than Solidarity leader Lech Walesa, for the presidency. Those shifts were attributed to the financial pain Poles were experiencing as a result of the economic "shock therapy."

In 1997 voters such as Ms. Czolnik seemed to be telling pollsters that they were worried about something beyond their pocketbooks. Opinion polls found that people did not believe Poland's drive toward economic health could be derailed, no matter what party came to power. Instead, they were registering increasing dissatisfaction with the balance of power in government and were expressing support for measures that would revisit the fears of their communist past. Indeed, candidates in the 1997 election were required to declare in writing whether they had ever cooperated with the communist- era secret police, statements that were to be reviewed for veracity after the election by a panel of judges.

The Polish political establishment has generally embraced the reform program. Despite sometimes wild campaign promises, all Polish governments since 1989 have pursued vigorous programs of economic change. Although there was great anxiety when the ex-communists gained power in 1993, this is no longer an issue. Their economic policies turned out to be closer to the values of the market than to the teachings of Marx, as has been the case in other countries in the CEE region. The polarization of Polish politics is more apparent than real. When it comes to economic policy, what was once the left is now right-of-center, and what was once the right is now left-of-center.

For their part, the leaders of Solidarity can no longer be viewed as untested demagogues. In the 1980s Solidarity, backed by 10 million anti-communist Poles, symbolized Western values of freedom and opportunity. However, since then many Poles have come to identify the "American model" with excessive income differentiation and economic pain. It is true that the country's successful reforms have generated impressive growth rates. But the widening gap between the rich and the poor continues to create uncertainty and frustration. Despite sustained economic growth in Poland, by 1997 opinion polls indicated that the Polish populace was not especially optimistic about the future. Only one in five Poles believed that the economic situation had improved, while nearly half said it had not changed.

The liberalization program embodied in the Balcerowicz Plan laid the groundwork which made successful private sector development possible in Poland.

No other country in the CEE region embarked on such a bold plan and yet reaped such benefits. Legal and regulatory reforms cleared the way for the massive creation of new firms. The liberal environment allowed manufacturers to locate factory space, buy used equipment, secure working capital, and obtain intermediate inputs without major difficulties. At the same time, many of the new entrepreneurs initially faced serious difficulties in a recessive economy. The rapid liberalization forced domestic producers to compete in world markets without the benefit of basic business knowledge. In Hungary and the Czech and Slovak Republics exposure to world markets proceeded more slowly, but with no more successful consequences for private sector development.

According to World Bank reports, Poland remains the fastest-growing of any major European economy, and certainly of all CEE countries, even if its growth has slowed somewhat in comparison with its record 1995 performance, when the GDP grew at a 7 percent rate (World Bank, *Transition*, 1997). The following year it grew slightly less, at 6.1 percent—largely owing to a 10 percent growth in consumption and 19 percent growth in investment spending—and 5.6 percent in 1997. By 1997 Poland's real GDP far exceeded its pretransition peak although the structure of the economy has changed dramatically since 1990. The share of services in the economy rose from 35 percent to 53 percent, while that of industry and construction shrank from 52 to 39 percent. Agriculture's contribution to GDP fell from 13 to 8 percent even though farm employment still represented one-quarter of total employment. Other sectors where adjustments still had a long way to go included heavy industry, particularly coal mining.

Prospects for continued economic growth in Poland in 1998 and beyond appear to be quite good. The OECD forecasts a still strong growth of 5.4 percent in 1998, compared with 3.9 percent for Hungary and only 1.7 percent in the Czech Republic. Most observers expect the EU economies to begin to grow at a faster rate. Although world trade growth is projected to slow, it should remain buoyant relative to global output growth, as further liberalization occurs. This would be supportive of Polish exports. Domestic investment and consumption are likely to continue to grow. The former will be sustained in part by foreign inflows as foreign direct investment continues to accelerate. And Poland's growth record, OECD membership, and EU accession prospects are likely to ensure continued Western business interest. Bank and government officials warn, however, of the danger of the economy overheating. Poland's ballooning trade deficit ($6.4 billion by November 1997) was a sign that the consumption boom would likely be unsustainable.

Small and medium-sized enterprises have fueled the remarkable growth which Poland has experienced over the past few years, even though there has been no strong political lobby in support of the SME sector.

Piotr Dominiak and Franciszek Blawat (in Piasecki and Fogel 1995) have argued that the macroeconomic situation in Poland has not favored small businesses. They note that high inflation and low savings levels were factors that tended to discourage start-up businesses in the early 1990s. SMEs managed precisely because of the gaps in the market which could not be filled by either large firms or by imports. The increase in the number of small firms was simply testimony to their resilience. Being aware of the spontaneous resistance of SMEs to unfavorable conditions, the government had neglected to devise a policy that would suit the needs of the sector. Dominiak and Blawat (1995) go so far as to state that there has not been, nor is there likely to be a clear government policy towards SMEs in Poland. Tax policies, for example, have tended to ignore the fact that small businesses have contributed significantly to employment creation.

As Krajewski and Piasecki (1997) point out, the Polish government's SME policy was initially geared toward eliminating barriers hampering the sector's growth and development and creating the appropriate institutional and legal framework for its operation. The relative success of the SME sector has been due mainly to microeconomic conditions rather than to a conscious government policy of SME promotion. Poland now has the possibility of assuring sustained economic growth by developing a comprehensive policy that aims specifically at maintaining SME development. At the same time, numerous foreign organizations providing assistance to Poland have recognized the SME sector as a priority for development and have committed resources to them.

The Polish government appears to have finally taken steps to improve the environment for SMEs while the private sector is beginning to realize the importance of lobbying for their interests.

In the spring of 1998 a special task force was appointed with a charge to cut bureaucratic red tape by reducing economic quotas and simplifying the business licensing process. Composed of representatives from both the public and private sector, this task force has the mandate to examine all existing business laws and make recommendations to the cabinet and parliament. Several changes figured on the task force's agenda. The licensing process in the transportation and tourism sectors were to be the first to be examined. Next, the tax system required simplification. Then, the number of licenses for various economic operations and the number of import quotas needed to be reduced. The only quotas that warranted retaining were those resulting from international trade agreements.

Also on the agenda was the simplification of privatization procedures and the publication of the list of firms slated for privatization. Ms. Henryka Bochniarz, a former government minister and presently head of the Polish Business Round Table, has expressed the sentiment of many in the private sector, arguing that present laws allow for too much interpretation by government officials. She is leading a drive to introduce stricter lobbying regulations with the idea of making negotiations between business and government more binding and transparent. Her Business Round Table is working to create a lobbying group in order that all businesses be able speak to the government with one voice. Although the Business Round Table consists only of larger firms, Ms. Bochniarz has indicated that smaller firms are represented by such groups as the Business Center Club and many regional organizations who also need to belong to a private sector lobbying organization.

REFERENCES

Berg, Andrew, and Olivier Jean Blanchard 1994 "Stabilization and Transition: Poland, 1990-1991," in Olivier Jean Blanchard, Kenneth Froot, and Jeffrey Sachs eds. *The Transition in Eastern Europe: Volume I: Country Studies* Chicago: University of Chicago Press.

Davies, Norman 1984 *Heart of Europe: A Short History of Poland* Oxford, England: Oxford University Press.

Dominiak, Piotr and Franciszek Blawat 1995 "Small and Medium-Sized Enterprises and Their Regional Contribution to Employment Generation in Poland," in Piasecki and Fogel *Regional Determinants of SME Development in the Central and Eastern European Countries* Lodz, Poland: Lodz University Press.

Gati, Charles "The Smart Money Is on Poland" *The Washington Post* September 17, 1997.

Harvard Business School 1993 "Prochnik: Privatization of a Polish Clothing Manufacturer," Case No. 9-394-038 Boston: Harvard Business Press.

Johnson, Simon and Gary Loveman 1995 *Starting Over in Eastern Europe: Entrepreneurship and Economic Renewal* Boston: Harvard Business School Press.

Krajewska, Anna, and Bogdan Piasecki 1997 "Small and Medium Size Companies as Factors Stimulating Competitiveness and Generating Jobs in

Poland," paper presented to the Polish Academy of Sciences in Warsaw October.

New Europe "EU, Poland Meeting Will Be Fruitful" May 4-10, 1997.

New Europe "Polish President Pushes for Deadline in EU Negotiations" April 5-11, 1998.

Piasecki, Bogdan, and Daniel S. Fogel eds. 1995 *Regional Determinants of SME Development in the Central and Eastern European Countries* Lodz, Poland: Lodz University Press.

Reuters News Agency, May 27, 1998.

Spolar, Christine "Applicants Offer Lots of Heart but Few Arms" *The Washington Post* June 17, 1997.

Spolar, Christine "Poles Enthusiastic About Entry, Czechs Ambivalent" *The Washington Post* June 18, 1997.

Spolar, Christine "Solidarity Ousts Left In Poland: Bloc Begins Search For Coalition Partner" *The Washington Post* September 22, 1997.

Spolar, Christine "Coming Back, Retooled, to Save Poland: Six Years After Unhappy Exit, Finance Czar Returns With Same Goals but New Image" *The Washington Post* March 30, 1998.

Thomas, Scott 1993 "The Political Economy of Privatization: Poland, Hungary, and Czechoslovakia, in Christopher Clague and Gordon Rossiter, *The Emergence of Market Economies in Easter Europe* Cambridge, MA: Blackwell Publishers.

UNIDO, 1996, *A Comparative Analysis of SME Strategies, Policies and Programmes in Central European Initiative Countries, Part III: Poland.* Geneva.

U.S. Department of State 1994 *Background Notes: Poland*, Bureau of Public Affairs, August.

The Warsaw Voice "Polish Entrepreneurship, Dutch Technology" April 26, 1998.

Webster, Leila 1993 *The Emergence of Private Sector Manufacturing in Poland* World Bank Technical Paper No. 237.

World Bank *Overview of the Polish Economy*, 1997.

World Bank 1997 *Transition Newsletter* "Domestic Consumption Drives Economic Growth in Poland" Vol. 8, No. 1.

CHAPTER 6

Romania

ROMANIA

Romania Profile

Area: 237,500 square kilometers, slightly smaller than Oregon
Bordering countries: Bulgaria, Hungary, Moldova, Serbia and Montenegro, and Ukraine
National capital: Bucharest
Population: 22,463,077 (July 1997 est.)
Population growth rate: -0.28% (1997 est.)
Ethnic groups: Romanian 89.1%, Hungarian 8.9%, German 0.4%, Ukrainian, Serb, Croat, Russian, Turk, and Gypsy 1.6%
Religions: Romanian Orthodox 70%, Roman Catholic 6% (of which 3% are Uniate), Protestant 6%, unaffiliated 18%
Languages: Romanian, Hungarian, German
GDP real growth rate: 4.1% (1996 est.)
GDP per capita: purchasing power parity ($5,200 1996 est.)
Inflation rate—consumer price index: 56.9% (1996 est.)
Unemployment rate: 6.1% (1996 est.)
Administrative divisions: 40 counties (*judete*, singular—*judet*)
Natural resources: petroleum (reserves declining), timber, natural gas, coal, iron ore
Independence: 1881 (from Turkey; republic proclaimed December 30, 1947
National holiday: National Day of Romania, December 1, 1990
Constitution: December 8, 1991
Chief of state : President Emil Constantinescu (since November 29, 1996)
Head of government: Prime Minister Radu Vasile (since April 1998)

Source: U.S. State Department

Romania

THE HISTORIC AND ECONOMIC SETTING IN ROMANIA

> It was in this square that I was born again, among those who fought
> and sacrificed themselves for freedom.
>
> —Emil Constantinescu of the Democratic Convention (CDR)
> Party *In Review,* Bucharest (December 1996)

Although Romanians are passionately committed to joining Western
Europe, they have lagged behind in the transition to a market economy.
With nearly 23 million people, Romania is the second most populous
country in the Central and Eastern European region after Poland. While
most of the population is ethnically Romanian, minorities consisting of
Germans, Jews, Armenians, Gypsies, Bulgarians, and Greeks make up
about 12 percent of the population. The dominant feature of Romania's
geography are the Carpathian Mountains that separate Moldavia and
Wallachia in the east and south from Transylvania in the west and the
Black Sea on the east. The great Danube River flows eastward, forming
Romania's southern border with Bulgaria.

Romanians trace their ancestry back to the Dacians, who formed a
state in the region known today as Transylvania. In the second century
a.d., Dacia was in turn conquered by the Romans and remained under
Roman rule for a century and a half; thus the Romans gave the country
its present-day name. More than any other country in the region,
Romanians today reflect a Latin heritage in their language and names.
Indeed, Romania is often referred to as "a Latin island in a Slavic sea."
During the centuries following the decline of the Roman Empire, the

Dacians did come under Slavic influence, however. Subsequently the Romanians suffered waves of invasions of the barbarians from Central Asia. Three major regions came to constitute the Romania of today: Wallachia, Transylvania, and Moldavia. The area eventually came under the successive domination of the Turkish Ottoman Empire, the Hapsburgs, and then the Hungarians.

Despite opposition from Transylvania, which had a large ethnic Hungarian population, Romania adopted a new constitution after World War I, making it a centralized state for the first time in history. The government embarked upon a program of industrialization for which the peasant population had to bear the burden. During World War II, the Romanian government joined the Axis powers and from 1941 to 1944 the country was governed by a military dictatorship backed by German troops. In 1944 the government was ousted by an alliance of political parties who in turn declared war on Germany.

Prior to World War II, the Communist Party was weak and ineffective in Romania and was outlawed by the government in 1924. There were two groups of communists during the 1930s and 1940s— the "home" communists who were behind bars in Romania, and the "Muscovites," who had fled to the Soviet Union to avoid being jailed and persecuted. In 1945 the communists began a campaign of agrarian reform which they hoped would bring them to power. That year several people were killed in a communist-supported demonstration, prompting the Soviet Union to force the resignation of the government. Although the new government included both communists and non-communists, it was dominated by "Muscovites" supported by the Soviet Union. By 1947 the communists had eliminated opposition from the other political parties and the following year formed a constitution declaring Romania a people's republic.

Immediately after World War II, a land reform program provided for the expropriation of all real property. Collectivization of agriculture was begun in 1949 and completed in 1962. The state purchased, processed, and distributed most agricultural products. Starting from a fairly low productive base in 1948, Romania began an industrialization program using the Stalinist command model which resulted in one of the fastest growth rates in the world. The major industries during this period included oil refineries, chemical plants, metalworking, and machine-building enterprises.

Primary political power was exercised by Gheorghe Gheorghe-Dej, head of the Communist Party, for most of the next two decades. Upon his death in 1965, Gheorghe-Dej was succeeded by his protégé, Nicolae Ceaucescu, one of the most heinous rulers in modern times. Accumulating a host of offices and powers, Ceaucescu fashioned a full-blown cult of personality accompanied by advanced nepotism. During the 1980s, Romania recorded the slowest growth of all the countries in Eastern Europe, thanks in large part to Ceaucescu's insistence upon paying off all foreign debt. Romania was able to pay off its hard currency debt in early 1989 only by dropping the standard of living to the lowest in Europe. During Ceaucescu's final years food was rationed, cities were unlit at night, and gas and electricity were available only on a limited basis. The Ceaucescu regime was finally swept away at the end of 1989 when Ceaucescu himself was summarily killed by a firing squad following a popular revolt, after he had rejected calls for economic and political reform. Ceaucescu's megalomania is reflected today in the massive People's House, with hundreds of meeting rooms and halls, which had been completed shortly before his demise and now stands scarcely used.

Romania's recent history has been perhaps the most painful among the countries of the CEE region. Romania was the last country in the region in which Communist Party cadres lost power, in the elections of November 1996, and was among the slowest reformers among the post-communist economies of the CEE region. Policies designed to prop up the statist structure held economic reform in check in the years following the demise of Ceausescu. A lack of effective economic restructuring and privatization of large state-owned firms kept unemployment rates low in comparison with other countries in the region. Many of these firms continued to register financial losses while operating with excess labor. And yet, Romanians showed themselves to be among the most ardent supporters of membership in NATO and the European Union.

The new government that succeeded Ceaucescu was comprised of a coalition headed by Ion Iliescu which was at first made up of former establishment figures—remnants of the Communist Party—who had fallen out with Ceaucescu . A group calling itself the National Salvation Front emerged as the new political leadership in the country. While the old Communist Party structure had collapsed, a large portion of its members simply transferred their loyalties to the front. In May 1990, Iliescu was elected president and the National Salvation Front took a majority of seats in the National Assembly. The two main opposition parties had argued for a rapid transition to a market economy within two years.

It first appeared that Romania might follow the rapid reform model of Poland. During the summer of 1990 legislation was passed encouraging the creation of small businesses and authorizing the government to privatize state-owned enterprises. Other legislation authorized the sale of government-owned apartment houses built after 1948. However, bureaucrats quickly found ways to frustrate the intent of these legislative initiatives. One set of actions did have the intended effect. One-third of the country's arable land was redistributed to private farmers, resulting in an unusually good grain harvest and an increase in meat and fresh products on the market.

Nevertheless, the degree of economic liberalization in Romania during the first seven years after the downfall of Ceaucescu was among the lowest in the CEE region. Douglas Graham summarizes Romania's halting reform process through 1996 as follows (in Meyer, Chapter 2, 1997). There was a sharp decline in GDP accompanied by a shrinkage in real credit. From 1990 to 1992, the decline in the economy was more pronounced than any other country in the region, registering negative growth ranging from -5.6 to -13.8 percent. There was little meaningful policy initiative to reform and restructure state-owned enterprises or to privatize them. This in turn slowed the privatization of the state banking industry linked to these industries. The bias in favor of state enterprises meant that the small and medium-sized firms received a smaller portion of bank financing than did the larger firms.

From 1989 to 1993, industrial output fell by more than half while unemployment and inflation began to rise. Romania registered the largest drop in output during the first half of the 1990s and the highest rate of inflation in the region. Subsidies on basic food products were phased out, leading to increases in the prices of bread, eggs, and meat. There was a drop in the general standard of living of most Romanians as inflation outpaced wage increases. Graham (1997) notes, however, that the deep declines in output likely applied only to the formal economy. While inflationary finance allowed state enterprises to keep workers on the payroll, production output declined. There was a corresponding increase in private sector output in the unrecorded (or informal) sector that cushioned formal sector declines.

Not until 1994 was there a visible decline in Romania's high rate of inflation, due primarily to pressure by the International Monetary Fund and the World Bank, and the standby facility to help straighten out the country's finances. This resulted in declines in inflation in the following year. Unemployment rates, meanwhile, had remained among the lowest in the region until 1994 when they began to rise as a result of the stabilization program. Despite modest economic reform initiatives, popular dissatisfaction continued to mount because of inflation, unemployment, and economic uncertainty.

Finally, on November 17, 1996, Romanians went to the polls in a runoff election to choose a new president which would bring an end to communist domination *(In Review* December 1996). That night, tens of thousands of revelers crowded into Bucharest's historic University Square to greet Emil Constantinescu, the candidate of the opposition party (the Romanian Democratic Convention, or CDR), as the victor. Constantinescu and his party had defeated President Ion Iliescu's ruling Party of Social Democracy (PDSR). The CDR was an umbrella group of parties which had received only 16 percent of the vote in the 1992 elections, compared to 34 percent for the ruling PDSR. Constantinescu had been a university rector with little political experience, whereas Iliescu of the PDSR represented the successor to the National Salvation Front of Ceausescu.

Many Romanians thought that this election constituted the "real revolution," in reference to the internal coup that brought down Ceausescu in 1989. They were hopeful that the new government would speed up the implementation of policies to promote the private sector. The CDR claimed to favor clearing the way for private enterprise by reducing bureaucracy and taxation and by liberalizing legislation to attract foreign investment. For its part, the ruling PDSR had won the 1992 elections by promising gradual reforms. But under its administration, reforms had come slowly and Romania continued to lag behind other countries in the region.

The Romanian economy managed to show a 1 percent growth in GDP in 1993, after three years of spectacular decline. By the time of the 1996 elections, economic results were mixed. Real GDP growth slowed to 4.1 percent from 6.9 percent in 1995, although per capita income increased (to $1,510 from $1,450). Inflation increased slightly to 38.8 percent, while unemployment was lower, hovering around 6 percent for most of the year. By March 1997, the average monthly wage was 93.3 percent higher than it had been a year earlier, although there was a real 26.8 percent fall in purchasing power over the year because of inflation (World Bank 1997).

Shock Therapy: World Bank and IMF Measures in Romania

Prime Minister Victor Ciorbea presented the new government's long-awaited shock therapy program in the spring of 1997 (World Bank 1997). The government imposed a stringent austerity plan in an attempt to comply with International Monetary Fund and World Bank benchmarks mandated under their assistance agreements. In mid-April 1997, Romania signed an initial letter of intent with the IMF regarding reforms. On April 23, the IMF approved a 13-month standby agreement for Romania including credits totaling $430 million. The first installment of about $86 million was made available immediately, and four additional quarterly installments of the same amount would be subject to the observance of performance criteria. These measures were not directed at promoting Romania's long-shot bid for membership in NATO.

The government expected a rise in unemployment to about 8 percent in 1998 from the 1997 rate of 6 percent. Over 10 percent of GDP was to be channeled into a social program to compensate those most affected by the austerity measures. The average monthly wage was expected to rise by more than 30 percent from 329,000 *lei* ($53) to 430,000 *lei* ($70). The government hoped that this increase would compensate for the price hikes. The minimum taxable salary was to double from 97,000 lei (about $16).

On June 3, 1997, the Ciorbea government, having swallowed the bitter pill of adjustment, saw the World Bank approve three loans totaling $550 million in support of its reform policy to alleviate poverty and to get the economy moving again (World Bank 1997). The new loans were to finance social protection ($50 million), the agricultural sector's adjustment ($350 million), and improvements in Romania's highways ($150 million).

The price of fuel, electricity, public transport, and telecommunications had already surged in February, following the government's decision to withdraw subsidies for them. As a result, consumer prices rose steadily. The main objectives of the government's program were to reduce monthly inflation to about 2 percent in the second half of the year and to increase foreign exchange reserves. Romania formally accepted the IMF's Article VIII in August and then was to consider a trading band for the *lei*. Romania's monthly inflation fell to 6.9 percent in April from the all-time high of 30.7 percent in March; the country's current account deficit narrowed to $182 million in the first two months of 1997 from $291 million in the same period the previous year. Foreign direct investment increased to $191 million from $26 million during the same period. It seemed at long last that Romania was beginning to catch up to other CEE countries.

PRIVATIZATION AND ECONOMIC GROWTH

Prior to 1989, the private sector accounted for less than 10 percent of the total GDP in Romania. Its share rose from 39 percent in 1994 to 45 percent in 1995, yet was still among the lowest in the CEE region. The growth of the private sector has been concentrated mainly in agriculture, trade and services, although there is potential in agro-processing and manufacturing. Only modest progress was achieved in privatization under the initial reform program.

An ambitious privatization program initiated in 1992 resulted in the divestiture of 30 percent of the equity of state-owned enterprises to five private ownership funds. In this program, the equity in a large number of enterprises was distributed to the population through vouchers. Despite this system, designed to allow employees to "buy out" their company, the transfer of ownership frequently meant that the majority of shares would go to a few individuals within the company. Furthermore, the high rate of inflation undermined the voucher system. The pace of privatization thus soon lost momentum.

In March 1994 a Privatization Program aimed at some 2,400 commercial companies was published and approved by the Romanian parliament (European Bank for Reconstruction and Development 1995). A new Restructuring Agency was established to cooperate with the State Ownership Fund in order to assist large state-owned companies to speed up the restructuring process. A list of 288 medium and large commercial companies—mainly in industry, agricultural services, and food processing—was sent out to potential foreign investors. The size of companies to be privatized was expected to increase. Only one thousand small and medium-sized industrial companies, representing 16 percent of industrial production and worth around $200 million, had been privatized by April 1995.

In September 1994, the Romanian government submitted new proposals to the parliament to speed up mass privatization. The proposed value of the new nominal coupon was 875,000 *lei* for each Romanian citizen 18 years or older. In some cases individual citizens would be able to invest up to 60 percent in a specific commercial company, although in most cases the employees would have priority. In March 1995, 200 companies were offered for privatization through public offerings and a list of 75 large state-owned companies was published by the Restructuring Agency.

According to State Ownership Fund data for 1995, the privatization program was overwhelmingly focused on small and medium-sized commercial companies. Out of a total of 1,495 in the program, 1,345 were classified as small, 135 as medium, and only 15 as large. The small companies were concentrated in agriculture, trade, tourism, and industry, while most of the medium-sized and large firms were in agriculture and food processing. In terms of average capital value, however, the large firms represented the greatest volume.

Not until 1996, through the Financial and Enterprise Sector Adjustment Loan (FESAL) program financed by the IMF and World Bank, was there a serious effort to implement wide-ranging privatization of large and medium-scale enterprises. As a result of this extensive exercise, the pace of financial reforms and privatization of some state-owned banks began to speed up. As part of the reform program agreed to with the World Bank and IMF in June 1997, the government pledged to privatize about three thousand enterprises and at least two banks by the end of 1997, close down or auction off 10 industrial enterprises that accounted for 7.5 percent of all state-company losses, and shut down a further 20 unprofitable state-owned farms. Exchange controls were lifted, tariffs and price controls cut, and an inflated exchange rate abandoned. The government also invited foreign companies to buy stakes in state utilities, communications groups, and oil companies that were to be privatized. Foreign investors in Romania, whether their interest was in partially or entirely foreign-owned businesses, would be entitled to own the land required for their activities.

In August 1997, Prime Minister Ciorbea announced a list of 17 large, state-owned businesses that were to be shut down—forcing thirty thousand Romanians out of work—and beginning what he promised would be Polish-style economic shock therapy. Although a former union activist, Ciorbea made it clear he that wanted all-out privatization, despite the prospect of temporary social pain. Due to the continued dominance of the remnants of the Communist Party in power, Romania had delayed restructuring and privatization on any significant scale until that time.

LOOKING TOWARD EUROPE

> For us, it is an identity issue—being in the NATO club.
>
> —Sorin Ducaru, Romanian Foreign Ministry's NATO Department.

Romania is NATO country, with a zeal only the Marlboro Man could envy (Cody 1997). Left out of the Western alliance's first wave of expansion at the Madrid summit conference in July 1997, Romania nevertheless continued making an all-out effort to see that it would be on the second list of expansion countries scheduled to be named in April 1999.

When its neighbors—Poland, Hungary and the Czech Republic— were invited to join NATO at the conference in Madrid in July 1997, Romania was left out. It was far behind in economic and political liberalization, although it displayed the most zeal to be admitted. Economic growth had been lagging as measured in percentage change in gross domestic product, where Romania is among the lowest in the region. Romania was only just beginning to privatize state enterprises in earnest.

Although opinion surveys show that enthusiasm is highest in Romania, the campaign for NATO membership is part of a widespread desire across Eastern Europe to join the winning side of the ideological struggle that concluded at the beginning of the decade. Membership in NATO is seen as a path toward sharing in the free market riches of the evolving European Union. A poll conducted for the European Commission in March 1996 found Romanians the most eager to join NATO (95 percent) , compared with Poles (92 percent), Lithuanians (83 percent), Estonians (78 percent), Slovenians (71 percent), Slovaks (63 percent), Czechs (59 percent), Hungarians (59 percent), and Bulgarians (52 percent).

In some ways, Romania failed to make the first cut at the Madrid meeting of July 1997 because it started from so far behind in terms of economic reform. However, the government that arose from Romania's 1989 revolution quickly began to reform the military and point toward NATO. For example, it was the first to sign up for NATO's Partnership for Peace program in 1994. But along with Slovenia—the other candidate wait-listed at Madrid—Romania still had the lowest percentage of production from the private sector among major NATO contenders when the invitations were made. This was identified as the main reason for leaving Romania out of the club. Although half of

Romania's overall economic activity has now moved to private hands, 80 percent of large-scale industrial production still comes from state-owned enterprises.

Leading up to Madrid, President Constantinescu's government waged a quixotic campaign for admission, backed by France but with little chance of success. The U.S. decision to limit the first cut of NATO expansion to Poland, Hungary, and the Czech Republic which was formalized at Madrid did not generate the resentment in Romania predicted by some. Instead, Romania redoubled efforts to cement close strategic ties with the United States, recognizing Washington's determinant role in NATO as well as its interest in East European and Balkan stability. At the same time, officials in Bucharest followed NATO integration closely in Poland, Hungary, and the Czech Republic, with an eye to imitating what had worked well there and avoiding what had failed.

Romanian determination to join the North Atlantic Treaty Organization rises almost to the level of national obsession. More than desire for NATO's nuclear umbrella, the eagerness reflects a desire to see Romania anchored once more in the West after a generation of communism and dictatorship. Romanian troops or military medical teams have participated in international peacekeeping in Bosnia, Albania, Rwanda, Angola, Somalia, and the Persian Gulf over the last few years. The Defense Ministry came home from Madrid and began a military assessment of what needed to be done by 1999 to make sure Romania gained admission to NATO.

European integration represents a key external policy goal for Romania. Its status as an associate member of the European Union became effective in February 1995. Even though Romania was left off the initial list of countries invited to begin negotiations, it continues to hope for full membership in the European Union.

THE ROLE OF SMES IN THE ROMANIAN ECONOMY

The private sector has expanded rapidly in Romania since 1990, as measured by number of registered firms, persons employed, and share of total output.

—Richard Meyer et al. *Small Business Finance in Romania,* 1997

Because the process of privatization in Romania has proceeded so slowly, the development of the private sector has been all the more important. Several surveys have been conducted on this new private sector. An extensive study of banking services and the small business sector funded by USAID was undertaken by Richard Meyer and his colleagues at Ohio State University in 1996 (Meyer 1997). The objective of the study was to observe how new private firms were being financed in Romania and to identify constraints to their growth. Drawing upon documents from the Romanian Development Agency and CRIMM Foundation, the Meyer study noted that the private sector in Romania had risen to 45 percent of the GDP by the end of 1995 (Chapter 3, "The Private Sector and SMEs in Romania"). However, the importance of the private sector varies widely by subsector. For example, the private sector share of industrial GDP was still only 16 percent in 1995, an increase of 3 percent over the year before. The share of private enterprises in other sectors was considerably higher: 79 percent for agriculture; 70 percent for trade, hotels, and restaurants; 69 percent for retail trade; and 30 percent for total external trade. By the end of 1994, the private sector employed 1.1 million workers, roughly half of total employment.

Already by 1993, over 97 percent of all registered enterprises in the Romanian economy were private, representing only 28 percent of turnover. Even though only 1 percent of all industrial firms were state-owned, they still accounted for over half of total employment and turnover. Only 10 percent of the private sector enterprises were in industry, representing less than 5 percent of total employment and turnover. The trade sector, on the other hand, was heavily represented by private firms: 70 percent of the firms in the sector, accounting for 16 percent of employment and 19 percent of turnover. State-owned enterprises are generally quite large. In 1990, the average number of employees in these enterprises was 3,400, However, with restructuring and downsizing, that figure had declined sharply to 2,400 by 1994. Cooperative enterprises followed a similar pattern although they employed considerably fewer workers.

The state sector had traditionally dominated the economy of Romania. Prior to the reforms, the state ran all economic activities and owned most of the assets of production. The only exceptions were small cooperatives and individuals working in handicrafts and the arts. Then, with the reforms came a rush to create new businesses. The rapid expansion in private sector growth in Romania is owed directly to the registration of new firms as opposed to privatized state enterprises. By the end of 1991 there were some 83,000 new companies registered, and

240,000 added in 1993 and 1994. As in other countries in the region, however, these figures are somewhat misleading, since the number of companies actually operating is unknown. Registration reached its peak in 1994, declining to 65,000 in 1995. The most common juridical form chosen by registrants in Romania has been limited liability, with nearly 80 percent opting for this type. This is likely due to the fact that liability is limited to the capital contributed by each shareholder and the required sum for registration is as little as 100,000 *lei* (US $33).

The definition of the term *small and medium enterprises* used in the CRIMM Foundation's *1995 White Book* is a firm with five hundred employees or fewer. That report noted that SMEs accounted for the bulk of the private sector in Romania: about 70 percent of the total number of enterprises in Romania, 25 percent of total employment, 30 percent of aggregate turnover, 11 percent of fixed assets, and 40 percent of total fixed investments. The heaviest concentration of SMEs is in the service sector, where two-thirds of them are to be found. Service firms account for some 60 percent of total SME employment and 84 percent of total turnover. Manufacturing firms follow at a distant second, with one-quarter of the enterprises and employment.

The Meyer study makes particular note of the extent of microenterprises in the Romanian economy. By 1993, nearly 90 percent of all enterprises in the Romanian economy were micro-enterprises (fewer than 10 employees). Small enterprises (10 to 99 employees) comprised some 7 percent of private enterprises while less than a half of 1 percent were in the medium-sized category (100 to 499 employees). Only 8 percent of state enterprises were classified as micro-enterprises. Almost 25 percent of state enterprises were small, 40 percent medium-sized, and only 30 percent large (500 or more employees).

Almost 75 percent of the microenterprises were concentrated in the trade sector, as were 44 percent of small enterprises and 25 percent of the medium-sized firms. This was due in large part to the relative ease of getting started in trade, where capital requirements are lower and turnover more rapid than in other sectors. Enterprises in manufacturing and construction, on the other hand, require a minimum size in order to produce at competitive quality and cost.

While large state enterprises are being downsized and losing workers, small businesses are creating new jobs. While the average number of employees per state enterprise fell by one-third from 1990 to 1994, state enterprises still have a much larger number of employees than the average private firm. Within the SME sector, the micro-enterprise contribution to employment generation is heaviest in the trade sector, where they represent two-thirds of the total, and in services, where they account for half. As might be expected, micro-enterprises are least represented in the construction and industry sectors. Small firms are responsible for nearly half of industrial employees, while over 60 percent of the construction employees are in medium-sized firms.

Difficulties identified by Romanian entrepreneurs in various surveys bear similarities to those in other countries of the CEE region. Two studies conducted in Romania in 1991 and 1992 focused on the SME sector. An EU PHARE survey of 166 firms conducted for the Romanian government drew from a sample of firms with fewer than two hundred employees, half of them microenterprises. The second study, funded by the United Nations Development Program (UNDP), was undertaken by the National Agency for Privatization, and involved interviews with fifteen hundred enterprises.

These two studies identified similar problems. These included bureaucratic red tape, difficulties obtaining permits and licenses, raw materials, and financing. Problems related to locating premises were associated with high rents and insecurity due to the short-term nature of rental contracts. The greatest difficulty SMEs had regarding raw materials had to do with state companies retaining monopolies over them. State firms tended to give priority to other state enterprises in the allocation of centrally distributed raw materials. Most of those interviewed expressed a desire to improve their equipment and production technology, but they lacked information about technologies in use in other countries. With respect to start-up capital, well over half of those interviewed in one study reported that they had used personal financial resources exclusively. In the other study, nearly half said that they had benefitted from bank credit in starting their businesses. Problems associated with bank credit included high interest rates, complicated procedures, small loan size relative to need, and high collateral requirements.

The CRIMM Foundation 1994 Annual Report on SMEs included survey results based on nine thousand businesses. Regarding business financing, the most frequently cited source of funding was informal and personal sources, followed by supplier credits; bank credit was listed last. In addition to high interest rates and collateral, respondents mentioned that developing a business plan for the loan application was a less serious problem. More than one-third of them reported applying for bank credit within the last year, and 90 percent reported success. As might be expected, the rate of success was directly related to size: highest for medium-sized firms and lowest for micro-enterprises.

The Ohio State study was conducted in two stages in 1996. The first involved collecting data from banks, nonbank financial institutions, and donor agencies, while the second consisted of interviews with SMEs. To obviate lack of cooperation from interviews, the Ohio State team collaborated with five business centers, three in Bucharest, one in Alba-Iulia, and one in Timisoara—all funded by USAID or UNDP. The respondents were selected randomly from the clientele of the business centers in the food, wood, textile, trade, and service subsectors. A total of 68 entrepreneurs were interviewed. This approach elicited good responses from the entrepreneurs and facilitated the collection of sensitive information on marketing and financing strategies they would not otherwise have likely obtained.

The profile of the Romanian entrepreneur that emerged from the Ohio State study bears many similarities with that from surveys in other countries of the region. The typical Romanian entrepreneur was a highly educated young male who had acquired management skills in his previous employment, but was likely to be lacking in direct production experience. He might have more than one business as a risk diversification strategy to cope with an uncertain environment. The typical Romanian firm in the Ohio State study experienced a long gestation period from the time of registration to the time operations actually began. The average age of the firm was only three years. While half the firms studied employed an average of 23 workers, over one-third were micro-enterprises employing an average of six workers. The medium-sized firms had an average of 147 employees. The trading and service firms tended to be micro in size while the manufacturing firms were mostly small and medium-sized.

The highest sales reported by the Romanian entrepreneurs were in the trading subsector, followed by the food subsector. Micro firms in the food sector reported the highest sales, while the highest sales in the wood sector were reported by the medium-sized firms. Small firms registered the highest labor productivity, compared with both micro and medium-sized firms, suggesting greater efficiency.

The typical Romanian entrepreneur in the Ohio State survey relied upon his or her own resources initially for financing the business. However, nearly all respondents had borrowed from external sources including banks, suppliers, government agencies, customers, and friends to finance their activities. Banks were cited as the most common source, mainly in the manufacturing sector, for purchasing fixed assets such as land and buildings. Supplier credits and grants were most frequently used to purchase inputs, machinery, and equipment. The banks were the only type of source to explicitly charge interest and require collateral. The majority of the firms interviewed serviced only domestic markets.

The Ohio State study also explored the determinants of firm growth in Romania. Interestingly, it found that female entrepreneurs were associated with firms that have experienced significantly higher growth. This was interpreted as a sign that the business environment is conducive to women entrepreneurs, at least in the subsectors chosen for the study. Entrepreneurs who owned and operated only one business at a time also experienced significantly higher growth. Those businesses in Bucharest grew faster than those located outside of the capital city. The use of loans to purchase fixed assets and inputs was actually shown to be associated with reduced firm growth. This suggests that cash flow problems can arise with borrowing because of the inability of banks to match the term structure of loans with the type of asset financed, or because of the firm's financial mismanagement.

BANK AND NON-BANK SOURCES OF FINANCING FOR SMES IN ROMANIA

> There was a noticeable shift in credit and deposit balances away from state firms to private sector businesses from 1991 to 1995.
>
> —Graham and Nagarajan, "The Romanian Banking Sector" in Meyer
> *Small Business Finance in Romania* (1997)

Banks in the communist era in Romania were owned by the state and there was little competition among them (Graham and Nagarajan, Chapters 4 and 5 in Meyer, 1997) . They served as financial conduits for budgetary resources of central planning agencies to service expenses of state enterprises. These so-called loans were often not repaid, but the banks in question were not concerned, since they received new budgetary allocations each year. No screening of clientele was required. Therefore, few of the banking skills and regulatory framework required in Western banking were present in the Romanian banking system.

There has traditionally been a lack of credit available to the SME sector, although major changes introduced into the banking system in 1990 are beginning to have a positive effect on the sector. A two-tiered banking structure was established consisting of the central bank and several state-owned commercial banks. Although interest rates were formally deregulated, there continued to be informal pressure to maintain low rates until 1994. Not until 1996 was most of the relevant regulatory framework in place to supervise and regulate the banking system.

Among the significant changes in the system has been an increase in long-term credit to private sector businesses, due in large part to the directed donor programs launched in 1993. In addition to the bilateral programs such as the Romanian-American Enterprise Fund, there are several multilateral programs. Principal among them are the EBRD, the World Bank, and the European Bank for Investments. The World Bank has provided two special credit lines to state and private banks aimed at private farmers and SMEs engaged in agro-processing and exporting. The EBRD has also provided credit lines to Banca Agricola, the Romanian Development Bank, and Bank Coop to make medium and long-term loans to SMEs engaged in production and exports. However, with the exception of the Romanian Development Bank, very few banks have utilized these credit lines to make SME loans. The low utilization of these funds has been due to the stringent conditions applied for selecting borrowers. For example, by the end of 1996 the Romanian Development Bank had utilized less than half the funds that were allocated to it in 1993.

Graham and Nagarajan concluded from their study of the banking system that heavy political intrusion still prevails. The extent to which authorities can effectively implement bank examinations and take corrective action to forestall losses is still open to question. Short-term credit for trade predominates, reflecting inflation and growing risks, rather than for manufacturing. Most of the longer-term credit is still going to state firms. That which is reaching the private sector comes from the international donor lines of credit channeled through state-owned banks. However, the shift in credit and deposits toward private firms underscores the growth of the private businesses in Romania rather than the growth of "privatized" state enterprises.

Whereas at the end of the communist era there were only five state banks operating in Romania, by the end of 1996 there were some 32 registered commercial banks. State banks still dominated the system in terms of volume of business, number of branches, and employees. In 1995 they represented 67 percent of assets held and 84 percent of loans made by all 30 commercial banks. The Romanian Development Bank (RDB) has been the most successful in diversifying its portfolio to include short-term commercial banking activities for private businesses. When completed, the RDB will be the first state-owned bank to become successfully privatized through injections of foreign and private domestic capital.

The growth in private banking in Romania has come through the growth in new private banks, not through the privatization of state banks. There were 23 private banks operating in Romania by 1995. The seven foreign banks, which have only recently been opened, perform a limited range of banking services for international clients. Five of the remaining 16 private banks—Dacia Felix, Credit Bank, Bank Coop, Ion Tiriac, and Mind Bank—have the longest history of implementing private sector practices. With a German capital base, the Ion Tiriac Bank has registered the most consistently positive performance among these banks. Most of its business consists of financing export-import trade between local businesses and Western Europe.

Loans to the trade sector were found to be the most significant in the Ohio State Study. Ninety percent of lending to the private sector goes to companies engaged in trade, while only 10 percent goes to SME manufacturing firms. Nominal rates of interest range from 47 to 70 percent with positive real rates of interest ranging from 15 to 30 percent for most banks. Collateral-based lending is widely used by Romanian banks to screen loan applicants and enforce contracts. Collateral value reaches up to 200 percent of the value of the loan for both state and private banks. The use of credit guarantee programs in quite limited. The only two such schemes with loans for SMEs has not been commonly used by the banks. Normal bank loans require collateral of up to twice the value of the loan and the payback periods are between one and three years, even if the capital equipment in which the money is invested has an expected useful life of 10 years. This results in high payback amounts in a short time frame, which seriously impacts cash flow, which is a key factor for a business's operational sustainability.

Even with the rapid expansion in banking, the quality of human capital in the banking sector is not high. The private banks exhibit a risk averse behavior toward lending, while state banks engage much more extensively in lending. One of the most serious deficiencies in private banking is insider lending to directors and shareholders beyond the maximum loan size limits. The most serious problem among the state banks is their under-performing loan portfolios with state enterprises. They should be downsized, restructured, or privatized and made to compete by the standards applied to private banks.

The state of the banking sector in Romania is one of the critical issues the government of Prime Minister Ciorbea had to concentrate on in order to spur investment. In spring 1997 the government planned to introduce or revise up to eighty laws in order to attract direct and portfolio investments from the West. All five state-controlled commercial banks were included in proposed legislation. Bureaucratic procedures were to be cut back. Romanian authorities were to allow foreign banks to acquire up to about 95 percent of the capital of state banks and to develop capital markets.

In addition to the formal banking system in Romania, a number of nonbank financial institutions (NBFIs) are beginning to emerge (Nagarajan, Meyer, and Graham, in Meyer, et al. Chapter 7). These institutions—some of them profiled below—often offer unique products and services not provided by banks, including investment options through capital markets, long-term credit through guarantee schemes, leasing options, micro and small loans with training programs funded by donor agencies, and informal savings mobilization. The NBFIs are beginning to offer a range of deposit and lending services aimed at specific market niches. The formal NBFIs include capital market institutions such as the stock market, mutual funds, and venture capital companies.

The mutual fund industry has functioned in Romania since 1993, with the objective of offering high returns on investments and alternatives for portfolio diversification. They are licensed and supervised by the National Securities and Exchange Commission and managed by boards of directors elected by their investors. However, the mutual funds have not been able to offer attractive investment options thus far, and the National Securities Commission has not been effective in curbing insider lending activities. Equity financing, such as that provided by the Romanian American Enterprise Fund, has had very little impact on private firms. The loan guarantee programs have also had limited outreach and have yet to achieve subsidy independence. Intended to encourage banks to make larger and longer-term loans than they would otherwise, the guarantee programs make their financing decisions based more on the cash flow of the business than on collateral as do the banks. Thus far, however, they have had a small volume of activities.

Donor assisted and semiformal NBFIs are also quite limited and inadequate to the needs of SMEs in Romania. These programs are designed to service the thousands of micro- and small enterprises that have no access to formal banking services. They are highly donor dependent and do not provide deposit services. The PHARE Program is the most prominent of the donor agencies. The World Council of Credit Unions (WOCCU) has established an office in Bucharest with funding from USAID and is working with eight member-owned and managed savings and credit associations. Two U.S.-based non-governmental organizations—World Vision and Opportunity International—have initiated micro-loan programs in Romania aimed at businesses with fewer than 10 employees. Both of these organizations are experimenting with group lending procedures for their beneficiaries, who are primarily women.

In addition, there are a number of indigenous self-help groups formed among factory workers or retail traders in order to mobilize savings and make short-term loans to members for personal and business needs. Because of problems of handling large amounts of cash, some of these groups are being converted into more formal credit unions with the help of WOCCU. Another form of savings and credit association in Romania, known as *rotas,* or "gypsy wheels," has reemerged in the 1990s after decades of suppression. They traditionally functioned mainly to finance consumption needs and were considered illegal. These *rotas* experienced a contraction in the mid- 1990s because of one pyramid scheme in which many people lost money. However, the *rotas* are now growing among workers in both private and state-owned enterprises, but are not a significant source of business loans for their members.

GOVERNMENT AND DONOR AGENCY ASSISTANCE TO SMES IN ROMANIA

It is essential that SME loan funds require a minimum equity prior to any loan. . .To do anything less is to place start-up businesses in a false world.

—Robert Tolar, Washington State University, Director of International Small Business Development Program, 1996

Romanian Government

Despite a late start, the Romanian government has come to recognize that it has a responsibility to channel resources to facilitate the development of the private sector. The basic legislation regarding incentives to support the establishment of SMEs in Romania was approved by the parliament in 1993 (Economic Commission for Europe 1996). This act defined the scope of SMEs as follows: small (up to 25 employees) and medium (26 to 200 employees). The ordinance had as its purpose to create new jobs and to promote production in areas such as industry, construction, tourism, and services having value added by providing special incentives to SMEs. These were to include lending and guarantee schemes, leasing schemes, funding for industrial research, support for subcontracting to larger firms in production and services, and facilitating access to information on foreign markets.

In 1995 the Department for European Integration of the Romanian government elaborated a national strategy for preparing the country's integration into the European Union. Small business development represented a significant part of the strategy and was perceived as a priority for economic reform. In practice, this strategy has depended to a considerable extent on the support of the EU PHARE program and other donor agencies.

The primary government agency responsible for promoting small businesses is the SME division of the Romanian Development Agency (RDA), formally established in 1995 (UNIDO 1996). The SME division is charged with coordinating and implementing programs and keeping grant records. It also prepares proposals regarding SME policies and strategies and collaborates with various other ministries. An RDA Strategy for Economic and Social Reform provided for a regional development plan to foster the growth of SMEs, especially in areas with high unemployment. Among the elements of the strategy was the establishment of small business development centers and business incubator centers with donor support and integrated national networks. These centers were to build a standardized information system for SMEs and facilitate access of entrepreneurs to building sites and equipment. While the strategy had lofty objectives, it encountered existing local authorities and laws that ran counter to them. The SME division has cooperated with the ROM-UN Center in setting up 10 local development centers, providing logistical support to the CRIMM Foundation, and publishing articles on SMEs.

Small Business Development Centers

By the end of 1996 there were some 40 business development centers throughout Romania, funded by a wide variety of sources, such as the United Nations Development Program, the PHARE Program, and U.S. and German bilateral agencies. The centers typically involve a consortium of local institutions, universities, and firms, and provide a variety of services, including business advising and consulting, training, and market information. They also serve as a point of access to sources of grants and loans. One of the main distinctions among the various approaches is the nature and extent of income generated by fees charged to clients. In general, they will need to seek alternative means of achieving sustainability or risk going under when donor funding ends.

The ROM-UN Center

Established in 1991 by the Romanian government with funding from the United Nations Development Program, the ROM-UN Center was among the first (Allen 1996). Additional funding has come from the Dutch government and the British Know-How Fund. The executing agency is the United Nations Industrial Development Organization (UNIDO). The ROM-UN Center has assisted in the establishment of ten autonomous county business development centers and provided training for 60 small business counselors, including some who work with other programs such as EU PHARE. By 1994, the center reported having counseled over six hundred clients and processed 91 loan applications, and having organized 27 seminars and workshops for entrepreneurs. Success of the ROM-UN Center is attributed to its cost-effectiveness, dynamic and continuous management, and the commitment of the staff and consultants.

The CRIMM Foundation

Established in 1993, the CRIMM (Romanian Center for SMEs) Foundation was the implementing authority for the 1992-1995 PHARE Program for small businesses. The foundation set up five local small business development centers and four business incubator centers during this period, all within a support network. CRIMM activities included business consultancies, a grant scheme for SMEs, and economic and legal analysis. The grants were for machinery and equipment and required no collateral. The foundation has also developed a special program to support women entrepreneurs.

Centers for Business Excellence

Funded under a grant from USAID's Management Training and Economics Education Project, Centers for Business Excellences (CBEs) were established by Washington State University (WSU) in 1991 (Tolar 1996). USAID funding for the project ended in 1998. A significant feature of this program was that it involved universities along the lines of the Small Business Development Center model in the United States. Initially WSU worked with the Polytechnic University of Bucharest in setting up a Center for Business Excellence, to provide business counselor training, management training for privatization, and information resource development. Three other partner institutions of higher education were added, eventually forming a network of CBEs. The counselor training for university faculty members involved several modules, including marketing, management, finance, planning, and personnel. Lessons learned from the CBE experience, according to WSU, include the need for caution in exposing small business owners to grants without requiring them to make equity investments for a loan. New business owners who were required to attend regular counseling sessions in order to receive PHARE grants tended to avoid these pitfalls.

Donor Agency Assistance Programs

The PHARE Program

Funded by the European Union, the PHARE program aims at preparing countries in transition for eventual membership in the EU. The PHARE program in Romania was limited mainly to critical aid agricultural restructuring in its first two years (1990-1992). A first loan in the amount of 375 million ECU was approved in 1991 under the Stand-By Agreement with the IMF. Private sector development and enterprise support began in 1992. A financial scheme developed by the CRIMM Foundation under the PHARE program offered grants to SMEs of up to 50,000 ECU or half of the funds needed to purchase new manufacturing equipment. This program ended in 1995. Although PHARE contributed to the preparation of financial recovery plans for heavily indebted state enterprises, the plans were not implemented.

In 1995 PHARE also began a three-year assistance program for the development of SMEs through support for a network of business advisory centers backed by a grant aid scheme. This initiative was intended to support business incubation centers that were created beginning in 1992. The grant facility was established to provide grants to SMEs engaged in manufacturing and trading. These grants cover half of the cost of equipment and machinery imported or purchased locally by the beneficiaries. They are heavily concentrated in the Bucharest and Timisoara areas and are accessed through small business centers. More than half of the firms that have benefitted from the grants thus far are small (employing six to 25 workers) and a quarter of them are micro-enterprises employing fewer than six workers. In addition, PHARE has financed an assistance program for banks to help them conduct business with SMEs.

Romanian-American Enterprise Fund

In mid-April 1997, the Romanian- American Enterprise Fund (RAEF) and the Banca Romaneasca announced the establishment of a Small and Medium Loan Program. The RAEF Board of Directors approved a five million dollar investment in the program to be run through the Banca Romaneasca branches in Bucharest and Pitesti initially. Loans are to range from $20,000 to $100,000 and are for expansion of businesses, not start-ups. Initially RAEF limited its small loan program to the city of Cluj.

The European Bank for Reconstruction and Development (EBRD)

In the context of the preparation for Romania's strategy for European integration and application for full membership in the European Union, the EBRD has focused its support on privatization and industrial restructuring, stepping up its assistance in response to the government's request since 1995. The first major transaction under the EBRD's Investment Led Privatization Program was completed in May 1995. Support for the Mass Privatization Program (MPP) is aimed at increasing public awareness to maximize understanding and involvement in the process. The EBRD has also collaborated in establishing a Post-Privatization Fund (PPF) to provide equity for newly privatized and new private companies. The Fund involves close cooperation among Romanian authorities and the EU PHARE Program. Furthermore, the EBRD is providing support for the restructuring of the light source sector, and the agro-machinery and truck manufacturing industries in collaboration with the World Bank and EU PHARE program.

The World Bank

World Bank lending to Romania aims to sustain the implementation of the country's economic reform program while developing an effective social safety net. Bank-assisted projects are helping to prepare investment lending to increase the efficiency of energy production and use, and to maintain adequate infrastructure to support economic growth. Since Romania joined the bank in 1972, commitments have totaled $4 billion for 45 operations. The central element of World Bank assistance has been the $400 million structural adjustment loan, approved in June 1994, to support Romania's economic stabilization efforts. In January 1996, the Bank approved a US$280 million Financial and Enterprise Sector Adjustment Loan (FESAL) to support privatization, enterprise restructuring, and financial sector reforms.

PROFILES OF SUCCESSFUL ROMANIAN ENTREPRENEURS

Regardless of their previous employment and formal education under the former economic system, Romanian entrepreneurs are having to swim upstream against formidable odds in order to succeed in today's environment. Some are doing so successfully, including a few women.

Sarmstil 92, Timisoara

In Timisoara, where Washington State University collaborated with the chamber of commerce in establishing a Center for Business Excellence (CBE), one of the most interesting stories is that of Sarmstil 92. Although the company was registered in 1992, its clothing manufacturing operations did not begin until 1994. At that time the company operated out of a two-room apartment in a block. The space was so small that to accommodate the four sewing machines, the firm's manager made the apartment kitchen into his office. At that time, the only other equipment at the company's disposal was a van to ensure that it could get its products to the customers.

With the help of the Timisoara CBE, Sarmstil 92 received a 24,000 ECU grant from the PHARE program to purchase equipment for sewing, cutting material and drying. They also rented a workshop that was four times the size of the old apartment and began to expand their activities. The new equipment increased their output, but more importantly, the company doubled the number of its clients. The workforce was increased from six to 26.

Sarmstil 92 appeared on Romanian television twice to display its products on a popular show for young audiences that covers fashion. As a result of its success and overall exposure, Sarmstil 92 was invited, along with the country's largest fashion house, to visit the World Trade Center in New York City. Sarmstil product lines were presented to potential customers from around the world. As a result, the company now supplies an upper-end retail store in Strasbourg, France, and is working to finalize a contract for distribution in Germany.

Matei Construction

Matei Construction began operation in June 1992 with a capital base of 100,000 *lei* and 10 employees. By 1994, owners Elena and Mihai Matei had built their railway and road construction company to 29 employees with sales of 500 million *lei*. Satisfied with neither the numbers nor the profitability of the company, the Mateis planned their next step, to purchase improved equipment to replace what they had been leasing. In the process, they sought to cut production costs, maintain competitive prices, and increase their profit margin.

With assistance from the Center for Business Excellence, they put together a successful business plan and application for a PHARE grant. There were two conditions: that Matei Construction increase its social capital, and provide proof that it had the necessary funds for half of the equipment cost. The supporting documentation and revised business plan were subsequently approved. However, the Mateis still had to provide proof of payment to the equipment supplier. Only then would PHARE release its funds via wire transfer. The documentation for this phase was delivered in person to the local CRIMM office by the CBE counselor, who waited for a final response from CRIMM representatives regarding the credit. The PHARE credit for 30,000 ECU ($42,000) was approved. By March 1996, sales for Matei Construction had risen to 1.5 billion *lei,* the number of employees had increased to 150, and profits were growing.

SC Misy Prodimex, Craiova

SC Misy Prodimex is a computer software and services firm in the industrial city of Craiova founded and managed by Emil Ionescu. He attended a conference in Bucharest featuring well-known computer experts and participated in discussions regarding the use of the Internet to support scientific studies. This led Ionescu to wonder whether the internet might be a profitable business in Romania. He consulted the Craiova CBE to investigate potential opportunities in this area and to help him determine the feasibility of such a venture. Together with his CBE counselor, Ionescu developed a marketing study to determine the possibilities of internet use in Craiova, evaluating the market potential, competition, and financial prospects. The analysis showed that a great opportunity existed in this field. In November 1996, Ionescu began providing internet services in Craiova with Center for Internet Services and Instruction (CISNET), employing a young and energetic team. The demand was there, and the firm has expanded rapidly. Ionescu has found it necessary to invest additional resources in the business. Quick recovery of his initial investment allowed Ionescu to look toward even greater success with more clients.

PRINCO Group, Bucharest

The PRINCO Group, a father-son furniture manufacturing firm, decided to compete head-on with the Western European furniture products in January 1994. However, one essential piece was of their strategy was missing: a specific type of equipment needed to improve the quality of finish on the PRINCO product. With assistance from the Polytechnic University of Budapest CBE, Cosmin Constantin Florescu, the Deputy Manager of PRINCO, produced a business plan designed specifically to obtain the PHARE grant he needed for the purchase of the Italian-made finishing equipment. Florescu was successful in his bid for the grant, and by March 1995, the furniture-finishing equipment was delivered to the company's factory. Within a few months PRINCO had doubled monthly production and the number of employees. The cost of the finishing operation decreased by 30 percent and the sales price was increased to reflect the higher quality. Nearly all production was exported to companies such as IKEA in Sweden, as well as major importers in Italy, Austria, and Germany.

THE POTENTIAL FOR SME GROWTH IN ROMANIA

Even with the free market reforms proposed in the spring of 1997, economists expected Romania's GDP to fall by 1 to 2 percent. The country's annual foreign debt servicing totaled about $900 million in 1997. The IMF Resident Representative in Romania told an investors conference in Bucharest that this figure would likely grow to $1.6 billion between 1999 and 2001 due to short-term borrowing. He said that most of the country's resources for debt servicing in 1997 would come from foreign loans. And he predicted that the budget and current account deficits would steadily improve, allowing the state to pay for the higher debt servicing in the near future with little borrowing. Modest GDP growth could be expected by 1998 if only the promised free market reforms were in place. There was a wait-and-see mood of caution in the private sector, including SMEs, and as a result there was little growth in 1997 (*New Europe*, April 5-11, 1998).

But after a three-month political crisis that stalled reforms and paralyzed government activity, Prime Minister Ciorbea was forced to resign in March 1998. He also announced the resignation of his entire cabinet. Ciorbea had been under increasing pressure from within the parties of the governing coalition because of failure to implement the reforms. The Liberal Party, allies in the coalition with the Christian Democrats, joined the main opposition Social Democrats in calling for the resignation. Even dissidents within Ciorbea's own Christian Democrats joined in the chorus. The IMF team in Bucharest reportedly expressed concern that the political crisis would have further negative effect on the reforms.

Ciorbea had been unable to solve the prolonged crisis that had prompted the concerns of the IMF. The crisis had crippled foreign investor confidence and led to a decline in economic indicators. Inflation, instead of being brought down, had risen to over 150 percent by the end of 1997. Unemployment edged toward 9 percent, an increase of 3 percent over the previous year. The GDP actually declined by 6.6 percent, in contrast to positive growth of 4.5 percent in 1996. Clearly, the Romanian government had to devise a medium-term policy framework to stabilize the economy and bring down inflation. A tight and disciplined budget and renewed privatization were necessary to restore multilateral confidence.

The economic environment in which SMEs operate in Romania has not been especially favorable at any time and may be headed for even harder times. A private sector is emerging in spite of the slow progress of the government in dismantling the state sector. In the absence of a sustained program of privatization, however, the newly created SME sector has managed to account for much of the modest growth in the Romanian economy. In principle, the Romanian government has adopted a commitment to supporting small businesses, as evidenced by the growing number of agencies and programs. The system of small business development centers funded by donor agencies is widely used by small business owners and managers, both for access to grant and loan assistance and for business advisory services. The sustainability of these centers beyond donor funding, however, remains a critical issue. The legislation introduced by the Ciorbea government in 1997 began to make the banking system more responsive to private sector interests. Meanwhile, non-bank financial institutions are playing an important role in complementing the services of the formal banking sector. But the question remains as to whether these institutions are cost-effective and sustainable without donor assistance. In any case, the new legislation is needed to provide a more favorable environment for private sector development.

The support system for small businesses is still modest in comparison with the needs of the SME sector. Access to grant funds and bank loans among those entrepreneurs in recent surveys does not appear to have been a critical problem. This may very well reflect the fact that most of them were drawn from the clientele list of business centers, which is certainly a biased sample.

The banking system in particular could be made more effective in addressing the financial needs of small businesses. The Meyer study (1997) concluded with several suggestions for banking reforms, including:

- Banks should offer more long-term loans to obviate debt repayment problems. While many entrepreneurs appear to have been successful in obtaining financing from institutions, most loans are short-term.

- Conflict of interest laws and lending limits should be strictly enforced. The most serious deficiency in private banking is the damage caused by insider lending to directors and shareholders beyond the maximum loan size limits set by regulatory authorities.

- State-owned enterprises must reduce their under performing loans to eliminate soft budget constraints.

- Nonbank financial institutions should be encouraged to test alternative lending technologies such as cash flow and group lending for micro and small borrowers.

At the same time, Romania has a number of advantages that could provide the basis for renewed growth in the short term. The labor force is literate and skilled, and wages are relatively low by international standards, allowing for a competitive advantage in a number of exports. In the early 1980s, Romania was a competitive exporter of textiles, wood products, machinery, and light consumer goods. Romania could recapture some of those lost market shares. The new generation of entrepreneurs has already targeted these sectors and begun to succeed in reaching them.

Important changes are underway in the Romanian agricultural sector. The land reform of 1990-1991 led to an initial sharp decline in agricultural production. Since then, however, the government has directed considerable resources to the sector, and output has increased since the mid-1990s. Romania has become a net grain exporter. Presently, agricultural products and tourism have the highest potential for generating foreign exchange. While it may be some time before Romania is asked to join the European Union or even NATO, there is evidence that Romanians are committed to working toward European integration. Developing a vibrant and dynamic small business sector will be one of the chief cornerstones of that commitment.

REFERENCES

Allen, John 1996 "The Experience of the ROM-UN Center in Romania" in Jacob Levitsky ed. *Small Business in Transition Economies*. 1996 *Small Business in Transition Economies* London: Intermediate Technology Publications.

Cody, Edward "Romania Steps Up Efforts To Secure Spot in NATO" *The Washington Post,* August 26, 1997.

CRIMM Foundation 1995 *The Private Sector of Small and Medium-Sized Enterprises in Romania: Annual Report 1995.*

CRIMM Foundation 1995 *The White Book of Small and Medium-Sized Enterprises in Romania Annual Report 1995.*

European Bank for Reconstruction and Development 1995 *Strategy for Romania* Update, BDS/RO/95-1, June 15.

Economic Commission for Europe 1996 "Small and Medium-Sized Enterprises in Countries in Transition" IND/AC.3/1, February.

European Commission 1996 *The PHARE Program Annual Report 1995* Brussels: November.

Graham, Douglas 1997 "Economic Reform and Stabilization in Romania: A Precis" Chapter 2 in Richard Meyer ed. *Small Business Finance in Romania: Banks, Businesses and Business Centers in a Transition Economy.*

Graham, Douglas, and Geetha Nagarajan 1997 "The Romanian Banking Sector: An Analysis of Structure, Performance and Change," Chapter 7 in Richard Meyer, *Small Business Finance in Romania: Banks, Businesses and Business Centers in a Transition Economy.*

In Review December 1996/January 1997 Issue 12 Bucharest.

Meyer, Richard ed. 1997 *Small Business Finance in Romania: Banks, Businesses and Business Centers in a Transition Economy*, study prepared for the Bureau for Europe and the Newly Independent States of USAID, Ohio State University, March 31.

Meyer, Richard and Geetha Nagarajan 1997 "The Private Sector and SMEs in Romania" Chapter 3 in Richard Meyer *ed. Small Business Finance in Romania: Banks, Businesses and Business Centers in a Transition Economy.*

New Europe "PM Resigns to Save 1998 Budget," April 5-11, 1998.

Romanian Development Agency 1995 *Small and Medium-Sized Enterprises: Strategies, Policies, and Programmes* Bucharest.

Tolar, Robert 1996 "Higher Education Institutions' Involvement With Business Development Projects in Romania and Russian Federation," in Jacob Levitsky ed. *Small Business in Transition Economies* London: Intermediate Technology Publications.

UNIDO 1996 *A Comparative Analysis of SME Strategies, Policies and Programmes in Central European Initiative Countries, Part III: Romania* Geneva.

World Bank 1997 "Milestones of Transition" *Transition Newsletter* Vol. 8, No. 3. April.

CHAPTER 7

The Slovak Republic

SLOVAK REPUBLIC

Slovakia Profile

Area: 48,845 sq km, about the size of New Hampshire

Bordering countries: Austria, Czech Republic, Hungary, Poland, Ukraine

National capital: Bratislava

Population: 5,387,665 (July 1997 est.)

Population growth rate: 0.12% (1997 est.)

Ethnic groups: Slovak 85.7%, Hungarian 10.7%, Gypsy 1.5% (the Gypsy/Romany community may be over 500,000), Czech 1%, Ruthenian 0.3%, Ukrainian 0.3%, German 0.1%, Polish 0.1%, other 0.3%

Religions: Roman Catholic 60.3%, atheist 9.7%, Protestant 8.4%, Orthodox 4.1%, other 17.5%

Languages: Slovak (official), Hungarian

GDP real growth rate: 7% (1996 est.)

GDP per capita: purchasing power parity ($8,000 1996 est.)

Inflation rate consumer price index: 5.5% (1996 est.)

Unemployment rate: 12% (1996 est.)

Administrative divisions: 4 departments (*kraje*, singular -*kraj)*

Natural resources: brown coal and lignite; iron ore, copper and manganese ore; salt

Independence: January 1, 1993 (from Czechoslovakia)

National holiday: Slovak Constitution Day, September 1, 1992; Anniversary of Slovak National Uprising, August 29, 1944

Chief of state: President Michal Kovac (from February 8, 1993 until March 1998);

Head of government : Prime Minister Vladimir Meciar (since December 12,1994)

Meciar also assumed presidential powers in March 1998.

Source: U.S. State Department

The Slovak Republic

THE HISTORIC AND ECONOMIC SETTING IN THE SLOVAK REPUBLIC

It is better to see something once than to hear about it a hundred times.

> —Old Slovak proverb, quoted by President Michal Kovac, inviting investors to come to the Slovak Republic Bank Austria, *Eastern Europe: East-West Report Extra* 1996.

The Slovak Republic, created in 1993 out of the dissolution of Czechoslovakia, has registered respectable economic growth yet has failed to gain the respect of the international community. It is primarily a mountainous and hilly country defined geographically by the western spur of the Carpathian Mountains, which stretch from north to south, and the Danube River on its southern border. The highest peaks of the rugged High Tatras are found in the north central region of the country on the border of Poland. The southern and eastern parts of the country are lowlands significant for agriculture. Slovakia is bordered by Hungary and Austria on the south and west and Ukraine on the east.

The Slovak Republic has a population approaching 5.5 million. As its name implies, Slovakia is a land of Slovaks, members of the great Slavic language group, who comprise 86 percent of the total population. There are, however, three minority nationalities that make up a small percentage of the Slovak population. The Hungarians, numbering slightly more than half a million, are concentrated in the southeastern part of the country. There are smaller numbers of Poles in the northeast and Ukrainians in the east. Slovakia also has a sizable number of Gypsies (Roma) that do not show up in official statistics because they are not recognized as a separate nationality. Slovakia is predominantly Roman Catholic (60 percent), with a minority of Protestant (8 percent) and Orthodox (4 percent) adherents.

Although Slovakia as a political entity is one of the youngest in Europe, the people living there have ancient roots. The history of the Slovak peoples is traceable to the fifth century a.d. when a group of west Slavic tribes settled into the area that has come to be modern Slovakia. The establishment of the Moravian Empire at Nitra in the ninth century marked the rise of a western Slavic nation which was associated with Christianity, brought to them by Saints Cyril and Method. Although the empire lasted only a century, it was important because the western Slavs were converted to Christianity during this period.

All of the Slovak lands were brought under Magyar control by the year a.d. 1000, the date traditionally used to indicate the beginning of the Christian era in Hungary. For the next thousand years, until 1918, the Slovaks remained under the Hungarian crown. They shared the Roman Catholic faith with the Hungarians, but most of the Slovak population were serfs living on lands owned by Hungarian nobility. In the sixteenth century Hungary became a possession of the Hapsburgs, whose main seat was Vienna. Most of Hungary was eventually overrun by the Turks. For 150 years the seat of the Hungarian government was Pressburg, known today by its Slavic name of Bratislava, which came to be the capital of Slovakia.

The social revolution that swept across Europe in the mid-1800s also aroused Slovak nationalism. Interestingly enough, it was among Slovak emigres living in France and the United States that this sentiment eventually found its strongest champions. The Pittsburgh Agreement, signed in June 1918, expressed support for the union of Czech and Slovak lands in an independent state. A few months later, on October 28, 1918, an independent Czechoslovak Republic was proclaimed. It was not to be an altogether happy marriage for its duration over the next twenty years, however. It was an unequal relationship in which the Czechs enjoyed the upper hand in education and economics, and Slovaks came to harbor several grievances. There was no official recognition of the Slovak language in schools, Slovaks were in the distinct minority among civil servants, and most industries were being built in the Czech part of the country. Many Slovaks came to believe that they were being treated as a colony.

In 1938 Hitler was able to capitalize on Slovak grievances by urging them to declare independence from Czechoslovakia. The Slovak parliament unanimously adopted a declaration of Slovakian independence. For a brief period from 1939 to 1945, the Slovak Republic existed as a virtual puppet state of Germany, which declared the new republic a protectorate and sent in troops to maintain order. These troops were not to leave until they were forced out in 1945 by the vanguard of the Soviet army. Plans were soon underway for reconstituting the Czechoslovak state.

Three months after the communist seizure of power in Prague in 1948, a new constitution was issued which created a highly centralized state with most of the power concentrated in Prague. Although the constitution technically provided for autonomous status for Slovakia, in practical terms the Communist Party that ran Slovakia was merely a branch of the Czechoslovak Communist Party. Leading Slovak Communists were eventually purged to the extent that no ethnic Slovaks were in leadership roles in Slovakia. The general Slovak population remained alienated from the new Czechoslovakia, and the issue of Slovak autonomy refused to die.

The Velvet Revolution of 1989 in Czechoslovakia which spelled the end of Soviet domination and opened the door to reform also unleashed ancient Czech and Slovak rivalries. Upon Slovak insistence, the name of the country was changed to the Czech and Slovak Federal Republic. As new political parties were organized to contest the 1990 elections, separate parties emerged in the two parts of the country. Economic reform was the issue that galvanized the Slovak population. Many feared that the rapid implementation of the market system being advocated by the new Czech leaders such as Vaclav Klaus, the new minister of finance, would have a negative effect on the Slovak economy. These fears were manifested when Czechoslovak President Vaclav Havel was booed by thousands of Slovaks when he came to visit Bratislava in 1991. Havel was increasingly forced to act as mediator between Czechs and Slovaks.

Slovak Premier Vladimir Meciar took up the Slovak nationalist cause. Opinion polls showed that only a small minority of Slovaks were in favor of continuing the federation. In the 1992 elections votes broke down along national and ideological lines, with the Czechs voting for reform and anticommunist candidates and the Slovaks voting against reform and in favor of nationalist and leftist candidates.

When Klaus and Meciar met after the election to discuss the formation of a new federal government, Meciar made it clear that he would not accept a federal state that could dictate policy to Slovakia. Furthermore, he demanded that the Slovak Republic be authorized to establish its own army and issue its own currency. He also insisted that subsidies to state industries be restored, social benefits be increased, and privatization slowed. None of these demands was compatible with the free market orientation of Klaus. This scenario appeared increasingly like grounds for divorce, which was soon to come.

The Velvet Divorce between the Czech and Slovak Republics, which became effective on January 1, 1993, represented yet another watershed event in Slovak history. It was negotiated by the parliaments and governments of the two republics without being put to a referendum. Prime Minister Vladimir Meciar formed a governing coalition comprised of his own Movement for a Democratic Slovakia and the Slovak National Party, as well as the Worker's Union. Meciar subsequently found himself often in conflict with Slovak President Michal Kovac, who represented a more European-oriented perspective.

With the separation leading to Slovak independence, the Czech Republic succeeded in halting the decline in its GDP, while the Slovak GDP continued to fall at almost 5 percent (Svejnar 1995 23). Although the Czechoslovak GDP per capita in 1990 ranked along side that of Venezuela and Yugoslavia, it was already in decline. However, most indicators suggested that the Czech Republic would fare well after separation while the Slovak Republic would flounder. Indeed, at independence, many observers thought that Slovakia would be unable to survive without the Czechs. Tourism and other services were creating enough jobs in the Czech Republic to absorb workers being laid off from heavy industry. Official unemployment was only 2.3 percent. In contrast, the unemployment rate in Slovakia had risen to over 10 percent by the end of 1992 and would jump to over 14 percent the following year (Gray 1996).

However, by 1994 Slovakia had embarked upon a period of strong economic growth initially supported by export activity (Bank Austria 1996). Slovakia achieved an impressive GDP increase of 7.4 percent in 1995, the highest in the Eastern European region for that year, and a still robust 6.9 percent in 1996. Domestic demand, as reflected in private consumption and gross capital investments, grew strongly in 1996. Real industrial output grew a remarkable 8.3 percent in 1995, dipping to 4 percent in 1996. In the first half of 1997 the Slovak GDP grew at a slightly more modest rate of 6.2 percent while industrial output was 3.7 percent. Consumer prices rose by only 6 percent, over the 12-month period to July 1997, quite low compared to neighboring countries. In 1995 Slovakia was the only country in the region that managed to achieve a balance of trade surplus. The central bank had a solid monetary policy that had pushed inflation down to merely 7 percent in 1996 and 1997, among the lowest in the region. The country's foreign debt was also among the lowest in Central Europe.

Thus, by 1997 the Slovak economy was registering signs of resurgence, while neighboring Czech Republic was beginning to experience a downturn, quite the opposite of conditions only a few years before. Among transition economies, only Estonia and Poland were growing more rapidly than Slovakia in 1997.

However, there were also negative signs on the Slovak economic horizon. Despite the increase in industrial growth, unemployment continued to remain at a rate of nearly 13 percent, the highest among the countries of the CEE region (Wyzan 1997). Slovakia also had a large and growing budget deficit, much higher than that of Poland, Hungary, or the Czech Republic. The main cause for alarm, however, was the foreign sector. The current account balance imbalance was the highest among the Central European and Baltic economies. The initially favorable balance of trade surplus began to disappear and in 1996 the foreign trade situation worsened considerably. While imports continued to soar, exports weakened, resulting in a substantial balance of trade deficit. The decline in exports was due mainly to the economic cycle in Western Europe, which accounted for more than one-third of Slovak exports. Slovak products are low-tech and commodity-based, while imports are primarily capital and consumer goods.

Slovakia has remained a relatively unattractive country for foreign investors. While the Czechs began to attract large-scale foreign investment immediately after the fall of communism, no such deals had been realized by Slovakia by the mid-1990s. By 1997 the Czech Republic had secured a total of $7.6 billion in foreign direct investment since 1990, while the Slovaks had attracted only $887 million. By mid-1996, Slovakia's per capita foreign direct investment stood at only $150, compared with over $1,000 and $586 in the Czech Republic (Wyzan 1997). The largest transaction was the Volkswagen investment of $90 million in Bratislava's vehicle plant (BAZ). Volkswagen began producing VW Passats from kits in 1992, and two years later moved into gearbox assembly and production of VW Golfs (Bank Austria, 1996). There have been a few other notable investments, such as Whirlpool's acquisition of Tatramat, which now makes washing machines for the export market.

In the spring of 1997, Prime Minister Meciar's government sought to push through an enterprise revitalization law that would allow over two billion dollars in enterprise debt to be written off (*Business Central Europe*, April 1997). Under the legislation, struggling companies in areas of high unemployment could apply for government debt write-offs and tax deferrals. It would keep weak firms out of bankruptcy and their workers employed. But the proposed revitalization did not exactly encourage companies to do what they had heretofore failed to do: restructure. Industrial production had failed to keep pace with increasing wages. The proposed scheme was criticized by a local economic think tank as an attempt to channel even more taxpayers' money into the pockets of a narrow privatization lobby.

There is a significant risk that the economic choices made by Slovak economic planners and policy makers will not be sustainable. Unsound practices, such as excessive manipulation of exchange rates and balance of payments and the continued government subsidies to large inefficient public companies, illustrate a need for a more informed understanding of the economic consequences of policies. There is danger of soft credits being lavished on companies close to those in authority. Not only have these policies been questioned within the international donor community, but also by some of Slovakia's neighbors who have pushed forward on reforms more aggressively.

PRIVATIZATION AND ECONOMIC GROWTH IN SLOVAKIA

By the end of the communist era the Czechoslovak economy was geared toward heavy industry operated by state-owned enterprises. The private sector was virtually nonexistent, accounting for no more than 3 percent of the GDP. During the decade from 1978 to 1988, Czechoslovakia was the world's eighth largest weapons exporter and the global leader in per capita terms. More than 100 large plants produced weapons of various types, mostly destined for Warsaw Pact partners and Third World countries. Many of these plants were located in central Slovakia, the center of the country's arms industry. By 1989, military goods accounted for 60 percent of total industrial production in Slovakia and provided employment for more than one hundred thousand persons. The town of Martin north of Bratislava, for example, was the site of a tank plant that employed eleven thousand workers. In many of the small towns of Slovakia, a single factory would be the sole source of jobs.

After the fall of communism, Slovakia was spurred to rapid economic changes under the Czechoslovakian union. The new government's stated aim was to privatize the economy as quickly as possible. Two months after the November 1989 revolution, the Czechoslovak foreign minister announced that his country was ending its trade in arms. It became obvious that political and economic decisions would be intertwined when the old system began to be transformed. Many of the jobs dependent upon arms production were in central Slovakia. Fears about the fate of the heavily subsidized arms industry therefore helped fuel a Slovak separatist movement. Many of the state-owned firms were grossly over staffed, and there was concern that privatization would lead to high unemployment (Fisher 1995).

At the time of the divorce between the two republics on January 1, 1993, one statistic spoke volumes about their economic orientation: just over 5 percent of the Slovak industry had been privatized, as compared to 25 percent for the Czech Republic. Even so, the new Slovak government began to slow down economic reform and turn back the clock on many of the transition programs begun after 1989, particularly privatization. The Slovaks feared the massive downsizing of their heavy industries that would accompany the aggressive privatization envisaged for their region of the union.

The first wave of the Czechoslovak privatization program, launched in 1991, was small-scale privatization of small businesses, shops, and restaurants (Marcincin 1994). This involved public auctions to domestic investors. In Slovakia, nearly ten thousand were sold off, most of them in the domestic trade and distribution sector. By the time this program ended in March 1994, only fifteen hundred units remained unsold. A second form of privatization was restitution, under which property was returned to its pre-1948 owners. By the end of 1992, over twenty-five hundred applications for restitution had been filed and property claims settled in Slovakia alone.

However, large-scale privatization—focused on the voucher program—moved rather more slowly. The first wave of coupon privatization ended in December 1992. In the Slovak Republic, there were 503 companies offered for sale, and more than 2.6 million Slovaks took part in the program. When Meciar came to power in June

1992, this first wave of coupon privatization was well under way. The Meciar government began to slow the sale of property that had already been approved. By late 1993, many projects remained incomplete. The privatization program stagnated as controversy developed over how to carry out the second wave. While the Czech government forged ahead with its second wave of large-scale privatization, the Meciar government chose to use methods other than the voucher system, which lent themselves to political manipulation. It was argued that the voucher system would allow firms to be sold at market value, which would in turn ease the entry of foreign capital. However, the standard approaches required capital from either domestic or foreign sources, both of which were lacking in Slovakia.

Responsibility for privatization was transferred to the Privatization Ministry (headed by the prime minister himself), which showed little interest in speeding the process. In June 1993, Meciar announced that the second wave of large-scale privatization was being prepared and that six hundred firms were ready to be sold. Nonetheless, the Privatization Ministry indicated that it would wait until the right buyers came along. Meciar's government made little progress in privatization during 1993. Controversy over control of the privatization process led to the fall of Meciar's government in March 1994. Only then did privatization resume under the new government of Prime Minister Moravcik. But the second wave of coupon privatization under the Moravcik government was short-lived. Although Moravcik succeeded in increasing the growth of the private sector, Meciar vowed to cancel the program and accused the government of buying votes. Meciar was returned to office in December 1994 and quickly began to reverse the Moravcik government's program, once again delaying the second wave of coupon privatization.

By 1994, the Slovak private sector accounted for 44 percent of the GDP, compared with 56 percent in the Czech Republic (Bank Austria 1996). The private sector share of employment had only risen to 32 percent, the lowest in the region and far less than the nearly 50 percent in the Czech Republic. And while the Czech Republic had completed the two wave voucher scheme that was the hallmark of its privatization by the end of 1994, Slovakia, like Hungary and Poland, still had substantial assets in state hands.

In July 1995, the Slovak parliament passed three new privatization acts (Bank Austria 1996). Among other provisions, the acts suspended coupon privatization. Slovak citizens were no longer entitled to exchange their privatization coupons for shares in state-owned companies. The rights of investment funds that had acquired a large number of shares in companies in the first wave of privatization were curtailed. As a result of these restrictions direct sales became increasingly important. Domestic investors, however, were given preferential treatment, especially with respect to existing management teams. The acts also listed strategically important companies in the fields of energy, gas, defense, chemicals, and telecommunications which would either not be privatized or be privatized only with limitations. The government retained a right of consultation in strategically important decisions in another 40 major companies, some of which had already been partially privatized.

Thus, with the abandonment of the voucher system the Slovak government focused on privatizing through direct negotiations, particularly by selling to management buyouts. For example, in mid-1995 a 39 percent stake in Slovnaft, the national petrochemical company, was sold to a management- and employee-controlled company at a discount to its book value.

It cannot be said that the rather remarkable turnaround in the Slovak economy was associated with the process of privatization of large-scale enterprises. On the contrary, in contrast to the Czech Republic, the Slovak government under Premier Meciar made considerable efforts to see that privatization proceed at a deliberate pace. Economic growth in Slovakia since 1994 must be accounted for by other factors.

LOOKING TOWARD EUROPE

> It's now out of the question that Slovakia will be invited to join NATO in the first round of enlargement.
>
> —President Michal Kovac, after the NATO referendum vote of May 1997

Less than five years after the Czech and Slovak Republics went their separate ways in 1993, the Czech Republic seemed to be on its way to integration with the West, while Slovakia was often shunned (Stephenson 1997). The Czech Republic was the first former communist country to join the Organization for Economic Cooperation and Development (OECD), an elite group of advanced market economies, but no date was set for Slovakia to join. In July 1997, when the Czech Republic, Hungary, and Poland were invited to begin talks on NATO membership, Slovakia was one of four other countries left off the list. A month later, the European Commission recommended that talks on joining the EU begin with the Czech Republic and five other countries, but again Slovakia was passed over because of its poor performance in building democratic institutions.

The very question of whether and how fast Slovakia should be fully integrated into Europe has been at the center of the country's politics since independence. Prime Minister Meciar has publicly stated that his country's foreign policy priorities are to join NATO and the European Union. Despite the country's economic turnaround since 1994, political issues have clouded the road to European integration. For one thing, the long-running feud between Meciar and President Kovac has hurt the country's image. Foreign diplomats have expressed dismay at Meciar's refusal to tolerate political dissent and his campaign to undermine his archrival. Citing instances in which the Meciar government has ignored democratic rights, the U.S. State Department issued a stinging attack on Slovakia's failure to respect the rule of law, thus hindering the very international structures the government aspires to join. Also contributing to Slovakia's bad human rights reputation is its poor record of treatment of ethnic minorities such as the Hungarians.

The successive rapprochement between Slovakia and the European Union and the OECD has produced demands on Slovakia in terms of adhering to democratic principles, freedom of the press, and protection of minority rights. The government record of economic reforms has done Slovakia's chances of joining the OECD little good. In order to meet some OECD requirements, the Meciar government modified laws, but the larger issues have yet to be addressed. An OECD official was quoted as saying that, "As long as the Slovak government does not prepare answers to questions regarding privatization and foreign trade liberalization submitted in 1996, negotiations on Slovakia's admission to OECD will not move ahead" (*Business Central Europe,* October 1997).

The Meciar government has pursued a foreign trade policy that has left room for doubt about its commitment to integration with Europe. Its most important relations are with its erstwhile nation-mate, the Czech Republic (accounting for 25 percent of Slovakia's imports and 35 percent of its exports in 1996). Yet shortly after independence there was a drop of nearly 50 percent in exports to the Czech Republic, and an even greater drop in imports. The common currency of the two countries collapsed within two months. The government also has undertaken interventionist and administrative measures to protect the domestic market from imports, a plan hardly designed to please free market advocates and gain points for eventual admission into the European Union.

The Meciar government's response to the trade problem has been mixed. On the one hand, the government sought to increase trade ties with Russia, even though in 1996 Slovakia's trade balance with the country was the worst among all its trading partners (Zemanovic 1997). On the other hand, alarmed by a huge trade deficit with Russia, Slovakia sought to swing to the opposite side of the trade balance pendulum by promoting more trade. Russian Premier Chernomyrdin visited Bratislava in April 1997, where he held talks with Meciar to increase trade. A spokesman for the European Commission made it clear that Slovakia would be obliged to renounce any such agreement if it were to join the European Union.

At the same time, Prime Minister Meciar complained of Slovakia's exclusion from the list of the first group of CEE countries to be admitted into NATO. Jozef Tuchyna, chief of Slovak armed forces, warned that this could only have negative consequences. A spokesman for the defense minister said that "soldiers might go into a very low psychological state, which could slide into passivity and a reduced interest in NATO" (Zemanovic 1997).

In May 1997 a popular referendum was held on two different sets of questions. (Drozdiak 1997). In two days of voting, Slovaks were supposed to be asked to address two issues: whether they wanted to join NATO and whether they wanted their president elected by popular vote instead of by parliament. The latter question was framed by President Kovac and his allies. As in other countries in the region, referendums on NATO membership were being employed to show the degree of popular support. The ballot became a test of strength between President Kovac, long-time supporter of NATO, and Prime Minister Meciar, ending in turmoil and virtually dashing whatever hopes the country had of being in the first group of nations joining NATO. The damage had been done even before the results were in. A widespread boycott by Kovac's supporters of the disputed ballot, because the government provided the ballots only with the first set of questions on NATO membership, discredited the outcome. Only 10 percent of the voters turned out.

Confusion surrounding the vote reflected the contrasting visions of Slovakia's future. President Kovac and his supporters favored rapid integration with Western institutions such as NATO and the European Union, whereas Meciar was more comfortable with an authoritarian style of government and continued relations with Russia. Under the existing constitution, parliament must elect the president by a 60 percent majority. Otherwise, presidential powers pass to the prime minister. The president's supporters feared that a divided parliament would allow Meciar to increase his power when Kovac's term ended in March 1998. They thought that a popular vote would favor Kovac and prevent Meciar from gaining too much power. Prime Minister Meciar had already come under criticism from the United States and other Western countries for restricting the media, intimidating political opponents, and slowing economic reforms. Although Meciar had stated publicly his support for NATO, he signed a military cooperation pact with Russia.

Meciar, for his part, had crafted the NATO question in such a way as to encourage negative votes. The ballot asked whether Slovaks would accept nuclear weapons and foreign troops on their soil, although neither condition is required for membership in NATO. On the eve of the referendum the interior minister, a Meciar ally, ordered the presidential question removed from the ballot even though the supreme court had upheld the validity of both questions. He claimed that the presidential issue was irrelevant to a vote that was supposed to focus on NATO. Many voters expressed outrage when presented with ballots that only dealt with the NATO issue and not the issue regarding presidential elections. There ensued recriminations on both sides, further damaging the country's already poor image of a laggard in establishing democratic standards.

In March 1998, the day after assuming most of the powers of the vacant presidency, Meciar canceled a referendum on seeking NATO membership and on holding direct elections for president. Twice in one year, the divided Slovak parliament failed to muster the two-thirds majority needed to elect a new president. These issues tend to form the major political fault line in Slovakia. The five disparate opposition political parties have formed the Slovak Democratic Coalition (SDK), whose stated purpose is to "re-establish the rule of law and respect for the constitution, maintain economic growth and guarantee qualification for the EU and NATO." (*Business Central Europe* October 1997). The coalition aimed at unseating the Meciar government in the elections due in September 1998.

THE ROLE OF SMES IN THE SLOVAK ECONOMY

As noted in chapter 3 on the Czech Republic, the Entrepreneurial Act of April 1990 in Czechoslovakia opened the door to the creation of a private sector (Webster and Swanson 1993). The act legalized the establishment of private firms, allowing them to employ unlimited numbers of workers and to produce a full range of goods. Commercial codes were amended to provide for the incorporation of limited liability and joint stock companies and partnerships. In 1991, a constitutional amendment accorded private enterprises equal status with state enterprises before the law.

Other changes also facilitated both the regulation and promotion of the private sector. In 1992 a new law required companies to obtain a business license before they could register with the Commercial Registry. An amnesty was accorded to private firms on profits taxes in their first year for reinvested profits up to $36,000. The maximum personal income tax rate was lowered from 55 to 47 percent. New bankruptcy laws provided for liquidation or negotiated debt reduction for insolvent firms. Self-employed persons were permitted unlimited access to foreign exchange for long-term financing and investment.

Private enterprises took one of two basic legal forms: sole proprietorship (self-employed) or incorporated, registered company (limited liability and joint-stock). Self-employed persons were required to register in the courts if they met one of three criteria: employment of more than 25 workers, a turnover of more than 540,000 crowns, or use of foreign currency in trading operations. Such firms were required to pay corporate taxes.

In the first couple of years after the passage of the Entrepreneurial Law, there was a profusion of new businesses started in Czechoslovakia. Statistics do not provide a breakdown between the Czech and Slovak Republics during this period. By the end of 1991, there were 1,175,700 persons listed on official registers as sole proprietorships, up from a mere 8,200 in 1989. That number had reached 1.4 million by mid-1992. The largest proportion of these businesses (26 percent) was engaged in production and repair, followed by construction and direct trade. However, as in other countries in the region, many who were recorded as self-employed actually worked in registered private firms and used their self-employed status to spare their employers payment of high labor taxes. In effect, they had a subcontractual relationship with the registered firm. Also at the end of 1991, the official roster recorded a total of 40,000 registered companies, three times as many as the previous year.

The first few years of transition to a market economy in Czechoslovakia witnessed a sharp decline in economic growth. While large state enterprises began downsizing and restructuring, the new private sector in Czechoslovakia began to create jobs and respond to pent-up demand for consumer goods. Nowhere in Central and Eastern Europe has there been a more dramatic economic turnaround than in Slovakia. The Gross Domestic Product of Czechoslovakia fell by 2.2 percent in 1990, and plunged to 14.6 percent the following year. Not until 1994 did the GDP reach positive growth (4.9 percent), followed by a remarkable increase of 7.4 percent in 1995. This economic rejuvenation can be in large part linked to the birth of new enterprises. The private sector in the Slovak Republic was virtually nonexistent at the time of the Velvet Revolution, accounting for less than 1 percent of employment in the economy. The Slovak economy in particular was characterized by the predominance of very large state-owned enterprises, many of them employing from one thousand to twenty-five thousand workers.

In 1995 the Commercial Register, which sets forth the legal character of business entities in Slovakia, defined the term *small enterprise* as a firm with one to 24 employees, and *medium enterprises* as those having 25 to 499 employees (National Agency for Development of Small and Medium Enterprises 1996). *Large enterprises* were defined as those with more than 500 employees. In that year, there were 275,000 registered firms in Slovakia, down slightly over the previous year. Furthermore, there was a significant cancellation of business licenses, especially after the imposition of sanctions upon entrepreneurs who violated the compulsory use of cash registers in their business. These involved unregulated licenses such as trade and services, as well as regulated activities such as crafts. Many of these activities were conducted on the side (in addition to a main job), or by retirees and students who worked out of their homes and had no other office.

Certain sectors such as freelance professions witnessed significant growth during the mid-1990s. For example, with the privatization of health services there was a marked increase in dentists, pharmacies, and manufacturers of medical instruments. Other sectors registering an increase were tourism and trade. The explosion of growth in small businesses was especially notable among the smallest ones, firms with 24 or fewer employees, whereas the same was not true of medium-sized firms those with 500 employees or fewer. By December 1995, there were 760 state enterprises registered in Slovakia, of which some 273 were reported to be in the process of liquidation. State enterprises included various district and municipal enterprises, as well as building enterprises and research and development institutes.

The private sector has come to account for more than half of all employment in Slovakia (52.2 percent in 1996, versus a meager 1 percent in 1989). Within the private sector, small and medium-sized enterprises are playing a significant role in employment creation in Slovakia. In 1995, there were just over two million persons employed in the national economy, an increase of 2.2 percent over the year before. While the number employed by large firms declined by 0.8 percent, those employed in small enterprises grew by 46.8 percent. Medium-sized enterprises also declined slightly. Over the first three quarters of 1996, overall employment grew by only 0.7 percent. For small enterprises the rate was 4.8 percent, while for medium-sized enterprises there was a decline of 0.7 percent (Economic Commission for Europe 1997).

By 1996, data from the Central Statistical Office indicated that the high rate of economic growth in Slovakia was due in large part to the increased economic activity of small businesses. Industrial production in Slovakia has registered impressive gains, as reflected in solid growth in the GDP. The fastest-growing sectors of the Slovak economy included consulting, advertising, real estate, and tourism. The SME share of total output was 4.8 percent in industry, 16.8 percent in building construction, 23.8 percent in retail sales, and 31.6 percent in market services. By comparison, medium-sized enterprises accounted for 23.3 percent of industrial output, 37.7 percent of building construction, 10.9 percent of trade sales, and 31.3 percent of market services. Thus, while larger enterprises continued to account for nearly three-fourths of industrial production, small and medium-sized enterprises were rapidly filling the demand for trade and services (NADESME 1996).

GOVERNMENT AND DONOR AGENCY ASSISTANCE TO SMES IN SLOVAKIA

Regardless of its shortcomings in various areas of economic and political reform, the Slovak Republic since its inception has acknowledged the importance of the small business sector to economic development. As early as 1992, in its resolution on the revival strategy of economic development the government of the Slovak Republic recognized the SME sector as one of the key sectors in this process. Shortly after Slovak independence in 1993, the National Council passed an act that became the basis for overall government policy on SMEs. The legislation defined a small business as one with no more than 24 employees, and a medium-sized enterprise as one with no more than 500 employees. The Program of Complex Support to Small and Medium Enterprises (Resolution No. 331 on May 25, 1993) established the institutional, financial, and legislative framework for government support to SMEs (NADSME 1996). The Ministry of Economy was given the primary responsibility for the formulation and implementation of government policy for SME development in Slovakia.

The main goal of the policy of support to SMEs is to ensure the growth of the sector by removing the barriers to its development. Not incidentally, SME policy is also linked to developing an enterprise environment which is required for eventual admission to the European Union. Such policy measures the creation of new jobs, the growth of regional economies, and the provision of business advisory services to SMEs. Toward this end, the Ministry of Economy authorized the drafting of the medium-term policy for support of SMEs in early 1997. This policy aims at legislative measures based on review of the concerns of entrepreneurs themselves regarding health insurance, taxes, and access to credit. The revised framework is to include new definitions of small and medium enterprises in line with definitional changes in the European Union.

The National Agency for Development of Small and Medium Enterprises (NADSME), established in 1993, is the agency charged with SME policy and promotion of SMEs in Slovakia. NADSME was created as a result of a joint initiative between the European Union's PHARE Program and the government of the Slovak Republic. The Ministry of Economy set it up as a foundation controlled by a managing board comprised of public and private representatives. Representatives on the NADSME board include key national institutions with an interest in SMEs, such as the Chamber of Commerce, the Association of Entrepreneurs, and the Union of Craftsmen. Although NADSME is viewed as being independent of the government, it acts in coordination with relevant ministries. NADSME works through a network of twelve Regional Advisory and Information Centers (RAICs) and four Business Innovation Centers (BICs), providing advisory, educational, and informational services to entrepreneurs. This constitutes a system of government support to specific industries, coupled with a loan guarantee scheme, a small loan scheme, and SME credit support programs.

Among other responsibilities, NADSME recommends to the government policies and strategies necessary for the development of the SME sector, identifying the barriers to enterprise development and suggesting ways to eliminate them. NADSME cooperates with financial institutions on credit and guarantee schemes to promote SMEs. Through the RAICs, NADSME offers management, marketing, financial and technical assistance to entrepreneurs. Other important functions of NADSME include cooperation with European information networks and databases in the field business and management of European Commission assistance to SMEs. Twice a year, NADSME also prepares for the government a report on the state of SME development and proposes necessary measures to address SME concerns. The first of these, submitted in 1994, included a census of Slovak businesses since 1990 by district and sector, as well as by type of ownership.

NADSME coordinates the assistance of government ministries toward SMEs. For example, the Ministry of Finance is concerned with tax incentives for SMEs and the Ministry of Labor is responsible for the provision of support for the creation of new jobs. Through its Fund For Employment, funded through a tax on employees, the Ministry provides interest-free refundable and nonrefundable grants for loans to SMEs. The Ministry of Labor also administers a regional development program, funded through the EU PHARE Program and the International Labor Organization (ILO) Which provides training for declining sectors such as mining.

NADSME acts as the intermediating organization facilitating the participation of the Slovak party in programs of bilateral cooperation. With the German government, this has involved organizing seminars for starting up and developing enterprises for the textile and clothing sector. Dutch assistance through NADSME has been focused on developing a unified model of accounting software for its network of regional centers. A French team worked with NADSME to develop a subcontracting exchange aimed at matching Slovak with French firms as industrial partners. Beginning in 1995, U.S. Peace Corps Volunteers were deployed through NADSME to work in selected RAICs and BICs, and several NADSME employees received personnel management training with USAID assistance.

FINANCING SMES: BANK AND NON-BANK SOURCES

There are three important dates in the history of Slovak banking. In 1845 the first European Credit Cooperative was established; in 1881 Tatra Bank, the first commercial bank, was founded; and in 1993 the National Bank of Slovakia (NBS) was established as the central bank (Bank Austria 1996). The first stage of banking reform in Slovakia took place in 1990 while Czechoslovakia was still intact with the splitting of the state bank which had a near monopoly in domestic corporate banking.

The National Bank of Slovakia is an independent financial institution whose primary function is to ensure the stability of the Slovak national currency. Its mandate is to support government economic policy, although it may accomplish this in a manner independent of the government. NBS also controls the money supply, administers the official monetary reserves, and acts as supervisor of the banking sector. In the field of foreign exchange policy, NBS sets the exchange rate between the Slovak *koruna* (crown) and foreign currencies, regulates foreign exchange operations of banks, and conducts operations in the international money and capital markets. NBS acts as banker to the Slovak Republic, providing cash management and accounting services, and is responsible for the supervision and operation of the banking system. All banks in the Slovak Republic are required to maintain an account with NBS.

The first task of the NBS was the peaceful monetary division of the Slovak and Czech Republics. Portions of preexisting notes were stamped to become legal tender, at which point the Slovak crown began its own life separate from the Czech banking system. The period of transition came to an end on February 8, 1993, when the Czechoslovak crown was replaced by the Slovak crown. NBS introduced a 10 percent devaluation in accordance with the recommendations of the

International Monetary Fund mission on July 10, 1993. The establishment of a national currency created the preconditions necessary for Slovakia to enter foreign capital markets, which it did in September 1993. The NBS is now a member of the IMF, the World Bank, and the European Bank for Reconstruction and Development.

With the break up of the state bank after 1989, its traditional areas of specialization were opened to competition. The state bank's operations in Slovakia were transferred to a newly created institution, *Vseobecna uverova banca* (VuB), with a network of more than 160 branches and outlets. VuB has remained the largest bank in Slovakia by assets and capital, and has a dominant position in the corporate loan market, with loans constituting over half of its assets. Since 1989, several new private banks have been established. By the end of 1995, there was a total of 31 commercial and savings banks operating in Slovakia, an increase of one-third in three years. In addition, there were eight banks with foreign capital shares, seven without foreign capital shares, and three state financial institutions. There were also 10 branches of foreign banks active in Slovakia.

One of the biggest problems facing Slovak banks in the period just after liberalization was that of bad loans (Gray 1996). Under communism companies had received perpetual credits—loans that never had to be repaid. Many of the borrowers ran into financial difficulties in 1990 and 1991. A special institution was created to absorb the bad loans and Slovak banks were issued fresh capital used to recapitalize troubled enterprises.

As in many countries, however, the formal banking system in Slovakia was not geared toward servicing small and medium-sized businesses, much less micro-enterprises. Would-be entrepreneurs found access to capital difficult, while banks contended that few businesses were able to provide sufficient guarantees when seeking loans. Recognizing the problem, the government began to set up programs to address the financing needs of small businesses. The first of these was an SME Guarantee Scheme established in 1992 with three million ECU in funding from the EU Phare Program and another two million ECU from the state budget. The Guarantee Scheme, implemented through the Slovak Guarantee Bank, guarantees credits to SMEs of up to 10 million Slovak crowns. The enterprise must have been in business for at least two years and employ fewer than 100 workers. The Guarantee Bank initially used nine employees as the cutoff for small enterprises and 250 for medium-sized enterprises.

In 1994 the Slovak government approved 600 million Slovak crowns for a Credit Support Program (NADSME 1996). Funds for the program were generated by contributions from the Slovak government itself, the EU PHARE Program (whose contributions were to be administered by NADSME), and three selected commercial banks (Tatrabanka, Pol'nobanka, and the Slovak Savings Bank). The average size of loans under the scheme was much smaller with Pol'nobanka than with the other two banks. This program was designed to help SMEs whose line of business involves production, services, crafts, and tourism and who intended to use local assets and environment. The loans were for up to five million Slovak crowns with a maturity of five years. The loans were designated for the purchase of machines and equipment or for the reconstruction of premises, as well as basic stock and raw materials. The first phase of the Credit Support Program was launched in October 1994 and a second phase a year later, owing to its revolving facility. By the end of 1996, the total amount of funds available under the program had reached over one billion Slovak crowns.

A second program, initiated in April 1994, was the Small Loan Scheme (one million ECU) a pilot project to finance small-scale entrepreneurs with soft loans. A borrower could apply for up to 800,000 Slovak crowns under the same terms as the Credit Support Program. By the end of 1996, the Small Loan Scheme had provided a total of 120 loans, allowing borrowers to create 664 new jobs. Business activities financed included civil engineering, goods processing, wood production, and services such as automobile repairs, laundries, and tourism. In the first quarter of 1997, a Micro- Loan Scheme for start-up businesses was launched as a pilot initiative in three Regional Advisory and Information Centers. The maximum amount available under the Micro Scheme was 300,000 Slovak crowns and the minimum 50,000 Slovak crowns. Loan maturity was for three years and collateral of 100 percent of the loan amount was required. A total of 19 loans worth five million Slovak crowns were disbursed in the first phase of the Micro-Loan Scheme.

A Start-Up Capital Fund has also been created to help SMEs in Slovakia. The fund, managed by the Seed Capital Company, was established by NADSME with financial support from the PHARE Program in October 1995 to provide start-up funds over a three year period. The Fund was authorized to make equity investments of up to five million Slovak crowns in companies in such sectors as production,

production services, and tourism. The Seed Capital Company invests in selected SMEs with fewer than two hundred employees, in which the Slovak share of ownership is at least 51 percent.

Among the more dynamic new banks is Pol'nobanka, founded in 1990 as the first private bank in Slovakia with an initial focus on serving agricultural enterprises. Major shareholders include the Slovak Insurance Company and the European Bank for Reconstruction and Development. Today Pol'nobanka is the fourth largest bank in Slovakia and has achieved important positions in financial and capital markets. Entrepreneurial activity constitutes 60 percent of Pol'nobanka's client portfolio. There is a concentration on successful small and medium-sized businesses, not just in the agricultural sector, to which Pol'nobanka offers a full range of services.

EU PHARE Program support to Slovakia began in 1990 under the Czechoslovak program (European Commission 1996). In 1992 funds began to be distributed separately into Czech and Slovak components. By the end of 1994, Slovakia had received 169 million ECU in grants through the PHARE Program and another 1,172 million ECU had been provided in the form of loans by individual member states. PHARE support in 1995 war concentrated mainly on the provision of know-how and investment to assist private sector development. In preparation for Slovakian membership in the EU, PHARE assisted a post privatization fund—a joint PHARE-European Bank for Reconstruction and Development initiative—which provided equity capital and know-how to medium-sized enterprises. Another program aimed at SMEs provided financial assistance and business counseling through a network of assistance centers. All together, the European Union and its members supplied 71 percent of all assistance to Slovakia.

PROFILE OF SLOVAK ENTREPRENEURS

The communist government in Czechoslovakia went further in eradicating the private sector than did the governments in neighboring Hungary and Poland. Those few small craftsmen operating in the private, or informal, sector were tightly regulated, heavily taxed, and subject to arbitrary decisions of government officials. The entrepreneur in Slovakia is, then, a most recent arrival on the economic scene.

The World Bank survey of entrepreneurs conducted by Webster and Swanson in Czechoslovakia (1993) described in Chapter 3 (the Czech Republic) applies to the Slovak Republic as well. At the time of the survey in January 1992, the economy had begun to stabilize and structural changes were under way. The initial round of sharp price increases had nearly ceased. Wages had fallen, but were also stable. Already the small privatization program had transferred thousands of small enterprises into private ownership.

It is unfortunate that the Czechoslovak survey sample of 121 firms included only 20 percent Slovak firms, and that Webster and Swanson's discussion of survey results provided little distinction between these firms and those in Czech regions such as Moravia and Bohemia. Regardless of their origins, nearly all of the firms interviewed had registered as private, limited liability companies: three in 1989, 24 in 1990, and 94 in 1991. Fifty-five percent were private start-ups while the remainder were privatize state enterprises and cooperatives. Two-thirds of the sectors surveyed were in textiles, clothing, plastics, metals, and machinery, while the remainder were in food processing and related industries. Slovakia had a disproportionately large number of clothing manufacturers and a paucity of textile and plastics producers. More than 80 percent of the firms employed fewer than 50 workers, although more than half employed at least 20 workers.

In 1992, manufacturers in the Czech and Slovak Republics were already reaching export markets. Nearly half of those interviewed were exporting some portion of their production, and one-third of the value of total sales was exported. The major trading partners were Germany and Austria. However, Slovak firms in the survey were less likely to be involved in exporting than were those in Bohemia and Moravia, both in the Czech Republic.

As might be expected in Czechoslovakia, few of those interviewed by Webster and Swanson in 1992 had had any prior business experience. However, they were uniformly well educated: half of those surveyed had university or college diplomas, while another 40 percent had finished technical or commercial secondary and post-secondary schools. It must be recalled that the survey was limited to manufacturing firms, excluding self-employed persons and firms engaged in trade or services. The authors noted that some entrepreneurs in their survey came to private business out of choice, while others entered business out of necessity. Nearly half of all those in the Slovakia sample said they felt pushed into private business, compared with only one in five Moravia entrepreneurs. In the overall sample, primary goals were listed as personal achievement, independence, and economic necessity.

The entrepreneurs interviewed were becoming keenly aware of competition in the marketplace. The collapse of the Council for Mutual Economic Assistance market had already occasioned layoffs and price wars in textiles and clothing in western Slovakia. Meanwhile, imports were pouring into the local market, causing local entrepreneurs to question whether to increase their prices in response to rising demand. The following are profiles of small businesses in Slovakia:

ProCS (Process Control Systems)—Sala

Located in the small town of Sala in western Slovakia, ProCS has become the number one power engineering firm in the country. ProCS is involved in process automation and measurement and control. The company was formed in 1992 as a privatized division of DUSLO Sala, the largest producer of artificial fertilizers and special rubber chemicals in Slovakia, employing six thousand workers. ProCS turnkey applications are provided in such fields as civil engineering, food processing, chemical industry, and biotechnology. According to Ladislav Major, quality and marketing manager and one of the founders of ProCS, the company started with some 30 employees and now employs 70 people. Most of them are young electrical and chemical engineering graduates, specialized in automation, and measurement and control, and who speak either English or German or both.

By 1994 ProCS began reaching exports markets in the United States, Western Europe, and Asia, and recently the former Soviet states. Its principal clients range from chemical and heavy industries in South Korea, Hungary and South Africa to power engineering and biotechnology in Slovakia, the Czech Republic and Russia for whom ProCS acts as a supplier. Sales grew 120 percent from 1995 to 1996, and today most are in export markets. As with many newer firms, ProCS has experienced growing pains. The rapid increase in growth has resulted in a shortage of experienced and qualified manpower, which is difficult to recruit locally. It has also occasioned the need to contract out to a local consulting firm to install a local area network.

ProCS was the first Slovak company to receive the ISO 9001 certification, which represents a model for quality assurance in design, production, installation, and servicing of the product supplied to the customer. In 1996 ProCS was approved by Lloyd's Register of Quality Assurance specifying quality management system standards. Prospects for the future success of ProCS seem bright, as management plans to extend its reach to Middle East markets as well.

Ceram Cab, Nove Sady

Ceram Cab produces ceramic devises used in electrical power generation, transmission and distribution, such as the insulation for power lines. Its plant is located in the small town of Nove Sady, not far from Sala. One of the first joint ventures formed in Slovakia in 1990, Ceram Cab was initially 67 percent Austrian-owned and is today wholly owned by an Austrian holding company listed on the Vienna stock exchange. The Ceram Cab production process consists of converting raw materials into final ceramic products using both conventional and isostatic methods. Both processes involve glazing, firing, cutting, grinding, and testing of the product. Ceram Cab applies Total Quality Management (TQM) tools in accordance with environmental protection standards.

Managing Director Ivan Kosalko started working with the company in 1980 as a chemical engineer when it was a state-owned enterprise. Since 1991, he has taken up managerial responsibilities and now sees himself as an international manager, willing and able to move to any one of the company's other six plants in Western Europe. Kosalko notes that Ceram Cab orders are often small and differ in design from order to order. Each entails the introduction of new technologies which are a challenge for engineers as well as for management. Ceram Cab sales have grown at a rate of some 30 percent over the past few years.

POTENTIAL FOR SME DEVELOPMENT IN SLOVAKIA

I am happy to say that the state of democracy in Slovakia is much better than generally expected and we in no way lag behind neighboring countries which have been invited for accession talks with the EU and NATO.

—Prime Minister Vladimir Meciar, April 1998

The government of the Slovak Republic continues to receive criticism at home and abroad for backsliding on political reform, despite the country's relatively good economic performance.

Prime Minister Meciar and his government remained the subject of criticism by the European Union and the United States who questioned his commitment to good governance and the rule of law. Slovakia was the only Eastern European state blocked from the first wave of EU entry talks because it had not met the criteria for civil and minority rights.

When President Kovac's term of office as president expired in March 1998, the presidency became vacant. Meciar first ignited a political inferno over presidential powers and then unveiled a controversial new election law proposal which engulfed his ruling coalition in a fresh wave of criticism (Nicholson 1998). The government maintained that the law was designed to restore order and consensus in parliament by reducing the number of small parties fighting to secure narrow interests. But the opposition claimed the measure would virtually outlaw coalitions, discriminate against independent candidates, and give an overwhelming advantage to Meciar's party. Independent legal experts pointed out that the proposal contained several articles that were in conflict with the constitution and which threatened to cause mass confusion during the September 1998 elections. In the first place, people who were in detention and awaiting trial would not be allowed to vote or stand for election. The second questionable provision of the new proposal was an article that required candidates for office to submit confirmation of party membership. If the article meant that one must be a member of an organized political party to stand for election, then it would be a clear violation of the constitution.

Meciar denied that there was a power vacuum in Slovakia, although the country remained without a president (*New Europe* April 19-25, 1998). Four attempts by the parliament to designate a new president failed, as the ruling coalition blocked candidates while not nominating one of their own. Mecia insisted that Slovakia was not "the enfant terrible" of Europe as was being suggested. Opposition parties maintained that Meciar really wanted to secure the presidency for himself, although opinion polls showed little support for his government.

Despite positive economic growth, there were signs of weakness in the Slovak economy. In an investors service report of April 1998, Moody's lowered the country ceiling for foreign currency bonds and notes due to Slovakia's consistently high fiscal and current account deficits financed increasingly by foreign borrowing (*New Europe* April 5-11, 1998). The high interest rates were increasing the burden of servicing domestic debt, forcing Slovak firms and banks to finance their operations abroad. The rating agency noted that Slovakia's good record on GDP growth, investment, and industrial growth was based on high levels of public spending and rapidly growing short-term foreign debt. The Moody report predicted pressure for devaluation of Slovak currency to grow in 1998, which could in turn lead to difficulties in private sector debt payments.

Standard and Poor's followed shortly thereafter by revising its ratings downward as well, with a triple-B-minus foreign currency rating and its single-A local currency rating on the Slovak Republic (*New Europe* April 19-25, 1998). This revision was a reflection of the country's overall external indebtedness and other economic performance indicators. The steep rise in corporate external debt, which could pressure the government to provide financial assistance, was seen as a troubling factor.

The overall economic and regulatory environment for SMEs in the Slovak Republic appears to be on a par with other countries in the region.

Political factors, however, seem likely to prevent Slovakia from early integration into the European Union and the presumed advantages that that would entail. Even though the economic growth picture for Slovakia is basically encouraging (positive growth in GDP, export success and a trade surplus, decreasing inflation and unemployment), many of these positive growth factors have been due to successful moves on the part of a few very large firms which were nearing production capacity. While macroeconomic aggregates appear to be improving, much more work needs be to done on restructuring and strengthening privatized enterprises on the one hand, while encouraging small and medium-sized enterprise development and democracy-building on the other.

As in other countries in the Central and Eastern European region, entrepreneurs in Slovakia are struggling to overcome a rather negative image within society. Profit-seekers were initially thought of in the transition period as selfish and greedy, and unmindful of the good of the community. They also still face a bewildering array of government policies and regulations that tend to dampen their initiative. Fortunately, changes on both of these measures are underway: an increasing number of Slovaks are engaged in some type of business activity which is coming to be seen, for better or for worse, as the reality of a market economy.

The entrepreneurs in the World Bank Slovakia survey (Webster and Swanson 1993) were asked to identify their three biggest problems. Those most frequently cited were excessive taxes, delinquent payments by state enterprises, and high interest rates. Heavy taxation had distinctly negative effects, leading many entrepreneurs to avoid payment of taxes whenever possible. The most highly resented of all taxes were labor taxes which totaled half of paid wages. The entrepreneurs felt that such high rates eroded their profits and created a disincentive to raising salaries. To avoid such taxes, entrepreneurs tended to subcontract portions of their production to workers registered as self-employed and who therefore are exempt from wage taxes. However, a new regulation was adopted in 1992 to limit subcontracting.

Turnover taxes were also very unpopular among Slovak entrepreneurs, especially since they involved an involuntary subsidy. Regulations required automatic payment of turnover tax on delivery of goods, regardless of whether payment had been received. As a result, turnover taxes were paid in advance of payment from state customers. In the event of late payment of such taxes, the authorities would charge interest. Tax on profits provided a disincentive for firms to grow. A common strategy for disguising profits as expenses was to order large inventories of raw materials at year-end.

Delinquent and frequent nonpayment by state enterprises was sorely resented by the Slovak entrepreneurs as well. Those who depended upon large orders by government clients were hardest hit. The obvious effect of this common practice was the erosion of the entrepreneur's working capital. Increasingly, entrepreneurs began to take steps to lessen their dependence upon the state sector, seeking new private sector clients. Some firms gave up on the domestic sector altogether and became subcontractors to foreign firms.

The third major concern of those interviewed in the Slovakia World Bank survey was high interest rates. At the time of the survey, the factors that likely influenced this attitude were tighter credit and a more commercial orientation of those banks willing to extend loans, declining inflation that increased real rates, and the perception that real rates had been lower. Added to these factors was the frustration with what the entrepreneurs called "red tape and fees." Paperwork was considered to be excessive, and those who could afford it hired lawyers to handle dealings with government agencies. The initial registration deposit of 100,000 crowns ($4000) was viewed as especially high. Other such expenses they cited were annual licenses for all formal activities, vague environmental impact assessments, and health and safety inspections. Lack of information about new laws and regulations was a serious handicap for many, particularly concerning tax write-offs for reinvested profits. Local officials were reported to be continuing past practices of clientelism and bribery.

The Slovak National Agency for Development of Small and Medium Enterprises (NADSME), responsible for SME policy and development, is among the more effective agencies in the region. NADSME does a credible job of representing the interests of small businesses and obtaining data on the performance of the SME sector.

REFERENCES

Bank Austria 1996 Eastern Europe: East-West Report Extra February.

Business Central Europe "Back to the Old Life" October 1997.

Business Central Europe, April 1997

Drozdiak, William 1997 "Clash Between Slovak Leaders Disrupts NATO Referendum" The Washington Post, May 25.

European Commission 1996 The PHARE Program Annual Report 1995 Brussels.

Economic Commission for Europe 1997, Slovakia: Country Study on Best Practices in Financing SMEs, Project on Financial Policies for Strengthening SMEs through Micro-credit and Credit Guarantee Schemes, Southeast European Cooperative Initiative, October.

Fisher, Sharon 1995 "Privatization Stumbles Forward," *Transition,* May.

Gray, Gavin 1996 Eastern Europe: Investing for the 21st Century London: Euromoney Books, published in association with Pol'nobanka (Slovakia).

Marcincin, Anton 1994 "The Political Framework of Slovak Privatization," Prague: CERGE-EI. .

National Agency for Development of Small and Medium Enterprises 1996 State of Small and Medium Enterprises 1995 Bratislava: NADSME.

New Europe "Moody's Downgrades Slovakia" April 5-11, 1998.

New Europe "Standard & Poor's Revises Slovakia Ratings Downward" April 19-25, 1998.

Nicholson, Tom "New Election Law Proposal Draws Criticism" *Slovak Spectator,* March 25, 1998.

Stephenson, Nigel "Slovaks, Czechs Diverge After Historic Velvet Divorce" *The Slovak Spectator* October 23-November 5, 1997.

Svejnar, Jan ed. 1995 The Czech Republic and Economic Transition in Eastern Europe San Diego, CA: Academic Press.

United Nations Industrial Development Organization 1996 A Comparative Analysis of SME Strategies, Policies and Programmes in Central and Eastern European Initiative Countries: Part III: Slovakia, compiled as a country report by the National Agency for the Development of Small and Medium Enterprises.

Webster, Leila, and Dan Swanson 1993 The Emergence of Private Sector Manufacturing in the Former Czech and Slovak Federal Republic: A Survey of Firms World Bank Technical Paper Number 230.

Wyzan, Michael 1997 "Is Slovakia's Economic Reputation About to Tarnish?" Vol. 1, No. 151 November 3, RFE/RL Newsline Dejanews website.

Zemanovic, Igor "Government Seeks Closer Trade Ties With Russia," The Slovak Spectator, April 24-May 7, 1997.

CHAPTER 8

The Potential for Small and Medium Enterprise Growth in the Central and Eastern European Region

In Chapter 1, six basic propositions regarding the growth and development of small and medium enterprises in Central and Eastern Europe were examined. In this chapter we look at current trends within the framework of these propositions, exploring the potential for small business expansion in the region.

The Central and Eastern European region continues to be in a transition mode from a communist command economy to a free market.

Macroeconomic trends in the Central and Eastern European region have registered modest success, at a time when East Asian economies are in a free fall and countries in the former Soviet Union are well behind in the transition process. Some countries in the Central and Eastern European region can rightfully claim to be well on the road to a free market economy. However, the road to a market economy has not been a smooth one. The term *free market* has tended to take on a distorted meaning in some transition economies. It has been interpreted as unbridled or unregulated, an economy in which anything goes. An effective free market should be governed by rules that are transparent, rules that the populace are willing to live by. But there has been a tendency in the region to live by only one rule: let the buyer beware! In the absence of a sound regulatory system and contractual law, there is often no guarantee of the quality or legitimacy of the products being sold in the market. The customer cannot be sure of the authenticity of a product bearing the familiar brand name of Singer or Pepsi Cola. Much less can she or he be assured that the Mercedes-Benz he is about to buy is not contraband. In countries tempted by this kind of free market, there is a need for rather more government intrusion into the market-place to protect the unsuspecting consumer.

Even though growth has slowed somewhat in recent years, the region continues to do much better than the economies of the Newly Independent States (NIS) of the former Soviet Union. The growth rate of CEE economies closed 1996 well behind 1995, with an average GDP growth of 3.4 percent, down from 5.5 percent the year before. Only in Poland and Slovakia did GDP growth continue at previous levels. Modest growth was reported in the Czech Republic and Romania, with negligible growth in Hungary. The most troubling reports came from Bulgaria where the gross domestic product (GDP) slid precipitously, due largely to a crippling burden of debt (Podkaminer et al. 1997).

Poland and Slovakia owed their stronger showing to a healthy rise in domestic demand, and particularly in gross fixed investment. The more cautious macroeconomic policies of the Czech Republic, and even more so of Hungary, resulted in lower rates of investment growth that led to lower growth in GDP. At the same time, net exports in the Czech Republic declined sharply. In Hungary, the level of net exports declined only slightly, so that the final level of GDP primarily reflected very weak domestic demand. The country's austerity program, begun in early 1995, placed a damper on growth that proved hard to shake. By the end of 1997 the Czech Republic had gone into an economic and political tailspin, two years after the government had boasted of having successfully traversed the transition to a free market.

In Romania and Bulgaria, progress was slowed by a lack of integration of the economic infrastructure and its evolving legal context. In Bulgaria especially, problems have been aggravated by a policy of high interest rates that have lasted far too long. A moderate decline in inflation continued in all of the more advanced CEE economies, although the low budget deficits and recent restrictive monetary policies have not brought about the rapid disinflation hoped for. Real appreciation of the domestic currencies, as well as rising competition, seem to have been important in the continuing reduction of inflation rates. Higher inflation did return to Romania and Bulgaria, where the problem verged on hyperinflation. It remained to be seen, however, whether the two countries would manage the necessary reform of their banking systems, which have accumulated large portfolios of bad loans.

Forces underlying economic performance in 1997 continued to be at work in 1998. GDP growth in the more advanced CEE countries was expected to continue to be moderate to low in the less advanced economies. Assuming only marginal improvement in the Western European business climate, there seemed likely to be little opportunity to boost exports in the CEE region. Structural changes—rising volume of both skill-intensive and research and development-intensive products—would be necessary for this to occur. For the countries that have made substantial investments in manufacturing technology in recent years, the payoff could be big, leading to improved export performance in 1998.

The advanced CEE countries were expected to try to prevent excessive increases in imports through additional devaluations, but short of the drastic Hungarian-style restrictions on domestic consumption and investment that seem likely in Romania and Bulgaria. In Slovakia, import levels could be slowed by limiting the pace of government investments in infrastructure.

On the whole, the countries of the CEE seem models of stability and growth when compared with those in the NIS region. However, the tremors shaking the economies of East and South Asia give the countries in transition pause to wonder what pitfalls may lie along the road to transition and beyond.

The assumption that the privatization of state-owned enterprises would be the key to successful transition to a free market economy has not proved valid.

Since most policy-makers and economists concerned with the CEE region tended to view privatization as the sine qua non for enterprise restructuring, most attention was on methods for privatizing. These included such methods as public offerings and mass privatization programs. In several instances, there was a rush to sell off small and medium sized state-owned shops and retail trade in the early days of transition. Small-scale privatization has proved far more successful than that of larger firms, although it has received less attention in the press.

The Czech Republic is generally accorded the best privatization record in the CEE, having carried out the most extensive program among the six countries examined in this book by the end of 1994. Until the Velvet Revolution, the Czech economy had been highly centralized, consisting primarily of only a few thousand state-owned enterprises and cooperatives. Until then only 1 percent of the labor force, 2 percent of all the registered assets, and a negligible fraction of the Czechoslovak GDP belonged to the private sector. Yet extensive privatization became the cornerstone of the Czechoslovak (later Czech) economic transformation. The program consisted of restitution of property to previous owners or their heirs, privatization of small units in public auctions (small scale privatization), and privatization of large and medium-sized firms. The most important program was that of large scale privatization. About four thousand firms out of a total of six thousand large firms were privatized in two waves of large-scale privatization by 1994.

However, six years after the reforms were begun in the Czech Republic, most large enterprises were still struggling with over employment (official unemployment was only 4.1 percent), low labor productivity, and low profitability. Microeconomic transformation—streamlining, rationalizing, and increasing productivity at the enterprise level—was required to improve the country's economic performance. Czechs found that political and macroeconomic stability and fast privatization of state enterprises—while important elements of successful reforms—were only the first steps toward industrial restructuring and maintaining high growth. It appeared that the economic slowdown might turn into a recession if drastic measures were not taken. A government reform package was announced in 1997 in response to signs of weak economic performance. This included stepping up the state's day-to-day control over enterprises in which it still retained a significant stake and accelerating the privatization of banks and of regional electricity and gas companies.

At the heart of the economic malaise was the the voucher privatization program, cornerstone of Prime Minister Klaus's economic policy, heretofore hailed as a success. Overnight the vouchers, which represented a stake in corporate ownership and were available to all Czechs at the equivalent of a little more than a week's salary, turned four-fifths of the country's citizens into equity shareholders—the highest percentage in the world, as Klaus liked to boast. But the vouchers were quickly bought up by investment funds, most of them owned by a handful of large banks that were still controlled by the state. Operating through the funds, the banks propped up industrial dinosaurs with easy loans, refusing to cut off the flow of cash or demand restructuring for fear of bankruptcies and loan write-offs. The result was hundreds of companies operating much as they had in the communist era, with bloated payrolls, incompetent management, and substandard production facilities. Exports slumped even as Czechs went on a buying spree, snapping up Western European consumer goods at a ferocious rate. By 1996 the trade deficit had swelled to six billion dollars—a huge figure in a country of just 10.3 million people. And 35 percent of all the bank loans were believed to have little chance of being repaid; a privatization success turned sour.

The Klaus government fell in the fall of 1997, and elections the following spring afforded Czechs the opportunity to reflect on the consequences of its policies. While Poland and Hungary had voted in and out left-wing governments since 1989, the Czech Republic had yet to see a shift in power. Although he usually kept above the fray of partisan politics, President Havel, in an interview before the June 1998 election, called for new blood to be injected into the troubled Czech political system.

In Slovakia, privatization has been mired in political controversy. When the Velvet Revolution took place in Czechoslovakia in 1989, the country's private sector was virtually nonexistent. While rapid privatization was one of the new government's main priorities, in the Slovak region of the country many state-owned enterprises were grossly over staffed. The employment issue was critical since in certain Slovak towns a single factory could be the sole source of jobs. Nevertheless, the Czech-devised plan for privatizing large firms through the coupon or voucher method was implemented in 1992. In Slovakia, political controversy over economic reform programs—and especially control of the privatization process—left Slovaks confused. Even though three-fourths of the population bought vouchers during the first wave of coupon sales, this did not reflect voter support for the government that implemented the program.

The political party that won the largest share of the vote in Slovakia had pledged increased autonomy from the Czech Republic, and the following year Slovak independence was declared. Coupon privatization was a critical issue in bringing the first Slovak government to power, but it brought the same party down in 1994 elections amid accusations that the government was abusing the privatization process. Despite the government's promises to speed up privatization by implementing a second wave of the coupon program, it was suspended at the end of 1994 and the start-up delayed several times.

Hungary is further along in the privatization process than many other countries in the CEE region, even though it has been gradual. Both the privatization process and the creation of new enterprises by domestic and foreign entities were off to a fairly good start beginning in the late 1980s. Legislation enacted in 1989 provided for both the creation of new domestic and foreign companies and the transformation of previous enterprise forms, including state-owned enterprises. Spontaneous privatization, where managers in state enterprises moved assets out of the firm into their own private companies, was common initially. But this practice occasioned public outcry, and the privatization process had already stalled by 1991.

The Hungarian government pursued a privatization model of individual corporate sale, generally through tenders, in which cash price was the key factor. Hungary did not implement a voucher or other popular privatization scheme, so the process has been slower and more difficult than anticipated. Although Hungary made good progress in the initial years of transition, the reform process slowed in 1993-1994, in part because of the May 1994 elections and the resulting change in government. By 1994 the privatization of state firms had ground to a halt. However, by 1997 the sale of large companies by the government was almost complete, with only 36 major firms remaining fully state-owned. As in many of the CEE countries, the sale of small enterprises to the private sector was initially more successful in Hungary than that of larger firms. Most of the shops under state ownership in 1990 had been transferred to private hands. Privatization of agricultural enterprises has been less successful.

While privatization in Hungary seemed to achieve the objective of putting the majority of resources into private hands, it did not translate into political success. The spring 1998 elections brought a change of government, as the center-right Fidesz-Hungarian Civic Party celebrated victory over the ruling Socialists, who had assiduously followed the privatization agenda. The full-fledged promotion of international investors and the attendant economic growth proved insufficient to please the majority of voters.

In Poland the first non-communist government assigned the highest priority to a privatization program, but the ambitious initial goal of 150 privatized enterprises was first scaled down to 50 and finally to only five by January 1991. Even though a third of the 8,500 state enterprises had begun some form of privatization by 1994, only 121 had actually involved the sale of equity to those who did not work in the company. Public reaction was against alleged sweetheart deals, in which managers would agree with workers to sell their own firms directly to foreign investors. The perception was that only former *nomenklatura,* black marketeers, and foreigners would benefit from these deals. Poland has privatized proportionately fewer of its large state enterprises than other countries in transition that have done less well economically. While more extensive privatization would probably contribute to greater growth, the fact remains that Poland's economic success has not been dependent upon it.

Privatization has been slow in coming to Romania. Despite the semblance of commitment, Romania delayed restructuring and privatization on any significant scale initially due to the continued dominance of the remnants of the Communist Party in power. An ambitious privatization program initiated in 1992 resulted in the divestiture of a third of the equity of state-owned enterprises to five private ownership funds, much of it distributed to the population through vouchers. Despite this system designed to allow employees to "buy out" their company, the transfer of ownership frequently meant that the majority of shares went to only a few individuals within the company. Furthermore, the high rate of inflation undermined the voucher system. The pace of privatization thus soon lost momentum.

In 1994 a privatization program was published and approved by the Romanian parliament, ostensibly aimed at the privatization of some twenty-four hundred commercial companies. An agency was established to cooperate with the State Ownership Fund in order to assist large state-owned companies to speed up the restructuring process. Only one thousand small and medium-sized industrial companies, representing 16 percent of industrial production worth around $200 million had been privatized by 1995. Not until a change of government in 1996 was there the semblance of a real commitment to privatization. The new prime minister announced a list of 17 large, state-owned businesses that were to be shut down, beginning what he promised would be Polish-style economic shock therapy. He made it clear that he wanted all-out privatization, despite the prospect of temporary social pain.

In Bulgaria, privatization has come late. The legal framework for mass privatization was not established until 1995. A list of more than one thousand enterprises was approved for the first wave of privatization, representing a third of the total amount of state-owned capital. However, within a year there had only been a little more than 100 privatization transactions, and only 65 of those involved whole enterprises of which 18 were sold by the Privatization Agency. The actual scope of "real" privatization was quite modest in terms of the number of transactions concluded. In fact, the transactions carried out in 1995 amounted to a fraction of that envisioned in the program.

The new center-right coalition United Democratic Front government which came to office in August 1997 seemed to succeed in facing the challenge of much-needed reforms (*New Europe* September 7-October 13, 1997). The new government was forced to fight the economic malaise of hyperinflation, an obsolete state-dominated economic apparatus, and a quasi-legal business mafia. A deal with the IMF was signed which had already produced its third tranche payment. The Currency Board stabilized the currency and inflation. Interest rates fell and the banking system appeared stabilized. Not until the end of 1997 did the new Kostov government manage to complete the first wave of mass privatization, long overdue. It also began to pursue the sale of large state enterprises to foreign investors. The parliament was beginning to address government legislative proposals for a wide range of policy reforms. New privatization amendments were intended to speed up trading in mass voucher privatization shares. Smaller enterprises were to be sold by the respective ministries, enabling the Privatization Agency to concentrate on the most profitable transactions.

Thus, in several of these countries privatization has been quite slow, getting under way only recently after years of posturing. When privatization has come, it has brought downsizing and dislocations in the labor markets leading to higher unemployment rates. Real restructuring in terms of amount of staff and productivity often does not take place. The majority of large companies remain saddled with huge debts which the banks tend to ignore. The owner is often not visible and does not take responsibility. Even when the process of privatization appears to have succeeded, it has brought with it questions about the consequences. Where programs of privatization have been the most advanced, as in the Czech Republic, they have not necessarily been associated with strong economic growth. Privatization, as it has been commonly understood, has not proved to be the panacea for the transition process that was hoped for and expected.

Several countries in the CEE region are now on track to join NATO and the European Union, a process that involves attaining certain standards including a healthy private sector.

NATO expansion has been one of the least partisan issues I've been involved with since I came here. There's a shared community of interests in NATO expansion for senators from both parties.

> —Senator Dan Coats (Republican of Indiana),
> retiring in 1998 after 18 years in the U.S. Congress

It is a moral obligation for us Germans to help (Czech Republic, Hungary, and Poland) return to Europe through membership in NATO and the European Union.

> —Foreign Minister Klaus Kinkel, referring to
> their support of German reunification in 1980.

We have to welcome the candidates (to the European Union) not only in principle but by showing them that the countries of Europe are prepared to change and reform.

> —British Prime Minister Tony Blair, on admission
> of new members to European Union

All the countries of the Central and Eastern European region are eager to join Western European institutions. Indications are that aspirations to join Europe are generally justified. Membership in the North Atlantic Treaty Organization (NATO) and the European Union constitutes a consummation devoutly to be wished. In the summer of 1997, Hungary, the Czech Republic and Poland were invited to begin negotiations for admission to NATO. Invitations to join the alliance, issued at a NATO summit conference in Madrid in July, were seen as a first step toward a historic expansion that in time could stretch from Estonia to Romania. Criteria for membership were economic, political, and military.

All three countries had freely elected their governments at least twice since the end of Communist rule in 1989. All had fledgling but solid free markets. Public opinion polls in Poland and Hungary showed strong public support for NATO membership. However, apathy in the

Czech Republic seemed to illustrate a lingering weakness of the democracies: relatively little public discussion or debate, even on crucial issues of national security. And when NATO does expand into the former Soviet bloc, its new members will have few military assets to offer and a multitude of logistical obstacles to overcome.

The United States, which has played a leadership role in NATO since its founding, is actively involved in issues concerning expansion of its membership. Romania waged a quixotic campaign for admission with backing from France but with little chance of success. The U.S. decision to exclude Romania in the first cut of NATO expansion did not generate the resentment there that was predicted by some. Instead, Romania redoubled efforts to cement close strategic ties with the United States. On the other hand, Slovakia, once part of Czechoslovakia, watched bitterly while the Czech Republic was invited in and yet was left out.

In March 1998, with little rancor or dissent, the U.S. Senate moved toward approving the most ambitious expansion of U.S. global commitments since the end of the Cold War, enlarging NATO to admit three former Warsaw Pact enemies (Lippman and Dewar 1998). Despite the scope of the undertaking, which would extend a U.S. defense commitment deep into Central Europe, few major treaties in recent years had stirred so little serious opposition in advance of a final Senate ratification vote. The partisan wrangling that usually characterizes the Congress was all but absent from the NATO debate.

Arguments against NATO failed to inspire a following in the Senate, where an unusual bipartisan alignment assured approval for expansion. The opponents wanted to attach conditions that would mandate a three- or five-year pause before any additional NATO enlargement. But what was remarkable about the Senate debate was the very absence of controversy. The Senate Foreign Relations Committee voted overwhelmingly to ratify amendments to NATO to include Poland, Hungary, and the Czech Republic, with support ranging from the committee's conservative chairman, Senator Jesse Helms (Republican of North Carolina), to Senator Richard G. Lugar (Republican of Indiana), a committed internationalist. The final Senate vote was a political triumph for President Clinton, who for more than three years had advocated expansion of the alliance as the cornerstone of European security.

Poland, Hungary and the Czech Republic were easy for the senators to accept as potential NATO members because they had strong

U.S. domestic constituencies, maturing democracies, and a history of courageous resistance to communist rule. NATO expansion transcended the ideological arguments of earlier battles over arms control, tapping into a half-century tradition of support for NATO by both political parties.

In Europe, to the delight of its proponents and the surprise of many, the treaty to expand NATO membership provoked even less dissent among member legislatures (Drozdiak March 27, 1998). Much of the credit for the smooth legislative ride in Europe went to Germany, where support for expansion was overwhelming. The lower house of the German parliament voted by an 89 percent majority to accept Poland, Hungary, and the Czech Republic as full NATO members in 1999, making it the fourth nation after Canada, Denmark and Norway to ratify the military alliance's treaty on enlargement. Germany's backing was rooted in a desire to see that its eastern borders no longer serve as the perimeter of NATO's security zone. There was also a deep sense of gratitude toward Poland, Hungary and the Czech Republic for their support for Germany's unification in 1990. All other legislatures in the 16-member NATO alliance were expected to approve the treaty by the summer of 1998—one year after it was signed in July 1997 in Madrid.

The two biggest U.S. worries about NATO expansion—Russia's opposition and the costs of integrating military forces of former communist states—had been mitigated. A permanent joint council was created to build greater trust and cooperation between NATO and Moscow, while alliance studies concluded that the cost of absorbing the three new members should be no more than $1.5 billion over 10 years, a fraction of some early estimates. Nevertheless, NATO Secretary General Javier Solana predicted that it would take 10 years to fully integrate the three new members.

Meanwhile, virtually all the countries in the CEE region actively pursued membership in the European Union (EU). In June 1997, the European Union invited Central and East European leaders to a special summit in Amsterdam to discuss the EU's preparations for admitting new members from among the former communist countries. The meeting followed EU approval of a package of reforms designed to prepare for an eastward expansion over the coming years.

Then the EU formally invited five formerly communist nations, plus Cyprus, to become candidates for membership on December 13, 1997 (Swardson 1997). Poland, the Czech Republic, Hungary, Estonia,

Slovenia, and Cyprus were asked to begin negotiations by March 1998. Five other CEE nations were given precandidate status (Bulgaria, Latvia, Lithuania, Romania, and Slovakia) and encouraged to keep the faith. Turkey, suffering low esteem for its record on Cyprus, human rights, and relations with Greece, was invited to join an affiliated conference, but only on conditions it might find difficult to accept. With the exception of former dictatorships—Spain and Greece—the European Union has expanded from its original six-nation membership in 1957 by adding long-time democracies.

The two-tier invitation was devised precisely because some countries were deemed to have prepared their democratic institutions and economies better and faster than others. Officials emphasized that all 11 countries were essentially on the same level, even though only six would begin membership discussions in the spring of 1998. Initially, EU leaders wanted to begin negotiations with the first group and leave the rest aside. But they found a way to include the others after fears arose that a new iron curtain would divide Eastern Europe into two groups. Leaders spoke in glowing terms of the European Union's first expansion to former communist nations. In the next few years, the EU would also be implementing its single currency, and that would require major economic adjustments.

For the applicants, the benefits of EU membership will be considerable. Generous farm and poverty subsidies, aid in developing industry, advice on economic restructuring and the pride of achieving Europe's first rank have made EU membership a high priority nearly everywhere in the former communist sphere. The European Union plans to spend more than $80 billion in the next six years to help the candidates make necessary reforms. The current EU countries can sell their products duty-free to these growing economies once they become members, and thus keep the fledgling democracies oriented toward the West and free markets. The thinking in Brussels has always been that it is better to have the relatively new democracies inside the circle than out.

The invitation to join the club of Europe's 15 wealthiest nations is the first official step in what promises to be a long process of negotiation and compromise. No candidate nation is expected to join the European Union before 2000, and likely even later. The candidates themselves, with a combined GDP equal to only 4 percent of the European Union's combined GDP, are generally unprepared for the competition of the group's open borders and free markets. And the

European Union itself is not ready. Past attempts at reforming EU rules, institutions, and financial systems have failed, and the current structure could not accommodate more than its 15 members. Such rules as unanimous decision-making block EU action in many areas, and agricultural subsidies are far too expensive to be expanded to a new batch of poor countries.

The main impetus for economic growth in the region is coming from small and medium-sized enterprises (the SME sector).

> The contribution of SMEs to employment generation and sustainable growth in the European Union is quite significant. Given the high levels of unemployment throughout Europe, SMEs will continued to play a role in stimulating economic recovery.
>
> —Christos Papoutsis, member of the
> European Commission, responsible for enterprise policy.

The European Observatory for SMEs is dedicated to monitoring their growth and development as well as their problems and prospects. In its annual report, the Observatory asserts that SME policy is becoming increasingly important for the creation of new employment opportunities. It indicates that the European Union is committed to promoting initiatives that will assure the development of the SME sector among its member states. What are the implications for the countries of the Central and Eastern European region that aspire to join the EU?

Building a new private sector from scratch has proved less complicated and faster than privatizing and restructuring state-owned enterprises. Early on, it became clear that economic growth was going to come more from new businesses than from the sale of state firms, many of them dinosaurs. Most of the countries in the region witnessed a veritable explosion of the formation of new businesses at the beginning of the transition period, which would inevitably taper off with the competition of the market place.

In Czechoslovakia, the number of registered private entrepreneurs grew quickly from fewer than 100,000 at the end of 1989 to 488,000 at the end of 1990. By the end of 1992, there were 1.4 million already listed on official rosters as sole proprietorships. Also by the end of 1991, some 40,000 registered companies had been created in

Czechoslovakia, although many were probably inactive. Of the 200,000 or so small firms that existed by the end of 1990, at least 80 percent were newly created, rather than privatized firms.

Perhaps the most important factor in the development of the Czech SME sector was in the program of restitutions and small-scale privatization which were unique in helping establish a foundation for an efficient market economy. Restitutions were not originally on the economic reform agenda, which instead focused on the privatization of large state-owned enterprises. In response to strong political pressure, however, several restitution laws were passed which provided for nationalized property to be restituted to original owners or their heirs. These restitutions were estimated at one hundred thousand, the majority of them in real estate.

In the early transition the private sector in Poland played a crucial role in the creation of employment. In the recovery process, the private sector comprised predominantly of SMEs has served as the key stimulus for economic growth. By 1997 it accounted for over 50 percent of total industrial output, over 90 percent of retail trade, agriculture, road transportation, and construction, 62 percent of exports, and 75 percent of imports. More than 65 percent of Poland's workforce (totaling 22 million people, or 57 percent of the population) is now employed in the private sector. By the end of 1996 the private sector was represented by over two million private enterprises.

In Bulgaria, by 1995 fully 90 percent of the 194,800 economically active registered firms were micro-enterprises with three or fewer employees. Only 1 percent had more than 50 employees. There were over 1.2 million people employed in the private sector. Small businesses were contributing up to 30 percent of the registered GDP and were helping to compensate for five years of decline in the public sector. However, with the political and economic crisis, heretofore resilient small businesses began to register a downsizing of their activities for the first time since the transition began.

In Romania the private sector has expanded rapidly since 1990, as measured by the number of registered firms, persons employed, and share of total output. Because the process of privatization has proceeded so slowly, the development of the private sector has been all the more important than it might otherwise have been. By 1995 SMEs accounted for the bulk of the private sector in Romania: about 70 percent of the total number of enterprises, 25 percent of total employment, 30 percent of aggregate turnover, 11 percent of fixed assets, and 40 percent of total fixed investments. The heaviest concentration of SMEs is in the service sector, where two-thirds of them are to be found. Service firms account for some 60 percent of total SME employment and 84 percent of total turnover.

In Hungary, by the end of 1995 there were just over one million enterprises, of which only about 10 percent were registered as legal entities. Of these, just over one thousand had more than 300 employees, six thousand had 50 to 300 employees, twenty-two thousand had between 11 and 50 employees, and the remainder employed fewer than 11 workers. Thus, the vast majority were illegal micro-enterprises. Nearly half of all enterprises are located in Budapest and County Pest and the capital city also has the highest ratio of enterprise to population. By 1993 the contribution of small businesses to the Hungarian GDP was a third of the total GDP. Together with medium-sized enterprises, small enterprises contributed 44 percent of the GDP in 1992 and 48 percent the following year. Altogether, the private sector accounted for about 60 percent of the GDP. Equally important was the contribution of Hungarian SMEs to the creation of employment. By 1994, private enterprises and associations without legal status had absorbed over eight hundred thousand employees (and assisting family members). The small enterprise sector employed about a third of all workers and the medium-sized enterprise sector accounted for another 15 percent, amounting to roughly half of the total employment in the business sector.

All across the CEE region small businesses have already begun to make a marked difference in the economic transition of the CEE region, creating jobs while large firms are eliminating them. Jobs in the SME sector are already beginning to account for a substantial portion of total employment in the economy. Small businesses are growing at a much faster pace than are large firms, responding to the latent demand for consumer goods. At the same time, they are providing an outlet for the pent-up entrepreneurial skills of ordinary citizens. And quite a few of them have managed to reach export markets with their products, thus bringing in hard currency and helping the country's balance of trade.

**Institutions and policies that promote the SME sector are
beginning to contribute to economic growth and social development
in the CEE region.**

Despite the contribution of the SME sector to economic growth in the
CEE region as borne out by the statistics, surveys of small business
owners indicate that they continue to face an array of problems. A good
many of these are related to the slow pace of change in government
regulations to promote the private sector. The initial opening of the
banking system to small borrowers resulted in a high loan default rate,
partly due to the lack of experience in dealing with credit. Bankers
understandably became more cautious in handing out small loans. And
anecdotal evidence indicates that many more start-up businesses fail
than succeed, as is the case everywhere in the world. But there is no
turning back in this transition to a market economy, and the small-scale
entrepreneur is essential to its success.

The majority of the countries in transition have acknowledged that
small businesses are critical to industrial restructuring and have
therefore formulated national SME policies and promotion programs.
There is an increasing number of bilateral donor assistance programs
and multilateral initiatives to promote SMEs in the CEE region. The
following are but a few of these programs.

The European Union PHARE Program

The European Union provides assistance through the PHARE Program
to countries that are considered potential members of the European
Union. The PHARE Program was created by the European Council of
Ministers at the Essen Summit in 1989, initially to provide technical
assistance to support the reforms undertaken in Poland and Hungary.
Since then, PHARE has been expanded to become the principal
instrument of the European Community for cooperating with the
Central and Eastern European countries. The program aims at the
development of a larger democratic family of nations within a
prosperous and stable Europe. Its objective is to help the CEE countries
to rejoin the mainstream of European development by building closer
political and economic ties that will eventually lead to membership in
the European Union.

The PHARE Program provides grant finance to support its partner
countries through the process of economic transformation and
strengthening of democracy. PHARE funding has as one of its goals the

assistance of CEE countries in reforming their own internal political structures. PHARE has been given the task of coordinating technical assistance to CEE countries with procedures for their accession to the European Union. PHARE attempts to work in close collaboration with its partner countries to decide how funds are to be allocated, within the framework agreed to by the EU. PHARE provides a wide range of assistance to non-commercial, public, and private organizations in the region. The main priorities of the PHARE program include restructuring of state enterprises, private sector development, institutional reform, legislation and public administration, and transport and telecommunications. Between 1990 and 1995, PHARE provided funds to 11 partner countries, making it the largest assistance program of its kind in the region.

Within the private sector development and enterprises restructuring portfolio, most of the funds have gone for privatization and restructuring, banking, public finance, and accounting. Only recently has PHARE begun to provide assistance earmarked for small and medium-sized enterprise development. In 1994, 10 million ECU was set aside on a regional basis for SME development while 18 million ECU was allocated for SMEs in Romania. The following year, a modest sum of 3 million ECU was allocated to SMEs in Poland. This represented a belated recognition of the importance of the role of SMEs in the economic development of the countries in the region. Only lately has PHARE support in preparation for accession to the EU taken account of the need for public support of SMEs. Thus, the PHARE program for 1995-1999 in the Czech Republic includes support for SMEs, export, and regional development.

In 1997 the European Commission began completely revamping its multi-billion dollar PHARE program aimed at getting the ten former communist countries ready for EU membership. The program had been driven by requests from the countries, resulting in a plethora of small projects, many run by outside consultants, and not always efficiently. Under the new system the fragmented aid programs are to be merged into a superfund, and decision making on development spending will be shifted from the region to Brussels. The European Union will draw up national programs with the countries being offered membership, and the money will be targeted directly at preparing the countries to join the EU.

United Nations Industrial Development Organization (UNIDO)

UNIDO is the agency of the United Nations dedicated to promoting sustainable industrial development in countries with developing and transition economies. It is the only worldwide organization dealing exclusively with industry from a development perspective; its services are nonprofit and neutral. UNIDO acts as a catalyst to help generate national economic wealth and raise industrial capacity through its roles as worldwide forum for industrial development and as a provider of technical cooperation services.

The vast majority of UNIDO's programs are targeted at the SME sector, addressing the need for a coherent sector development strategy. UNIDO seeks to ensure complementarity amongst the various national programs and institutions and to develop a coordinated structure to provide the most needed services to SMEs. It works to strengthen national capabilities to establish a policy and institutional environment for promoting the SME sector. Cooperation is promoted between government and industry associations, as well as between private and public technical and financial institutions. UNIDO services include:

- Assisting governments to formulate national strategies and programs to promote the development of the SME sector;

- Strengthening national capabilities in order to collect and analyze SME sector-related information, required to monitor the health of the SME sector as a basis for formulating and implementing of policies, strategies, and programs;

- Contributing to improve the policy and regulatory environment in which SMEs operate by facilitating access to technological information, technology transfer, inter-enterprise linkages, and partnerships;

- Assisting governments and their national institutional partners to develop mechanisms to ensure effective implementation and continued fine-tuning of strategies and policies.

One UNIDO research project has particular relevance to the development of the SME sector in the CEE region. In 1995 the Central European Initiative (CEI) Working Group on SMEs requested UNIDO to carry out a study of SME policies and programs in the region. It was to provide a systematic basis for identifying areas of mutual interest for cooperation. The UNIDO survey was conducted in close collaboration with the national institutions and agencies in six countries. The final report consisted of a comparative analysis of SME strategies and programs as well as a critical appraisal of them (UNIDO, 1996).

Central and Eastern European Privatization Network (CEEPN)

CEEPN, headquartered in Portoroz, Slovenia, is an international, intergovernmental organization established in 1991 at the initiative of privatization practitioners from the region with the mission of promoting regional cooperation and East-to-East technical assistance in privatization. CEEPN specializes in various areas of economic transition. In response to massive training needs of the countries in transition, the CEEPN Academy offers a practical and action-oriented training program on the management of transition. The program is based on the extensive hands-on experience in transition, which CEEPN has gained over the years of its cooperation with leading experts in the region and the support of EU-PHARE and the World Bank.

As a regional institution, the CEEPN Academy provides a focal point for training on privatization and post-privatization issues in the countries in transition and is used as a vehicle for the conduct of training offered by international development agencies. The World Bank has awarded a special grant to assist CEEPN in the establishment of the Academy. PHARE provides a few fellowships which are administered by CEEPN. The objective of the CEEPN program is to provide the participants with: good understanding of the overall privatization and post-privatization processes and related issues; opportunity for specialization in specific issues of economic transition; ability to critically compare examples of different technical solutions and learn from best-practice cases; and analytical, diagnostic, and problem-solving skills that will allow them to implement such decisions and programs in practice.

The curriculum and teaching materials are prepared on the basis of regional expertise on economic transition, technical know-how, and case studies from a range of countries, and are continuously updated to incorporate the latest developments in the field. The curriculum is organized in five-week modules which can be taken separately or all together as the complete academy program. They include Privatization Techniques Capital Market Development, Enterprise Restructuring,

Banking Sector Development special topics in economic transition such as Privatization of Public Utilities.

CEEPN fellows who have hands-on experience in various transition issues in the CEE and NIS, region assure the teaching individual modules and topics of the academy. The CEEPN program is primarily intended for professional staff of governmental institutions managing, supervising, and regulating privatization and post-privatization processes (e.g., various ministries of the government, privatization agencies, state holding companies, restructuring agencies, bank rehabilitation agencies, and securities and exchange commissions).

Southeast European Cooperative Initiative (SECI)

Twelve Southeast European states held an inaugural meeting in Geneva in December 1996, and formally adopted a statement of purpose, forming the Southeast European Cooperative Initiative (SECI). Participating states included Albania, Bosnia, Bulgaria, Croatia, Greece, Hungary, Former Yugoslav Republic of Macedonia, Moldova, Romania, Slovenia, and Turkey. The impetus behind SECI was to create a regional association aimed at encouraging cooperation among its member states and to facilitate their integration into European structures. SECI is not an assistance program, but aims at complementing other regional initiatives. SECI is endeavoring to facilitate close cooperation among the governments of the region and create new channels of communication among policy makers. It attempts to coordinate regionwide planning, to provide for involvement of the private sector in regional economic and environmental efforts, and to create a regional climate that encourages the transfer of know–how and augment investment in the private sector.

SECI intends to bring together regional decision makers to discuss mutual economic and environmental concerns through joint projects, meetings, conferences and project groups organized by the Agenda Committee, which will be the motivating force behind the initiative. SECI is cooperating with the United Nations Economic Commission for Europe (ECE), as well as the Organization for Security and Cooperation in Europe (OSCE). The ECE provides technical assistance to SECI and the needed expertise to the project groups. Initial projects identified at the first SECI Agenda Committee meeting early in 1997 in Geneva included training (centers of excellence, environmental education, vocational training, further education), information exchange, media, communication, conferences, privatization, technology transfer, economic potential, investment opportunities, legal structures, credit insurance schemes, tax advantages, and banking.

Among the projects discussed was financial policies to promote small and medium enterprises through micro-credit and credit guarantee schemes, under the coordination of Romania. The promotion of widespread entrepreneurship through the establishment of small businesses was seen as crucial for the transformation to a market economy and the democratization of society in some SECI countries. SMEs were becoming accepted as indispensable to economic growth and a source of sustainable development. It was felt that the establishment of SMEs could secure job creation and self–employment in the SECI region, where the estimated number of registered unemployed exceeds 4.5 million.

This project aims at facilitating the securing of capital which potential entrepreneurs need in order to obtain initial credit for starting their operations. The exchange of experiences and joint efforts of two or more countries in establishing credit schemes and providing credit guarantees could accelerate the process of promoting SMEs. The project will include governmental bodies dealing with entrepreneurship and employment, chambers of commerce, regional and local authorities, financial institutions and the banking sector. International financial institutions such as the World Bank and the EBRD will be invited to participate. The project will be developed on the basis of a review of the existing national policies concerning financial services and micro-credit guarantee schemes, and the first pilot project could be implemented within a year. The first project group meeting took place on 24 April 1997 in Bucharest.

The growth of SMEs reflects a global trend: the bigger the world economy, the more powerful its smallest players become.

The study of the small economic players, the entrepreneur, will merge with the study of how the big bang global economy works.

—John Naisbitt, *Global Paradox,* 1994, p. 4

John Naisbitt's propositions emphasize the importance of small actors in the global economy. The United States economy best illustrates this axiom although most large industrial economies are characterized by the preponderance of smaller firms.

In the United States, 53 percent of all nonfarm private sector employment in 1992 (the last year for which data was available) was in firms with fewer than five hundred employees, according to *State of Small Business 1995: Report of the President* (U.S. Small Business Administration 1996). From December 1993 to December 1994, the greatest gains in employment were in those industries with the highest percentage of employment in small firms. The service sector continued to be the largest creator of new jobs, a sector dominated by small businesses (defined by the SBA as having 60 percent or more of its employment in firms with fewer than five hundred employees). That sector showed the largest numerical gain in employment among small businesses with about 685,000 new jobs. Just as the manufacturing and finance sectors were downsizing, companies in the service sector were up sizing: many small firms were growing into large firms, and service industries previously dominated by small firms were becoming medium-sized. The next largest percentage gain in sector employment was in construction, where more than 88 percent of employment was in small businesses.

In other terms, the percentage rate of employment growth in small business-dominated industries was one-third higher than the national average and four times the rate in large business-dominated industries. The effect of downsizing was most evident in finance, insurance, and real estate. While the employment gain in the large business dominated sector of this industry was almost nil, the small business-dominated industries in the sector showed substantial growth in employment. Large businesses experienced their greatest job losses in manufacturing, particularly in the aerospace and defense industries.

And half of all U.S. exports are created by companies with fewer than 20 employees, while only 7 percent are created by companies with more than 500 employees. The Fortune 500 companies now account for only 10 percent of the GNP in the U.S., a decline of 10 percent in 25 years. Much of the balance of the GNP is produced by small and medium-sized firms.

Woman-owned firms in particular have registered phenomenal growth in the United States. During the decade from 1982 to 1992, woman-owned firms grew at a rate of 8.5 percent per year, more than twice the rate of all businesses. Women's share of total nonfarm businesses rose from 30 percent in 1987 to 34 percent in 1992. Most of the growth during that period was accounted for among self-employed women, micro-enterprises with only one employee.

One of the most common problems regarding small businesses is their high rate of failure. The U.S. Small Business Administration keeps track of business formation and dissolution. Over the past decade, the number of new small firms has increased at a rate of around 2 percent, about equal to the rate of growth of the general population and of the workforce. In other words, each year about 14 percent of small firms drop from the unemployment insurance rolls, while about 16 percent are added. This means that half of all listed firms either disappear or reorganize every five years.

Although the United States has no formal annual survey of new business formation, three proxies are used instead: change in the total number of tax returns filed, the number of new firms as measured by employer identification number, and the new business incorporation series of the Dun and Bradstreet Corporation. The Small Business Administration notes that business failures and bankruptcies have been declining in the United States over the past several years, in contrast to a trend of increasing failures in the early 1990s. Most firms fail during their early years. For a given cohort, about 20 percent of the remaining firms fail in each of the first and second years after start-up. The rate of failure decreases year by year, so that by the ninth or tenth year only about 7 or 8 percent of the cohort remainder fail. Fewer than half of all new firms are still in operation after five years.

And what of the social underpinnings of this trend in the United States? Entrepreneurs simply didn't count for much socially during the middle of this century (Richman 1997). Not many American parents who came of age during the Great Depression wished that their sons would become entrepreneurs or that their daughters would marry them. If entrepreneurs weren't actually disreputable, they were nonetheless suspect; they were the cultural misfits of business. That is not to say that there weren't entrepreneurs starting companies during the period beginning in the 1930s, but America wasn't exactly celebrating entrepreneurship.

But the mainstreaming of entrepreneurship in the United States isn't very surprising, considering that for the past 15 years or so there has been growth in both motivation and opportunity. There are several motives. The downsizing of large, established corporations has given many people reason to think about starting their own companies. The notion that smart people could join a big firm and be assured of making continuous progress has largely disappeared. So entrepreneurship is now seen as a viable alternative.

There are numerous examples of the negative effects of gigantism, when Naisbitt's axiom is not heeded. Japan has long been recognized as an industrial behemoth, and yet 99 percent of all Japanese manufacturers are classified as small to medium-sized, with fewer than three hundred employees (*The Economist*, April 26, 1997). In 1994, the latest year for which statistics are available, one out of every four of these Japanese firms employed fewer than 20 workers. Of the 10.4 million Japanese who were employed in manufacturing in 1994, 72 percent worked for small to medium-sized enterprises. Yet industrial policy in Japan has been mainly conducive to the growth of giant companies, while policies to promote entrepreneurship have been lacking.

Russia, for its part, is busy developing a system of oligarchic capitalism. Priorities among the economic and political elites in Russia have assigned small business the bottom rung (Hoffman 1997). President Boris Yeltsin's liberal reformers declared early in 1997 that Russia would take the path of "people's capitalism," promising to create equal rules for all, encouraging the middle class and letting small family businesses flourish. But the opposite is happening: the country's economy is characterized by the domination of giant conglomerates and a handful of wealthy tycoons who enjoy special privileges and a cozy relationship with the state. Unlike many of the more progressive nations of the CEE region, Russia is following the model which the conglomerates of South Korea practiced until recently: the big companies get bigger and bigger and the small ones scramble for survival.

Russia has some fourteen thousand medium-sized companies created as a result of privatization, many of them starving for capital. Most are not found on the stock market. Investors—especially the influential foreign investors—aren't interested in small companies, which often have opaque balance sheets or old-fashioned Soviet "red directors" in charge. Most smaller Russian entrepreneurs don't know how to raise capital, nor do they want to give up control in exchange for investment. At the same time, individual investors don't yet exist; most personal savings in Russia are still squirreled away under the mattress, or deposited in the state savings bank. The Russian banks have not offered to take risks on the smaller companies, choosing instead to feast on profits from ruble-dollar speculation and high-yielding, tax-free government bonds. Banks simply have not given long-term loans to business. According to the Central Bank, Russian bank assets total $155 billion, but last year banks lent only $9 billion to enterprises.

The countries of Central and Eastern Europe have thus far chosen a transition path that accommodates the growth of small and medium-sized enterprises, even if it does not yet make them the centerpiece of development. In this respect they deserve to be studied by the emerging nations of the former Soviet Union as models for their own development.

REFERENCES

European Commission 1996 *The PHARE Programme Annual Report 1995* Brussels: Com 96, 360.

Economic Commission for Europe 1996 *Industrial Restructuring in Selected Countries*, ECE/INDI/, Geneva.

Drozdiak, William "NATO Members Welcome Expansion: U.S. Senate Shaping Up as Proposal's Only Major Issue," *The Washington Post*, March 27, 1998.

The Economist "Japan's Minnows" April 26, 1997.

Hoffman, David "Russia's `People's Capitalism' Benefiting Only the Elite: Big Tycoons Squeeze Out Small Businesses," *The Washington Post*, December 28, 1997.

INC Magazine 1997 "Face to Face: An Interview with David Birch," State of Small Business in the U.S.

Levitsky, Jacob ed. 1996 *Small Business in Transition Economies*, London: IT Publications.

Lippman, Thomas W., and Helen Dewar, "Senate Giving NATO Expansion a Virtual Free Ride," *Washington Post*, March 8, 1998.

Naisbitt, John 1994 *Global Paradox* New York: Avon Books

New Europe September 7-October 13, 1997.

Podkaminer, Leon et al. 1997 "Year-End 1996: Mixed Results in the Transition Countries" Vienna: WIIW Research Report No. 233 February.

Richman, Tom "Issue: State of Small Business 1997" *INC Magazine*, 1997. p. 44.

Swardson, Anne "Ex-Communist Nations Receive Nod From EU 6 Countries to Start Membership Talks in March" *The Washington Post*, December 14, 1997.

United Nations Industrial Development Organization (UNIDO) 1996 *A Comparative Analysis of SME Strategies, Policies and Programmes in Central and Eastern European Initiative Countries*.

U.S. Small Business Administration *State of Small Business 1995: Report of the President*, Washington, DC: Government Printing Office.

CHAPTER 9

A Small Business Agenda for the Central and Eastern European Region

In 1986, I authored a book entitled *A Small Business Agenda: Trends in a Global Economy,* in which I ventured the proposition that small businesses were becoming the main source of economic growth and job creation. I discussed the "entrepreneurial economy" and the role of small business that was evolving in the United States, and suggested that it might be a model for developing nations. However, I was not prescient enough to foresee the eventual relevance of this thesis to those countries then behind the iron curtain. Today the relevance of this assertion is evident, and I am more than ever persuaded of its universal application.

In the preceding chapters, the notion that the privatization of large state-owned enterprises would be the necessary *and* sufficient condition for successful transition to market economies in the Central and Eastern European region has been challenged. None of the countries in the region has reached the promised land on the privatization express. The Czech Republic, for its part, followed a strict Thatcherite formula for privatization and an unfettered free market, and yet saw its economy go into a tailspin. Privatization has not proved to be the panacea that was hoped for. There is increasing evidence that the newly formed businesses in the small and medium enterprise (SME) sector are providing the leavening for economic development.

They are doing so despite the fact that most countries in the region are only now attempting to articulate policies and programs to support small businesses. Macroeconomic policies aimed at stabilizing the economy are usually of little help to small businesses, since they mainly depend upon consumption rather than on economic growth. They tend to benefit more from a contracting domestic economy than from international markets. Only a small percentage have reached export markets or benefit from subcontracts with multinationals. Thus, while macroeconomic reform is necessary to create the conditions for a market economy, it must be complemented by policies and programs for small businesses aimed specifically at mitigating its harsher effects and providing access to credit and training necessary for their development.

In this concluding chapter, a set of concerns and recommendations is put forward to suggest a small business agenda specifically relevant to the countries of Central and Eastern Europe, and to the Newly Independent States of the former Soviet Union as well.

AGENDA ITEM #1: THE NEED TO ATTAIN EUROPEAN UNION STANDARDS

The European Commission presented its Agenda 2000 to the European parliament in Strasbourg in July 1997, outlining in a single framework the development of the European Union beyond the turn of the century (*European Businessman*, Vol. 3, Issue 2, 1998). The main thrust of the document concerned a strategy for enlarging the European Union to include the countries of Central and Eastern Europe and the likely impact of this expansion on EU policies. Agenda 2000 also set out the new financial perspectives of the EU for the period from 2000 to 2006. In introducing Agenda 2000 to the parliament, Commission President Jacques Santer described a fast-changing Union which faced the challenge of adapting, developing, and reforming itself. He suggested that this was a historic opportunity to modernize key policies through enlargement as far eastward as the Ukraine, Belarus, and Moldova.

In order to attain EU status, the countries in the Central and Eastern European region must achieve certain standards. Some have already articulated an industrial policy aimed at creating conditions favorable to the development of private enterprise with integration into the European Union clearly in view. Such a policy sees modernization as necessary to enhance competitiveness and to increase value added. To attain membership in the European Union, it will be necessary to comply with the EU's prerequisite harmonization regulations.

To become fully integrated into Western Europe, the countries of the CEE region must introduce harmonization of the legal and regulatory environment into the areas of quality control and environmental protection. International product quality and standards control will have to be complied with in order for CEE exports to reach European markets. European standards are codified in the ISO 9000 series, which specifies requirements for each product sector for entry into the European market. ISO 9000 is a four-part framework developed by the European Standards Organization to assure defect-free production and assembly in an international production environment. The ISO system aims to assure organization-level accountability for and active management review of production systems. It emphasizes the importance of production according to documented quality systems and the overall harmonization of varying operational quality standards. Individual producers are certified by recognized external auditors using standardized procedures. A growing number of firms in the CEE region, recognizing the importance of European markets, are taking the necessary steps to obtain ISO certification.

Administrative burdens for enterprises will have to be reduced. Banking systems must be made more responsive to the needs of enterprises. More effective measures are required to reduce the informal (black market) economy. Cooperation with the European Union in research and development in management training must be pursued, especially for small and medium-sized enterprises.

AGENDA ITEM #2: THE NEED FOR SYSTEMATIC DATA ON SMES IN THE CEE REGION

The criteria for membership in the European Union are both economic and political. Essentially, the European Union expects its newest members to look like and behave like its other members. Western Europe may not offer a perfect model for development, but the European Union does have a system for accumulating and reporting on the small and medium enterprise sector. The European Observatory for SMEs publishes an annual report on the 16 member countries of the European Union. Through the European Network for SME Research, the European Observatory reports provide a comprehensive analysis of the perspective of SMEs in the European economy.

The European Observatory reports are based on the premise that the contribution of small businesses to employment generation and sustainable growth in the European Union is quite significant. And given the high levels of unemployment throughout Europe, SMEs will continue to play an important role in stimulating economic growth. SME policy is becoming increasingly important for the creation of new employment opportunities in Europe. The reports thus provide information not traditionally available, and therefore assist in problem solving and policy making among EU member states. These reports provide both quantitative and qualitative information in areas where data is scarce but necessary for effective analysis.

In order for the countries in transition to prepare themselves for entry into the EU, they need a similar database regarding the role of SMEs in their own economies. Definitions of employment categories differ from country to country. Data on the size of firms, employment, and contribution to the economy on the SME sector in these countries in its present form is often unreliable even when it can be found. A database is necessary for the elaboration of sound policies and regulations, as well as for programs of assistance. The existing information must be provided in a sufficiently consistent form so as to be useful to policy makers and interested stakeholders. With integration into Western Europe on the horizon, there is a need to benchmark progress in the CEE countries against the norms of the Western economies. There is also a recognition that adequate information for policy development should include analysis of the births, terminations, and growth, as well as the sectoral and regional performance of SMEs.

There has been an extraordinary growth within the micro-enterprise sector in all of the countries in the CEE region since 1990. On average, 90 percent of all registered enterprises fall into this category. The distinction between registered and unregistered firms is still somewhat blurred. The incidence of "inactive" firms is quite high, averaging as much as 20 to 30 percent of the total in the region. Significantly, the informal sector, consisting of unregistered firms, is estimated at between 10 and 30 percent of the GDP in countries of the CEE region. The size of the informal sector is seen as a problem by most of the governments in the region because unregistered companies in the "gray economy" are by definition escaping tax payment.

There is a need for a clear definition of SMEs along the lines of those proposed by the European Union, on which a proper framework of support for the sector can be based. ECE reports indicate that there is currently a wide range of definitions in use, and that often there is no official definition of *small enterprise* at all. Distinct official definitions are necessary so that programs, policies, and laws can be implemented with a well-defined target population. It is also important to begin to conform to international standards in order not to be excluded from capital and technical assistance accorded by donor agencies.

Currently, the Industry and Technology Division of the Regional Advisory Services Program in the Economic Commission for Europe (ECE) in Geneva is endeavoring to play this role in data-gathering and dissemination for the countries in transition. Its resources, however, are extremely limited. For the ECE to expand its present capabilities to bring them up to the European Observatory standard, additional funding would be required.

AGENDA ITEM #3: THE NEED FOR COMPREHENSIVE STRATEGIC SME POLICIES

Economic performance and growth varies considerably among the countries in transition in the CEE region (Szabo 1997). However, the 14 million unemployed are an increasingly painful problem, as traditional safety nets have been weakened under the pressure to reduce public expenditure. Eligibility rules for unemployment benefits have also been tightened. Inflation and economic uncertainty have eroded personal savings and people lack the financial reserves to start a business. Small and micro-enterprises can provide the way out of stagnation, especially in underdeveloped regions facing structural adjustment. They can play a significant role because they produce and distribute local products and provide services to a local market by generating jobs and creating income for the local population.

This potential is not yet fully recognized. Analysis by the Economic Commission for Europe indicates that governments of countries in transition have tended to focus more attention on questions related to privatization than on SMEs. In taking this approach, they run the risk of viewing privatization as the goal of the economic transformation process rather than as an instrument to make the economy more efficient through private initiative and real ownership. Such policies to promote small businesses as do exist usually fail to specify the contribution that they make to broader goals of productivity, employment, and economic growth. Furthermore, they are often characterized by frequent changes and a lack of coordination among government agencies.

The promotion of SMEs in the CEE region should be incorporated into a comprehensive approach to privatization and industrial restructuring. The promotion of small business in the region should be justified as part and parcel of privatization and industrial restructuring. In order to accelerate the transition process to a market economy, policies in support of the long-term development of SMEs should be integrated into the overall economic reform and industrial strategy.

The majority of the transition economies are beginning to acknowledge that small businesses are crucial for industrial restructuring, prompting them to begin to formulate enterprise development policies. The Czech Republic, Hungary, Poland, Slovakia, and Slovenia have all established policies for SMEs as a component of industrial restructuring. In each of these countries, the establishment and promotion of SMEs is becoming an accepted part of the privatization process and of economic reform.

Romania and the Baltic States of Latvia, Lithuania, and Estonia have begun to take modest steps toward formulating an SME policy as part of their economic reform. A coherent SME policy is still lacking in the countries of Southeastern Europe, including Bosnia, Croatia and the former Yugoslav Republic of Macedonia. The development of SME policy lags even further behind in the Newly Independent States, where the lack of legislation and understanding of entrepreneurship as well as inadequate infrastructure and financial means have been major obstacles to their further development.

In June 1995, a conference organized by the Committee of Donor Agencies for Small Enterprise Development was held in Budapest, the first of its kind in the CEE region. In attendance were representatives of small business associations, SME support agencies, and entrepreneurs, as well as donor agencies. Those agencies included multilateral ones such as the United Nations Development Program, International Labor Organization, United Nations Industrial Development Organization as well as bilateral aid agencies. Other sponsors included the World Bank, PHARE, and the European Bank for Reconstruction and Development. Conference participants discussed innovative approaches to financial and technical services for small enterprises. Four major themes were debated: financial support, technical and management services, policies conducive to SME development, and the focus of assistance by international donor agencies in promoting SMEs in the region.

Several general conclusions were drawn from the Budapest conference proceedings. Although there are many common features among the countries of the region, there are numerous historical, cultural, and political factors that also must be taken into account. The legal systems still remain inadequate to stimulate and protect small and medium enterprises and facilitate their growth. Entrepreneurs need advice and help in marketing their products to overcome the deficiencies of the distribution system and insufficient development of business linkages. The support framework needs to be assessed to ensure that local and regional support institutions are to be encouraged where there is sufficient demand for services. Training for SMEs is important, especially in marketing, financial accounting, and entrepreneurship development. More focus must be given to developing local case study materials and linking training with business consultancy.

In most of the CEE countries a strategic policy for SME development is still evolving. The Economic Commission for Europe attempts to track the resolutions and acts of government in each of the countries in transition pertaining to small business development and the authorities responsible for the formulation of SME policy. In the context of Central and Eastern Europe, SMEs have come to be seen as synonymous with the private sector, and by extension with entrepreneurship. The creation of a favorable political and economic environment for SMEs has become one of the tasks of the governments in the CEE region. The basic rationale for a strategic policy for SMEs, summarized in an ECE document (Economic Commission for Europe 1996), are similar to those in the countries of the European Union:

- SMEs contribute to employment growth at a higher rate than larger firms;

- SMEs can help in the restructuring of large state firms by enabling those firms to abandon or sell off non core production activities and by absorbing redundant employees;

- SMEs provide economies with greater flexibility in the provision of services and the manufacture of consumer goods;

- SMEs increase competitiveness of the marketplace and curb the monopolistic tendencies of large firms;

- SMEs act as a seedbed for the development of entrepreneurial skills and innovation, providing services to the local economy and contributing to regional development.

An SME policy agenda should include certain basic elements (UNIDO, 1996). It should:

- Spell out the relationship between national economic and industrial policy and that of SME development, specifying the rationale for intervention to promote the SME sector;

- Identify the departmental responsibilities within the government for SMEs;

- Indicate the role of SME policy regarding privatization and restructuring;

- Design and implement support policies for SME development.

AGENDA ITEM #4: NEED FOR INSTITUTIONAL SUPPORT FOR SMES

Support for small businesses involves a wide range of services to local agencies including exchanging information, updating on regulatory measures and lobbying for legislation favorable to small business, and providing access to donor assistance programs and special credit schemes. In most countries in the region there is a government agency charged with promoting small businesses, but these agencies often operate with very little authority and resources. In many cases SME programs administered by the Ministry of Industry or Economy were set up mainly to administer funds from the PHARE Program. In Hungary, the Institute for Small Business Development was established to monitor SME development and conduct policy research, whereas the Hungarian Foundation for Enterprises Promotion has a strong orientation to local enterprise support. An important issue is the extent to which such agencies are and should be autonomous from the government. Business owners themselves are less inclined to avail themselves of the services of an agency which they see as entirely government-controlled.

Also increasingly common are regional development agencies established in market towns to provide seminars and training and business centers. This initiative is usually associated with a policy of decentralization, providing more decision-making powers to the local authorities. Nevertheless, these networks of local agencies tend to look to the central government for support and are lacking in their own resources. The future of such agencies may be linked to the availability of funds from the European Union aimed at regional development.

AGENDA ITEM #5 : THE NEED FOR ACCESS TO CREDIT

Access to financing is an abiding issue for small-scale entrepreneurs, often linked to the financial instability of the countries in which they operate. The banking system in particular must be made more effective in addressing the financial needs of small businesses. The Ohio State study on Romania concluded with several suggestions for banking reforms which apply to other countries in the CEE region as well (Meyer, 1997):

- While many entrepreneurs appear to have been successful in obtaining financing from institutions, most loans are short-term. Banks should offer more long-term loans to obviate debt repayment problems.

- Conflict of interest laws and lending limits should be strictly enforced. The most serious deficiency in private banking is the damage caused by insider lending to directors and shareholders beyond the maximum loan size limits set by regulatory authorities.

- State-owned enterprises must be made to reduce their under-performing loans and to eliminate soft budget constraints.

- Nonbank financial institutions should be encouraged to test alternative lending technologies such as cash flow and group lending for micro and small borrowers.

AGENDA ITEM #6: THE NEED FOR A COHERENT TAX POLICY

Taxes are the universal plaint of businesses everywhere, and particularly small businesses. Corporate taxes were virtually unknown under the communist system, with notable exceptions. In Hungary, a civil law association, the Economic Working Community, was codified in the 1980s and actually subject to a three percent corporate tax! At the beginning of the transition tax legislation was typically contained in one thin book. Today the tax code is often so massive that it is increasingly easy for businesses to find loopholes in order to avoid paying taxes. Most governments in the CEE region are having serious trouble collecting direct taxes, especially the income tax on corporations.

A majority of governments in the region have been generally unsuccessful in establishing and implementing rational tax policies. For example, in April 1997, the Klaus government in the Czech Republic announced several economic measures aimed at addressing severe economic problems and reluctantly regulating the heretofore "free" market. Among them was greater discipline in the collection of taxes. If a firm was unable to pay its taxes or health and social security contributions, company management would have to declare bankruptcy. A new body to supervise tax collection and initiate relevant legislative changes was also established. The government would continue to reduce tax rates—the corporate tax rate would be cut from 39 to 35 percent. All this was a matter of shutting the barn door after the horse had gotten away. Within a few months, Klaus had been forced out of office.

The increasing presence of the informal sector is a testament to the tendency of small enterprises to avoid registering in order not to pay taxes. Even though registration of business and obtaining appropriate licenses has become relatively more easy in recent years, the number of enterprises opting not to register is alarming to tax collectors. Furthermore, a substantial number of businesses registered are simply on paper, a reflection of the attempt of some companies to avoid paying social security for employees who claim self-employment status.

Decisive measures to establish reasonable and stable tax policy and practices are needed in all the CEE countries. Often it is not so much the amount of taxes as the arbitrariness and cumbersomeness, the ineffective and inconsistent work of the tax authorities, that is at issue. It is imperative to abolish the practices of backdated taxes and the frequent amending of tax policies. Social security and labor taxes must be made less onerous. The tax structure must be changed by reducing direct taxes and increasing indirect taxes, as it the case in Western Europe. Ways should also be found to create deductions for institutions in the nonprofit sector.

TOWARDS AN ENTREPRENEURIAL CULTURE

The countries in Central and Eastern Europe continue on a path from state- controlled economies to free market economies. For several decades the Soviet system worked to uproot and destroy whatever nationalist sentiment managed to manifest itself within the residual artificial nation-states. The Hungarian uprising of 1956 and the Prague spring of 1968 were blips on the radar screen monitoring the health of nations in the intensive care unit of history. After a thousand years: alive and kicking. Furthermore, these nation-states were obliged to follow policies designed to snuff out any traces of individual initiative, much less entrepreneurship. Just as the economies of the Soviet system were organized for production of state enterprises to support Soviet interests, the individual worked for the good of the state. The nation was transformed into a unit of production for the Soviet empire.

Two important trends can be discerned in the region over the last decade since the disintegration of the Soviet Union. First, ancient pent-up sentiments and values have been unleashed. Nationalism is back in full force, characterized by an earnest desire to revive social, linguistic, and cultural identities. The nation-states of the CEE region are composed predominantly of linguistic and ethnic majorities with small minority populations. Long suppressed cultural, religious, and social identities are resurfacing, sometimes at the expense of the minorities living within their borders.

At the same time individualism is also making a re-appearance. Membership in *Komsomol* (communist youth league) and the Communist Party no longer define who one is or determines the degree of his or her privileges. Even though the governments of the CEE region have all opened the door to individual initiative and entrepreneurship, the regulatory environment and societal attitudes die hard. Prevailing attitudes toward entrepreneurs still tend to characterize them as self-centered profit seekers bent on evading the law. The growth of the mafia and flourishing black market operations does little to help this image. For their part, most small business owners feel that those who are responsible for operating the regulatory environment do not understand or care about them. Unquestionably, many of them view government as the enemy and seek to minimize their dealings with government agencies. Government is associated first and foremost with tax collection and regulation, and not with support to small businesses.

The countries of the region are at a crossroads where choices must be made. They can reassert nationalist values over regional and internationalist values or bend every effort to become European. The process of integration into the European Union will sorely test this assertion. The Slovak Republic has already paid a heavy price for its nationalist preachments. The ultra nationalism of the republics of former Yugoslavia has assured that they will be among the last to join the European family, if at all. The candidates for membership in the European Union are struggling with how much of their national identity to give up in return for European solidarity. Indications are that they will hold onto their newfound nationalist identities as long as possible while doing whatever is required to attain membership in the EU. The West should never underestimate the importance that people in the CEE region place on the security to be derived from membership in Western European institutions.

The second trend is toward choosing economic policies. The governments of the region can promote policies predicated on the assumption that bigger is better, as was done in the past. Transforming the old state-owned enterprises, they can create monopolistic *chaebols* through collaboration among the state, banks, and pseudo- privatized enterprises. Russia has thus far followed this path. They can opt for policy priorities that focus on attracting foreign investment as the primary engine of growth, creating "greenfields" or enterprise zones isolated from the local economy. Such policies have already led to economic growth without development, with negative political consequences. Or the governments can recognize the dynamic quality of the small business sector as the engine of growth, and create employment, provide an outlet for individual initiative, and promote subcontracting for the supply of parts and services to larger enterprises.

The wisest policy would be one that places emphasis on promoting an entrepreneurial culture. A set of policies that sustains an entrepreneurial culture will act as a steam valve for the pent-up ambitions and aspirations of the people. Such policies will allow for the possibility of business failure—including bankruptcy—and a second and third chance for those courageous enough to venture it. These policies must, however, ensure that small businesses operate within a legal framework, paying taxes and abiding by the regulations. They must embody respect for social values, a free market, and the adoption of European standards.

The promotion of small businesses in the CEE region should be incorporated into a comprehensive approach to privatization and industrial restructuring. In order to develop entrepreneurship and accelerate the transition process to a market economy, policies in support of the long-term development of SMEs should be integrated into the economic reform and industrial strategy of a country. The promotion of entrepreneurship through the establishment of small and medium-sized enterprises is crucial for the transformation to a market economy and the democratization of society. Small businesses are becoming recognized as an engine of economic growth and a source of sustainable development.

Within this sector, the small and micro-enterprise segment is of great importance because it is the cradle of entrepreneurship, particularly in environments facing high poverty and unemployment rates. These firms are especially crucial where there is a need for structural and social adjustment due to the restructuring of heavy machinery plants, military bases or the closing of worked-out mines. In those districts, small and micro-enterprises in particular can create jobs and provide income-generating opportunities to alleviate poverty.

Privatization has been wrongly seen simply as the transfer of existing enterprises from public to private hands. Many governments of the countries in the CEE region have tended to focus more attention on the privatization of state-owned enterprises than on small businesses. But privatization has far wider importance in that it expands the share of the private sector in the GNP and hence includes newly created enterprises as well. Privatization should be seen not only as an aim of the economic transformation process, but also as an instrument to make the economy more efficient through private initiative and real ownership. Small businesses in the countries of the region are the embryos of the new economic fabric of the market economy that transition aims to create and develop. They should therefore be recognized as engines of economic growth and a source of sustainable development.

REFERENCES

European Businessman: The Journal for Business in Central and Eastern Europe London Vol. 3, Issue 2 1998.

European Commission for Europe (ECE) 1996 *Small and Medium-Sized Enterprises in Countries in Transition* Technology Division of the

Regional Advisory Services Program in the Economic Commission for Europe, report IND/AC.3/1 February.

(The) European Observatory for SMEs 1995 *Third Annual Report 1995*, report submitted to Directorate-General XXIII (Enterprise Policy, Distributive Trades, Tourism, and Cooperatives) of the Commission of the European Communities by the European Network for SME Research, February.

Meyer, Richard ed. 1997 *Small Business Finance in Romania: Banks, Businesses and Business Centers in a Transition Economy*, study prepared for the Bureau for Europe and the Newly Independent States of USAID, Ohio State University, March 31.

Plumb, Lord 1998 "Agenda 2000, A Challenge for European Union" in *European Businessman: The Journal for Business in Central and Eastern Europe* Vol. 3, Issue 2.

Szabo, Antal 1997 "Microcrediting SMEs in Countries in Transition," mimeograph Regional Director Adviser on Industry and Technology, Geneva: Economic Commission for Europe January.

United Nations Industrial Development Organization (UNIDO) 1996 *A Comparative Analysis of SME Strategies, Policies and Programmes in Central European Initiative Countries: Part I* report of the Central European Initiatives Working Group on SMEs.

Index

Antall, Jozsef: Chairman of the
    Hungarian Democratic Forum,
    92; ailing former Prime Minister
    and support of Fidesz leader
    Viktor Urban, 123.
Association for Building
    Partnerships (BAP) in Bulgaria,
    42.

Balcerowicz, Leszek: Polish Deputy
    Prime Minister, author of
    "shock therapy", 6; Balcerowicz
    Plan and its effects, 136-138; as
    Minister of Finance, challenges
    Poland to achieve its potential,
    147-148.
Bank Gospodarstwa Krajowego,
    (Poland), manages loans to
    SMEs, 153.
Birch, David, research on small
    business in the U.S., 20.
British Know-How Fund, and
    support for Romanian ROM-
    UN Center, 191.
Bulgaria:
    historic and economic trends, 25-
        52: derivation of the name of

Bulgaria, 25; Bulgarian
    Communist Party, 26, 29;
    caretaker government and
    stabilization, 27-28; market
    reforms, 28-32; unemployment,
    27; GDP and private sector
    growth, 29, 31; economic
    policies promoting private
    sector, 30; agriculture in
    economy, 30.
privatization and economic
    growth, 32-35: employee and
    management buyouts, 33; small-
    scale, 33; municipal, 34; Mass
    Privatization Program, 32. *See
    also* MPP.
looking toward Europe, 35-38:
    Bulgarian participation in
    Partnership for Peace, 36;
    NATO and Bulgarian chances
    of joining, 35. *See also* NATO.
role of SMEs in economy, 36-39:
    definition of SME, 37; lack of
    SME legislation, 37;
    employment in private sector,
    38; hindered by economic
    destabilization, 38.